THE
HUNTER
ELITE

THE
HUNTER ELITE

INSIDE AMERICA'S SECRET FORCE AGAINST TERROR

LEON WAGENER

A KNOX PRESS BOOK
An Imprint of Permuted Press
ISBN: 978-1-63758-897-0
ISBN (eBook): 978-1-63758-898-7

The Hunter Elite:
Inside America's Secret Force Against Terror
© 2023 by Leon Wagener
All Rights Reserved

Cover art by Cody Corcoran

Permuted Press, LLC
New York • Nashville
permutedpress.com

Published in the United States of America
1 2 3 4 5 6 7 8 9 10

To My Wife and Collaborator Rochelle

CONTENTS

PROLOGUE

The line between war and criminality has traditionally been blurred in all-out war. There have always been incidents of atrocity: My Lai, Sherman's burning of Atlanta, and the Revolutionary War Boston Massacre. But in asymmetrical war it is the norm; there is no distinction between combatants and non-combatants.

That is the battlefield Hawkeye Counter Assault Team (CAT) and the Hunters were designed to fight on, and the counter-insurgency tactics they are taught to carry out—unfortunately for the civilian population, the battle will, of necessity, be fought on the streets of American cities, in extremis.

The good news for the country is that Hawkeye CAT is "the most elite unit of its kind in the world." Its members are in a sense the new soldiers, new policemen for the dark winter of the twenty-first century, but again they are a re-creation of the Praetorian Guard, the Roman Legion, warriors fighting savages, battling barbarians trying to storm the gates, kill our leaders, and sack our civilization.

The men and women of these elite forces are tasked with saving not only the president, but saving America from nuclear holocaust by ensuring the heads of government are kept safe from harm and able to continue to lead a retaliatory strike, in the event of a first-nuclear-strike attack.

I spent three years researching and writing this book and conducted over one hundred interviews with current members of Hawkeye CAT and the Hunters, as well as agency retirees and members of its elite, secret shock troops.

Hawkeye CAT is the last line of defense if a president is attacked by an organized terror force, heavily armed and determined to kill or even kidnap the president. Its members are not cops, don't carry handcuffs, and aren't in the business of making arrests. If they are deployed—which thus far in the forty years of their existence they have not been once—their goal is to destroy the enemy, at whatever cost.

This is the chronicle of the metamorphosis of the Secret Service agency from a strictly defensive organization that guarded the lives of the government's leaders, patiently waiting for an assassin to emerge from the shadows with a weapon, to a proactive, aggressive group of sleuths, who smoke the bad guys out of hiding and disrupt their plans *before* they have a chance to put them in motion.

In the past, the Secret Service wore black suits and were armed with .38 pistols. They were trained and equipped to confront and arrest a lone gunman—once a shot had been fired, or another violent crime committed.

Hawkeye CAT and the Hunters dress in black combat fatigues and are equipped with fully automatic weapons of war. They are prepared to take on teams of suicidal terrorists, who will also be equipped with weapons of war.

I appreciate all the interviews I was granted, but my premier sources, who go by code names Laredo and Ranger, were the two who took me inside the secret world of the elite shock troops and their methods, and often hair-raisingly dangerous assignments. A husband and wife team, they have thwarted countless plots against America and the nation's leadership.

They told stories of their adventures in great detail, based, in many cases, on previously highly classified episodes in which they prevented assassinations, as well as schemes to unleash deadly and highly infectious pathogens that could have sickened and killed untold thousands, including the inhabitants of the White House.

They also prevented the detonations of so-called "dirty bombs" that could have irradiated the White House and made the nation's capital uninhabitable for a hundred years.

Ranger and Laredo and their colleagues are the heroes of the new age of terror, and much is owed to them and their brave and patriotic sisters and brothers, who put their lives on the line daily.

Both are highly decorated veterans of the Afghanistan war. Ranger leads small bands of soldiers throughout the U.S. and the world, when need be, to break up and destroy terrorist groups with plans to harm the top leadership of the country.

Laredo has advanced degrees in biological, chemical, and radiological warfare and has prevented countless attacks that would have ended with apocalyptic loss of life.

This book is their story, as best as I can tell it, without giving away the identities of their families or their secret methods and tactics.

Ranger was on duty at headquarters, shortly into Donald Trump's presidency. He was doing paperwork, the bane of his existence, when a bulletin came from Secret Service Intelligence and Assessment, reporting a possible Level III threat in the wild mountains of West Virginia.

He remembers lighting up with an adrenalin rush.

The subject was a white male in his fifties, who was said to be holed up in a rustic hunting cabin in the steep mountainous countryside near Highway 50.

Ranger recalled: "He was identified as Jack Ford, although we were told he had several noms de guerre. He told several people that his son worked at the Trump Casino in Atlantic City and had become addicted to gambling and drinking. His son committed suicide and he blamed Trump personally for his death. He vowed to kill the president."

The subject was a trained Army sniper known to be heavily armed. State Police had credible intelligence that Ford had stolen army ordnance and possibly chemical weapons.

> I put together a team of four, including my wife Laredo and two guys with West Virginia mountain-hunting experience. One had hunted in the area with his dad since he was a teenager.

Reading the dossier on Ford, I realized we were up against a bad hombre. When the State and local police had asked to interview him, he said 'Sure, come ahead but at your own risk,' which the police took as a direct threat of violence. What made the situation even more treacherous was that this guy had mined his land with bear traps that could take off a man's leg.

That afternoon, we took a helicopter to the area and met with State Police, who promised they would erect a perimeter around the cabin.

Taking him would be my problem.

At dawn the next morning the quartet of Hunters were dropped in near the house, which they cautiously approached, wary of bear traps and slithering reptiles—including the official West Virginia reptile, the deadly timber rattler, which can grow as long as five feet.

Ranger announced on a bullhorn they were Secret Service and needed to interview him. A few seconds later several shots rang out and whizzed past them. Not a word had to be spoken.

The Hunters returned fire with P90 rifles, in bursts of three. The team fired more than one hundred rounds in about forty-five seconds. When there was no response, they rushed the house, still blazing away. After a quick search of the one-bedroom house—really a hunting shanty, perched on an escarpment—they realized the would-be assassin had escaped through an underground tunnel, obviously designed and built for that purpose.

"It struck me the whole thing was a loony game, set up by a very dangerous person, who, insanely, wanted us to come for him, knowing it would end with his demise. It was essentially a 'death by cop' ploy."

The Hunters began the search over some of the most forbidding terrain imaginable. For the next four hours, they trekked after their prey, well aware of the dangers every time they put a foot on the ground. The hope was that Ford would reach the police perimeter and be quickly captured. A Secret Service helicopter circled over the area. A marksman was on board with orders to use lethal force if necessary.

"There were a lot of snakes slithering around out there, so we had to watch our steps," Ranger later observed. "As we closed in on our man, he fired back in our direction. We answered with withering fire, but were obviously just firing in the general direction of his shots.

"After a grueling manhunt, I got word from the spotter in the chopper that he'd seen a man fall from a cliff and land nearly one hundred meters below in a rocky creek. When the state police got to the scene—pretty remarkable, admirable, police work—they identified the body as our villain. He was dead, so our job was done, the threat to the president was successfully neutralized. Usually in cases like that the call is that it was an accident. He died, after a fall, he wasn't shot. Not that we weren't trying.

"We returned to the house and searched it thoroughly, knocking down walls, digging up floors.

"There were several high-powered sniper rifles, including a Barrett M90 .50 caliber and a Barrett M98B .338 Magnum. They are both U.S. military-grade weapons."

The weapons cache was expected, but Laredo's sleuthing turned up a big prize. Laredo emerged from Ford's bedroom carrying a steel lock box that had been stashed under his bed. Ranger carried it outside and, while Laredo donned her hazmat suit, he gently pried the lock open with a Swiss army knife.

Safely covered, she slowly—almost with a drum roll—lifted the lid. But the lock box contained papers, and there was almost a collective sigh of relief and disappointment.

Laredo lifted a sheath of papers and her eyes widened. They were letters between Ford and various biochemists, mostly government employees, enquiring about variola, which is the virus that causes smallpox.

Laredo said, "So this is what this crazy bastard was really up to. I think the assassination threats were almost cover, in a completely insane way. I'm sure he wanted to kill Trump, because it would have made him infamous, and assuaged his guilt over his son's suicide, but that would have only been the beginning. He wanted to start a new plague, which, in effect, would have made him the new Hitler or Stalin."

She explained that back in the early '70s, after the smallpox virus was eradicated and the vaccine ubiquitous, both the Soviet Union and the United States preserved vials of the virus and freeze dried them for future research—or possibly for use as a bioweapon, perhaps in self-defense if the other guy shot first.

There were actually concerns in both countries of a bioweapon gap, a bizarre echo of Stanley Kubrick's 1964 movie *Dr. Strangelove.*

The vials, labeled "variola," plus other vials whose labels had deteriorated over the years, had been put in boxes, stored in freezers—first at the National Institutes of Health in Bethesda, Maryland, and later at the Food and Drug Administration—then largely forgotten.

But they were not forgotten by some rogue scientists, who recognized the value that vials of the deadly disease would have to terrorists, both domestic and foreign. When the FDA lab was moved to a different location, it was discovered that the boxes had been tampered with and there was apparently a number of missing samples of the frozen pathogens, at which point it was obviously too late to do anything about it.

The Hunters immediately recognized that Laredo's find was significant and could lead to the identity and the arrest of the rogue biochemists responsible for profiting from their sale to agents of terror.

Walking back to their helicopter, Laredo said, "I'm surprised Ford didn't destroy the letters before he left."

"With automatic weapons blazing away at your house all you can think of is to get the hell out," answered Ranger with a half-smile.

Exhausted, but glad to have survived their mountain wilderness expedition, the Hunters returned to the Capital, where the lock box was turned over to their partners at the FBI.

One of the most sinister plots against a U.S. President occurred shortly after Barack Obama's second inauguration in early 2013. Two men from upstate New York were involved; one of the men, Glendon Scott Crawford, was an admitted member of the Ku Klux Klan. The other, Eric J. Feight, was also a racist and a fierce foe of anyone of the Muslim religion.

The two had developed a remotely controlled device—an industrial-grade X-ray machine—and mounted it on the roof of a van. This one was designed to secretly irradiate people, many of whom would sicken and die days later. They referred to their device as a "death ray" and planned to park near the White House and aim it at the mansion with the goal of killing everyone inside.

Finding radioactive material is not nearly as hard as it sounds in the United States: according to the Monterey Institute of International Studies, there are over a million radiation sources used in industry, medicine, and research. Even worse is a report from the Nuclear Regulatory Commission that, in 2010 alone, a total of 262 devices containing radioactive material or medical radioisotopes were lost or stolen. And transporting highly radioactive material interstate isn't much of a problem, because only New York City and a few others have installed radiation detection equipment at their borders.

The intention was to attack and kill President Obama during the first months of his second term in office, then attack Islamic mosques around the country, possibly starting a war between the U.S. and worldwide Islam.

Crawford, then fifty-two, a Navy veteran with an engineering degree and extensive expertise on radiation dispersal devices, knew what he was doing and could conceivably have pulled off the plot. He explained to undercover FBI agents, who gained his confidence and trust, that he knew precisely what level of radiation was required to kill humans, and his often-repeated phrase was he "wanted to take my country back."

He contacted a Jewish organization in Albany, explaining he wanted to destroy "enemies of Israel" with his device and was seeking their help.

The organization immediately contacted the FBI, who in turn alerted the Secret Service.

The Hunters were immediately put in motion to work alongside the undercover FBI agents, and contacted the two would-be terrorists to offer assistance in locating sufficient fissile material to make the device operational.

The agents—including Laredo, for her expertise in radiological threats—kept the two in their crosshairs 24/7 and gave urgent warnings to the uniformed Secret Service and the D.C. police to be on high alert for a van with a weird device on the roof.

Upon his arrest, Crawford was the first to be charged under a 2004 law mandating a minimum twenty-five-year sentence for creating radiation dispersing dirty bombs. At trial, U.S. Attorney Richard Hartunian called it a "classic case of domestic terrorism."

Laredo said the damage such a bomb could render would be far beyond a mere explosion. "A small homemade dirty bomb would send four hundred radioactive isotopes into the biosphere. The result would be irreversible tissue damage to anyone exposed, malignant alterations to the bone structure and horrible chromosomal damage, plus a high probability of later developing lung cancer and/or leukemia."

But the worst part is that any person or animal exposed, would become, in effect, radioactive and spread the poison for as long as they lived, for up to thirty years. Each victim would become a super-spreader, infecting everyone they came in contact with. In the panic and hysteria that would inevitably ensue, it would be almost impossible for law enforcement to identify and contain all the people and animals exposed. It would become a malignancy that would metastasize all over the country, and the world. Many of the victims would remain healthy enough to continue infecting others with radiation poisoning for a long time. It would be almost impossible to contain.

"In the sick mind of a dirty bomb maker, that would, of course, be the desired effect."

Crawford was arrested and eventually sentenced to thirty years in prison. Co-defendant Eric Feight, who admitted to building the remote control for the X-ray device, was given a similar sentence.

After the trial, Laredo had the device transported to her lab where she dismantled it, and studied what she said was a "fiendishly clever" radioactive gun, capable of killing or damaging thousands of people who weren't even the intended targets.

She feared the publicity would lead to copycat radiation dispersal weapons that could be built by others with a grudge or random hatred against a score of targets. The story was classified for several years.

In 2002, then U.S. Attorney General John Ashcroft commissioned a study on "dirty bombs" or radiological dispersal devices (RDD), stating that they are the greatest terror threat facing the civilized world. He defined RDD as an exploding conventional bomb—probably regularly available dynamite—that "not only kills victims in the immediate vicinity, but also spreads radioactive material that is highly toxic to humans and can cause mass death and injury."

The greatest danger, according to A.G. Ashcroft's interagency task force, would involve a plan like that of Glendon Crawford's scheme to ignite such a device in an extremely crowded, televised event, like a presidential inaugural on the doorstep of the U.S. Capitol.

There would not only be mass casualties at the time, but radiation poisoning and contamination that would cause death for years to come and shatter public confidence in government's ability to protect us.

Jessica Satterfield defines a second type of RDD attack in her 2011 Georgetown University MA thesis *When Terrorists Fight Dirty.*

"A passive radiological weapon is commonly referred to as a Radiation Exposure Device (RED). Some analysts point to the 1995 discovery of a thirty-pound device containing radioisotope cesium-137 buried in the snow near the entrance to Izmailovsky Park in Moscow as a successful RED attack."

The radiological device was discovered when a Chechen terror leader told Russian TV reporters of its location—obviously to undermine confidence in government.

There are clearly two types of radiological attacks. Glendon Crawford fully intended to set off his "dirty bomb" at Barack Obama's inauguration, because he hated the notion of an African American being president.

The other type is the Chechen radiological device, which was meant to show what they are capable of and how the Russian government in that case was *incapable* of protecting her citizens.

Satterfield writes in her thesis that most terrorists intent on building a radioactive weapon are misguided, and likely incapable of creating a radioactive dispersal weapon meriting concern. But she warns that "a moderately competent terrorist...correcting past mistakes and carrying out a successful radiological attack...a malicious actor could successfully acquire these materials...and use them to construct a weapon."

★★★

In the months and years following the 9/11 attacks, President George W. Bush was convinced that more attacks—particularly against government officials, including him—were imminent.

José Padilla, also known as Abdullah al-Muhajir, was arrested in Canada and charged with plotting to obtain radioactive materials in Canada. He had been working with Ramzi bin al-Shibh, a key 9/11 architect. When he was arrested and returned to the United States, Bush designated him an enemy combatant, not entitled to a civilian trial, and ordered Padilla incarcerated at a maximum-security military prison in South Carolina.

The president ordered the joint task force of Secret Service hunters and FBI to give him daily updates on their investigations into the unfolding plot, which he was convinced would be carried by Al Qaeda operatives in the U.S.

Born in Brooklyn, N.Y. in 1970, Padilla had joined the Latin Kings street gang and had a long rap sheet of violent crime, including manslaughter as a fourteen-year-old. He had kicked a rival gang member to death.

While serving jail time for the killing, he converted to Islam and developed a relationship with peripheral members of Al Qaeda. In 2002, Padilla went to Afghanistan for training and to an Al Qaeda safe house in Lahore, Pakistan, where he was trained in the preparation and use of radiological weapons, and instructed to kill Al Qaeda's number one enemy at the time—George W. Bush. Training complete, Padilla traveled to Pakistan, Iraq, Saudi Arabia, and Egypt to meet with jihadi members, who planned to come to the U.S. to take part in the plot.

While in military custody in South Carolina, Padilla was visited by CIA operatives as well as Hunters, and subjected to "enhanced interrogation techniques" and additional "harsh techniques," including sensory deprivation (which gave the *New York Times* conniption fits, when a picture was printed).

The interrogation supplied some useful intelligence, but the Hunters also dispatched an operative with the nom de guerre Big Mac, who was a Muslim, and trained to befriend radical jihadis and gain their confidence. He had been recruited by the New York City Police Department Terror Intelligence Group and had been useful in supplying information regarding the first World Trade Center attack in 1993.

Mac was successful and got names of a group of four jihadis from Saudi Arabia and Iraq, who had been tasked with assassinating President Bush. They were promptly arrested, named as enemy combatants, and sent to military brigs for safe keeping.

Padilla was eventually afforded a civilian trial and sentenced to twenty-one years in federal prison.

Padilla and his mother Estela Lebron filed suit for damages against John Yoo, the U.S. government official and author of the so-called "torture memos." In May 2012 the U.S. Ninth Circuit Court of Appeals ruled against mother and jihadi, saying that "while his treatment may have amounted to torture, it was not defined as such legally in 2002–2003 when it occurred."

In 2009, Barack Obama declared war on the Mexican drug cartels. Fentanyl, heroin, and other drugs were streaming across the two-thousand-mile Mexican/U.S. border, causing an epidemic of misery, violence, and death in American cities.

In its wake came the cartels' savage means of enforcing their power: beheadings, savage beatings, and slashing machete attacks were common. Mutilated bodies were hung in public, in border cities, as a horrific reminder of the cartels' ruthlessness.

Even "no drama Obama" knew drastic steps had to be taken. He announced the spending of millions of dollars in equipment and that hundreds of additional personnel would be brought to bear, to seal the border, and rein in the drugs and violence.

In a rare case of cooperation between the drug lords, there was consensus they had to strike back in their traditional way: extreme violence. An *asesino* was to be dispatched to take out the American president, which would set a harsh example of the cartels' ruthless disregard for the power of the United States and its people.

Late in his second term, the Secret Service was alerted that President Obama was planning to play a round of golf at the Farm Neck Golf Club on Martha's Vineyard. That raised a red flag, because the Farm Neck Golf

Club is open to the public, and protecting Obama there during his annual summer vacations always proved to be a logistical nightmare at best. It's the opposite of Joint Base Andrews Golf Club in suburban Maryland, where they can lock down the entire base and deploy a small army to help protect the president.

"We were nervous about the situation to begin with, but then we got a Level III alert that a known assassin had arrived on the island at the same time as Obama," Ranger, who took part in the operation, told me. "He was a vicious Mexican drug cartel hit man, who had assassinated police officials and government reformers in Mexico. He had a lot of blood on his hands. He frequently beheaded his victims. His dossier was soaked in blood."

This information set off alarms on the bank of jumbo computer screens at the Secret Service Joint Operations Center on H Street in Washington, D.C. The duty officer in charge of the Intelligence and Assessment Division picked up his encrypted phone and alerted the deputy director of the Secret Service that they had a Level III threat—the most serious category—on their hands. Within minutes, word went out from the director of the Secret Service:

"Send the Hunters!"

The intel was that El Loco had a hard-on for Obama, obviously because he was hired to kill him, but it was also personal. He blamed the president for having deported him and his family of eight. He bragged that if he assassinated the American president, he'd become the most famous outlaw in Mexico.

"We weren't going to take any chances, so we flooded the island with Secret Service people, local Massachusetts law enforcement, and FBI. We were determined to flush this rat out of his hole no matter what it took," recalled one of the other agents, code-named Brownie, who was assigned to the operation.

"Naturally, Hawkeye CAT was there in force, ready to pounce. But the initial job was for the Hunters to track down the assassin and neutralize him.

"Incredibly, days went by and he couldn't be found. He was apparently still on the loose, either on the Vineyard or nearby. No one was willing to take a chance that he'd simply slipped away. That was not his M.O. He was a determined, savage killer and wasn't about to give up."

The Hunter, a combat veteran who, like Ranger, had served multiple tours in Afghanistan and Iraq, later recalled that when he read the dossier on the hit man, he felt his hands tremble slightly. That night he had a nightmare that the president was attacked by the man with a machete; he woke up from the dream covered in sweat.

"It's every agent's worst fear that harm will come to a person whose life is entrusted to him, and he will never be able to forgive himself for missing some clue that could have prevented it from happening.

"It was a very secret operation, and local law partners were only told El Loco was a 'person of interest.' But considering the number of local, state, and federal officers involved, it was remarkable that it stayed that way. I put together a team of my best men, including one of my friends, a Spanish-speaking man named Juan. I served with Juan in Iraq. He also had a great deal of experience serving as a U.S. drug enforcement agent in Mexico, working with the *Federales* down there. Juan had actually interrogated this individual during one of the times he was captured by the Mexican authorities and was quickly allowed to escape, probably due to a bribe, or threats to a Federal police officer's family.

"Unfortunately, when they say, 'we will kill your entire family,' they mean it, from a newborn baby to an aged grandmother, they will hack them all to death. It's a nightmare world, totally unfathomable.

"On the flight up to the Vineyard, Juan told me that the hit man was nicknamed El Loco, and that he was a master of disguise, who'd been an actor as a young man and did his own makeup. He was a big fan of John Wilkes Booth and often used the alias John Booth, among others. He spoke perfect English and had the ability to speak in accents from New England to a Southern drawl. A formidable adversary, and a dangerous psychopath.

"He was the personification of the cartel mentality.

"Despite being warned of the impending threat, President Obama insisted he was going to go ahead with his vacation schedule as planned. He scoffed at the idea that the virtual army we assembled to defend him couldn't hold off one crazed individual.

"The President was clearly calm and in good humor. He wasn't going to let the threat ruin his golf game or his summer vacation. We were the ones unable to sleep at night, putting in fourteen hour shifts and sweating bullets.

"But after days of an intensive manhunt, we still hadn't found El Loco. It was obviously a game to him, and he was very good at it. Many people were stopped and interviewed, and he was still on the loose.

"It was like searching for a ghost. Because he was known to be a master of disguise, every face was a suspicious one, even old ladies had to be looked over closely because he was known to disguise himself as one."

Finally, the Hunters got what they had been praying for: a tip that an undisguised John Booth had been spotted at a motel in Hyannis Port, just twenty-four miles of ocean away. The decision was made immediately not to alert local police and take the chance the killer would notice and vanish.

They sat in silence on the short Cape Air flight to Cape Cod Gateway Airport in Hyannis, hoping the break in the case would quickly end with the would-be assassins captured, and end the threat to the president, but both doubted the killer would sit around waiting for them to bust down his door in the harborfront tourist motel where he was holed up, just walking distance from ferries to the islands.

There was no need on the part of the two agents to articulate how unlikely it would be to bag their man easily.

Once they were wheels down at the small airport (that was used frequently by members of the Kennedy clan, coming and going to their famous Hyannis Port compound), they grabbed a cab, which dropped them a block from the hotel. Under cover of darkness the men approached the hotel from different sides, hands on their semiautomatic M11 Sig Sauer sidearms, hearts pounding, brows and armpits wet from perspiration despite the cool sea breeze.

Juan stationed himself in the darkness out of sight of the room, his Sig Sauer cocked and ready, while his partner Brownie approached the room and without a moment's hesitation kicked the flimsy door half off its hinges.

Aware that the situation reeked of a trap, Brownie backed off slightly to allow his eyes to adjust to the darkness. The situation was precarious because El Loco and his cartel were known to be aware of the existence of the Hunters, who had become a target of the drug gangs. While not on par with assassinating the leader of the Western world, killing a Secret Service operative would be a worthwhile appetizer for a cartel hit man, and a feather in his cap back home.

The two men instinctively crouched to present a smaller profile, and moved across the small, musty bedroom toward the closed door of the bath. Brownie stood quickly when he reached the door and with a practiced move put his 230-plus pounds and six-foot, five-inch frame into a solid kick, sending the door flying.

Juan shined his flashlight into the darkness, and both men reared back in shock: the bathroom was alive with dozens of snakes slithering to life, fangs bared and forked tongues waving. El Loco had left his calling card. The Hunters later learned that the hit man had tattoos of snakes on both arms and his chest.

Brownie told the author: "During three tours of duty in Afghanistan, I was seldom as scared as I was that night in Hyannis, Massachusetts. You expect any macabre shit to happen over there. But in Hyannis port?"

Animal control later reported they were non-venomous water snakes, but "the son-of-a-bitch had made his point."

Back at the Hyannis airport, both men had several double bourbons neat, before the flight back to Martha's Vineyard to resume their vigil, trying to save the president, and neutralize the would-be assassin.

"One of President Obama's protective Secret Service team told me that he'd overheard Michelle Obama arguing with her husband that he shouldn't go out and play golf while the threat existed. But Obama shrugged her off," said Brownie.

> When the day of the golf game came, we were at the highest state of alert. President Obama was covered by three times the usual number of guards. Hovering just behind the President and his team of protective detail agents was my team of four. I had a very strong feeling that El Loco was in the vicinity, had somehow penetrated all our security, and was set to strike.

Then, a man dressed as a groundskeeper suddenly seemed to appear out of nowhere and headed for the president. Juan spotted him, shouted, "That's goddamn El Loco!" Just as El Loco reached for his gun, all four of us pounced on him. Juan managed to wrest the weapon away and pinned him to the ground. He was unbelievably strong, but we got him handcuffed. It was the closest call I have ever seen to someone assassinating the president."

Incredibly, the president didn't appear to notice the scuffle, and continued with his game. The press was so concentrated on the president they barely noticed.

I was later asked by a reporter if there had been an incident. I said it was an unauthorized person who had to be removed.

The Hunters later learned that the would-be killer launched his clearly suicidal assassination attempt because he had been diagnosed with terminal cancer and wanted to die in a blaze of glory, and be a hero to the drug cartels all over Central America and Mexico.

He died before he could be tried.

As former Secret Service Uniformed Division Officer Gary Byrne wrote in his book *Secrets of the Secret Service*, "It was only luck and coincidence that so often saved President Obama's life. Many of those incidents were kept secret from President Obama, and they [were] surely being kept from Presidents Trump and Biden as well."

He writes about a harrowing incident when Obama was visiting the Centers for Disease Control and Prevention in Atlanta in 2014. An advance team from the agency screened "everyone...except the private armed security guards."

"A guard with a criminal history managed to get onto an elevator with the president—he simply walked past all of the Secret Service's security. He caught Secret Service's attention only when he started snapping pictures inches away from the president's face." Fortunately, Byrne writes, the man "who was armed with a handgun, wanted merely to snap a picture and not to shoot the president."

Threats against Obama were far more common than those of his predecessors, which analysts say is in some measure attributable to racism, but the other component was that his obvious, shining self-confidence spurred unstable people with little or no sense of confidence or self-worth to anger and rage.

A close friend of Barack Obama, who often slept in the Lincoln Bedroom during his presidency, said that Michelle had never wanted Barack to run for president, or any other electoral office.

> Michelle wanted Barack to be a rich, successful Chicago lawyer, not the most famous man in the world, who is loved and/or loathed by millions. She was not at all surprised that he became a magnet for death threats, both conventional and crazy, including attempts to get him with everything from ricin to pipe bombs and radioactive death rays.

> She saw it coming, and it became a major issue in their otherwise extremely happy marriage. She felt that he took far too many chances, especially when the Secret Service warned him that he was needlessly risking his life, and that there many bad players out to get him.

> Michelle often told him he should only play golf at places that could be completely secured, like Joint Base

Andrews. But he said he had complete faith in the Secret Service's ability to protect him.

Unfortunately, with all the nut jobs that were out to get him, the Secret Service couldn't pretend to be as confident as the President.

Michelle was wise enough to know that no security is perfect all the time, and when it came to his well-being, she worried a lot.

Michelle had a sometimes-contentious relationship with the agency, particularly when a guy who may have been controlled by Al Qaeda shot seven high-powered bullets toward the family quarters, while her mother and younger daughter were there alone.

But she worked hard to develop a relationship with the agency, and particularly the Hunters and Hawkeye CAT because she wanted—actually demanded—the unvarnished truth. Barack would often wave her concerns off, saying, "let them handle it, it's their job."

The Hunters, more so than the uniformed Secret Service, enthusiastically embraced Michelle's interest, because they wanted to know what the President and the First Lady were thinking. It's important they know the profile of the people they protect, and what their plans are in advance, so they can arrange security in a calm and measured way.

Michelle insisted that she be briefed on the threat levels, what attempts were intercepted, and how close they came to succeeding. She became their eyes and ears and did her best to convince Barack to take their warnings seriously, and even to modify his schedule to err on the side of safety. He went along with her at least some of the time, just to keep her happy.

The friend said that Obama did feel the pressure and the unique danger, and it took a toll on him.

Barack put his "no-drama Obama" face on in public and it was very convincing. But in private he showed the strain. He has a hard rubber ball that he pulls out of a drawer and squeezes extremely hard when he is under pressure. He puts on a face that the public never, ever sees—it reflects the angst in his secret soul. Then he bounces it off a White House wall and catches it. It's a way to ease the tension. It makes a tiny dent. One time I joked, "Dude, are they going to charge you for that when you check out of this place?"

The presidency is a cauldron of tensions that never eases up, day and night. He would get up in the middle of the night and wander around the family quarters, often squeezing the rubber ball.

Barack also occasionally took a small dose of edible marijuana to take the edge off. Obviously, he couldn't smoke anything because Michelle would have had a fit with the girls around, and it is illegal to smoke in the White House or any other federal government building, so he was very discreet about his use of pot.

Michelle once in a fit of pique said, "What's going to happen if you are high and a world crisis comes up?"

Barack quipped, "That's what Joe Biden is here for."

He certainly enjoyed the perks of the presidency and was proud to be the first black leader of the country, and hopefully a role model and inspiration to young black men. But toward the end of his second term Michelle was literally putting an X on her calendar when they had survived another day, and his presidency was soon to end.

When they moved out and into their own home on Connecticut Avenue, she felt like she was free again. It was a very happy day. Michelle was finally able to exhale. But then two years into civilian life she learned that somebody had sent a pipe bomb to their new address. It was, of course, intercepted by the Secret Service, but it was shocking to her that people were still out to get him.

She thought it was depressing and infuriating.

One of the most fraught jobs the Secret Service faces is protecting the president on overseas trips. Agents are routinely granted the right to carry weapons, and the president's limousine—the hugely fortified "Beast"—is allowed to be flown into all countries he visits. But for the most part, the job is only to react to a situation that is unfolding. The proactive stance is severely limited. The problem, especially in countries that bear hostility to the United States and her policies, is to know who are friends and who are foes.

Are there elements in the security forces of other nations that may have bad intent toward the president? That element, which must always be kept in mind, complicates the job tremendously. Agents must keep a suspicious eye on their host's armed security forces, as well as looking out for conventional dangers.

In most cases the Service is allowed to have advance men in place to examine the hotel where the president will stay. They also like to look at the names of people staying at the hotel while he is going to be there. But in some circumstances the hotel will refuse, supposedly for "privacy reasons."

The Hunters are a solution to much of the problems. Operating separately from the protective division of which they are a part, they can rely upon relationships with trusted local police and security, learn the chatter about possible threats, and be proactive about interfering in any plots.

During President Obama's first one hundred days in office in 2009, he attended a NATO summit in Strasbourg, France, before going to Istanbul, Turkey for the final leg of his trip. Ranger and several Hawkeye CAT men were in Istanbul in advance, leaving the relatively predictable and safe visit to France exclusively in the hands of the protective services.

> We had heard buzz that a Syrian man was going to be masquerading as an Al Jazeera journalist with phony credentials to infiltrate security. The report was that he had been sent by ISIS to assassinate the president. Turkish security had the man on their watch list, but when we arrived, had not made a move to detain and interrogate him.
>
> It was one of those infuriating situations where there is little you can do. We certainly weren't authorized to arrest the man if local authorities weren't interested in taking action.
>
> All we could do was watch him and hope he would do something to trigger action on the part of Turkish security. It was skating on the edge of a razor, because we couldn't do anything that would turn into an international incident. We knew the Turkish police and security were

very touchy about foreigners stepping on their toes, as was the Turkish government.

Relations between the two nations was never warm and fuzzy, despite Turkey theoretically being a U.S. ally and NATO partner, to say the least.

Our marching orders are always to try to work closely with the host country and to be respectful and restrained. But we had this guy in our crosshairs the whole time while we waited for the president's arrival. There was no attempt to not let him know he was being followed and surveilled 24/7.

We got into his trashy hotel room, rummaged through his belongings, looking for contraband that would force Turkish police to arrest him. But more than that, it was psychological war. We wanted to spook him.

It became a cat and mouse game. There were four of us and he was always being followed. Finally, he snapped and pulled a knife on one of the guys, screaming like a man possessed. We had driven him crazy. It happened in a bazaar and a police officer immediately nailed him.

We were assured he was in a Turkish prison and would be kept in very uncomfortable conditions long after President Obama was safely back in the White House.

Our job was over. The president arrived the next day without incident and we went home.

In early 2010, Osama bin Laden was desperate to turn the war in Afghanistan around. His forces were helplessly outnumbered, outgunned and were suffering unsustainable casualties.

His solution was to order his Pakistani lieutenant Ilyas Kashmiri to kill President Obama. The calculus was that assassinating Obama would make Joe Biden president, a job that Biden was "totally unprepared" to fulfill, according to the terrorist's assessment.

When the National Security Agency intercepted satellite telephone conversations alluding to the plot, an emergency joint committee was formed to oversee a defense against the scheme. Members of the FBI, CIA, and Secret Service met in a secure room at the FBI Bureau on Pennsylvania Avenue in Washington.

Kashmiri was said to be bin Laden's hand-picked successor and had been tagged as "the most dangerous man in the world" by CNN. The U.S. government and even the United Nations—normally reticent at riling state sponsors of terror—had officially designated him a terrorist.

The terrorist was responsible for ordering twelve coordinated shooting and bomb attacks in Mumbai, India, which killed at least 174 and wounded well over 300. Targeted were hospitals, movie theaters, hotels, and other soft targets.

All the attackers were killed by Mumbai Police and National Security Guards, but Kashmiri had made his point that he could send his troops on a mass murder mission anywhere in the world.

The late journalist Syed Saleem Shahzad called him "the most effective, dangerous and successful guerilla leader in the world." Shahzad was an investigative journalist based in his native Pakistan, who wrote extensively about Kashmiri and Al Qaeda for European and Asian publications and television.

On May 30, 2011 he was found dead in a canal in Northeast Pakistan. He had been tortured and mutilated, and clearly left to be a warning to others who wanted to "investigate" the "most dangerous man on earth."

The joint intel group was convinced that Kashmiri would never travel to the U.S. to carry out the crime himself, because he would almost certainly be nabbed going through customs. Instead, he would appoint an assassin, likely one who was already in the states. Someone well-trained and skilled, but who didn't have Kashmiri's notoriety, could fly under the radar. He would also probably be a jihadi. And there would probably be not one, but several killers assigned, operating independently, coming in waves, until the job was done. The assassination order clearly came from the top—bin Laden—and many of his soldiers would happily give their lives to carry out his wishes.

There was unanimous agreement that the president's security would have to be ratcheted up to unprecedented heights. There was also agreement that Barack Obama was going to be a very hard man to sell on living behind barricades and severely limiting contact with the public.

A Secret Service agent who was on Biden's protective team later said, "Biden wasn't convinced they would kill Obama and let him live and become president. He was convinced he was in mortal danger as well. Frankly, he was terrified and cancelled all public appearances, and refused to leave the Vice President's Residence in the heavily fortified U.S. Naval Observatory.

The Obama friend said, "Obama laughed at him saying, 'I'm the one they're after. I should be hiding out, not you.'"

Obama kept to his schedule because he was completely convinced his agents had his back. Biden disappeared from view for a long while.

"There is a steel and concrete fortified safe house in the VP mansion and he spent most of his time there, with it locked down as if there had been a nuclear exchange, for which it is designed."

The Hunters in the joint intel task force regaled their partners with tales of Obama's insouciance in the face of dire danger. The protection plan against the Kashmiri-led Al Qaeda onslaught would have to be largely a stealth project, done with little cooperation on the president's part.

One of the many concerns was the Obama family's quite reasonable, almost impromptu parties with actors, musicians, and various Hollywood friends and supporters, who often came with an entourage, frequently with little time for Secret Service vetting regarding security concerns. The dazzling star-studded parties included Hollywood's greatest stars, including Meryl Streep, Tom Hanks, Paul McCartney, Beyoncé, Usher, and Oprah. One Halloween, they threw a costume bash, with stars dressed in full, elaborately conceived costumes. George Lucas loaned the original Chewbacca costume to one guest, and Johnny Depp staged the Mad Hatter's Tea Party in the State Dining Room.

They were dazzling, almost *Great Gatsby*–like affairs, but a nightmare for security. Entourages, some of whom came into the White House and joined the party, were worrisome to the agency. The affairs often lasted until the early hours of the morning, which necessitated agents working very long hours. Also, many of the stars came with their own security details, who stayed outside with the limos but had to be watched constantly by Secret Service, simply because they were on White House grounds and hadn't been vetted.

At one Obama extravaganza, according to the *New York Times*, Leonardo DiCaprio, Ashton Kutcher, and Demi Moore were asked by Secret Service to wait outside of the mansion in the cold for additional security checks. The First Family expressed their displeasure, suggesting it had better not happen again.

Comedian Billy Eichner later explained to Ellen DeGeneres how amazing one bash was. "You're on-line going through security with David Letterman, Bruce Springsteen, Stevie Wonder, and Paul McCartney. It's two in the morning, and the president has his sleeves rolled up and a couple of buttons down, and he's, like, breaking it down on the dance floor. Questlove is blasting Kendrick Lamar in the White House, next to a huge picture of Mary Todd Lincoln."

CHAPTER THREE

The All New Osama Bin Laden

O n the other side of the world, Ayman al-Zawahiri, the new head of Al Qaeda, sat in his Karachi, Pakistan apartment where he lived under the protection of the feared Pakistani Inter-Services Intelligence (ISI). The terror chief was comfortably ensconced at the exclusive Rabia Enclave in a large apartment with marble steps and wrought iron fixtures, decorated rather bizarrely with French brothel-style furniture.

Zawahiri was born in 1951 in Egypt, south of Cairo, the progeny of a distinguished family, who grew up a pious boy immersed in strict Sunni Islamic religion. The family has long clung to the generationally repeated tale that they have ancestors from the Harb tribe in the Saudi city of Zawahiri, where in Muslim lore the Prophet Muhammad defeated the infidels and established the Islamic religion in the Middle East. The terror leader attributes the fire in his belly to his familial connections to the prophet. His grandfather Sheikh Ibrahim Al Zawahiri was, truthfully, revered in the Nile Delta city of Tanta, where a mosque still stands that bears his name. His grandfather was an Imam, and his father a professor of Pharmacology at Cairo University.

In short, he was neither poor nor put-upon. His terrorist zeal was born of religious conviction and a fierce belief in the righteousness that violence, however draconian and regardless of the innocence of the victims, is always justified when done in the name of Allah. Growing up, he became obsessed with the writings of the violence-imbued Islamic zealot Sayyid Qutb, who once declared, "In the world there is only one party, the party of Allah; all of the others are parties of Satan."

At age fifteen, he began working to create a movement to violently overthrow the Egyptian government and replace it with strict Sharia Islamic rule. Clearly Zawahiri took the words of Qutb to heart. At sixteen, he joined the jihad cell of Said Tantawi, where he learned to assemble improvised explosive devices and suicide vests, and gained an efficiency in handling the AK-47 automatic rifle.

Following the assassination of President Anwar Sadat, he was caught in a police sweep of known jihadis, imprisoned, and tortured, as was customary. Zawahiri cracked under the agony and gave up the location of a leader of the movement, al-Qamari, who was arrested and summarily executed. As a reward, Zawahiri was released, but soon was again arrested and imprisoned.

It is claimed by his supporters and acolytes that the guilt and pain he suffered over that youthful betrayal of one of his Islamic heroes spurs on an enraged inner demon to mastermind the next 9/11-style mega-tragedy. Plus constant plotting of assassinations, even a biological weapon holocaust—according to U.S. intelligence, including Secret Service Hunters' surveillance, is his favorite means of mass murder.

The humiliating defeat of Egypt in the Six-Day War in 1967 against Israel, when Jews and many Christian supporters volunteered to fight for the state of Israel, demoralized Zawahiri's generation. According to his memoir, the defeat radicalized many of his countrymen, and convinced him to become one of the architects, and arguably the mastermind, of the future ultra-radical, ultra-violent Al Qaeda.

In the years leading up to 9/11, Osama bin Laden would emerge as the front man, the voice, the firebrand, but Dr. Zawahiri would be the brains, spinning the web of monstrous plots.

★★★

As a youth, while professing to be at war with the government, Zawahiri attended Cairo University and became a physician and surgeon. And despite his murderous, fanatical loathing of the Egyptian government and sacred vow to destroy it and kill its officials, he joined the army and served with the Red Crescent in Pakistan during the Afghan War. It was claimed by both friend and foe that he wanted to be trained in military matters by the Egyptians, so that he could later use that knowledge against them.

Back in Egypt after the war, he continued his militant clandestine actions against the government—a true fifth columnist. During one of the endless dragnets that continued for years, by federal police in response to the assassinations and general unrest, he was again arrested, this time on firearms charges, and sentenced to three years in prison. He later said he had been tortured once again in prison, which added a red badge of courage to his reputation, elevated his stock among other young militants, and spiked his determination to violently overthrow the government.

When he was released, Zawahiri fled to Saudi Arabia and rekindled his friendship and camaraderie with wealthy and equally high-born Osama bin Laden, who had plans to create a world-wide terror organization called Al Qaeda, designed to spread chaos and bloodshed in both Muslim and non-Muslim countries, and to eventually establish a caliphate in the Middle East. Zawahiri signed on as the philosophical and propaganda leader in the terror organization and became highly involved in the planning of the bombing of the U.S. Navy destroyer USS *Cole*, as well as the attacks on September 11, 2001. After each murderous attack, it was Zawahiri's job to explain to sympathizers in the Islamic world why the slaughter of non-combatants, women, and children was justified, and why they should continue donating lucre, as well as their sons, to support more such atrocities in the name of Allah. His skill with words and mastery of several languages made him a natural as the official spokesman, apologist, and cheerleader for Al Qaeda, and to become bin Laden's number two. In May of 2011, with bin Laden's execution by Navy SEAL Team Six, he became the group's formal leader.

Almost twenty years later, al Zawahiri was watching U.S. cable news on a big flat screen TV connected to satellite, switching from MSNBC to Fox to CNN, occasionally stopping at the Cartoon Network, which made him giggle and sometimes nearly double over in hilarity (according to Secret Service intelligence, which closely monitored the terror chief). What caught his rapt interest was Joe Biden becoming president and the riots in the streets of American cities, and in the Capitol itself. His friend and mentor Osama bin Laden had assured him that Biden was incompetent and quite probably suffered from dementia. Bin Laden had at one time hatched a plan to assassinate Barack Obama with the sole goal of making Biden president.

Biden's election and the obviously chaotic state in America convinced Zawahiri it was time to strike a death blow to America and avenge the death of his mentor and brother-in-arms.

"Inshallah," he said with a broad smile and an ironic laugh.

Zawahiri had always been a virulent anti-Semite, who grew up despising the very existence of a Jewish state in the Middle East, in the heart of land that he believed Allah meant to be the soul and sacred heart of the Muslim homeland—the caliphate.

His goal had always been to violently push the Jewish nation into the sea and salt the land they had defiled, in his warped mind, for so long.

The terror leader was a secret admirer of Adolph Hitler, even though the Führer was an infidel. He had studied the Holocaust and wondered if, in a caliphate incorporating hopefully most of the Middle East, another such slaughter would be possible. Many of his followers agreed it would be imaginable to solve the Jewish problem in the region for good—by mass murder. He was convinced the only way to carry out mass genocide would be either biological or nuclear weapons, and he had jihadis from around the world working hard to bring both to him.

Al Zawahiri was convinced that reports that Biden had voted not to take bin Laden out when he was in the special ops crosshairs proved bin Laden's point that the new American president lacked the mettle to fight, and would cave when confronted with the magnitude of Zawahiri's plan for a final solution.

He even joked that if Biden had been in Dwight Eisenhower's shoes in June of 1944, he wouldn't have had the nerve to give the go-ahead for the D-Day Invasion. Terror-meisters ferret out weakness, and bin Laden and Zawahiri had sensed it in Joe Biden. With an American president who apparently had so little backbone, the golden age of terror could begin. Zawahiri reasoned that Al Qaeda could run rampant with Biden's unsteady hand on the tiller of the U.S. military and government.

But the new terror chief had a big problem: he was considered by many to be boring and uninspiring. He was considered a pedantic old uncle with none of Osama's sinister charm and menacing charisma. Even Zawahiri had to admit he wasn't a stirring speech maker and probably couldn't convince men to die for him. He needed lieutenants to accomplish that, which even he perceived as a personal weakness, inspiring fervent prayers to Allah to make him stronger and more inspiring.

In addition, the U.S. government was offering a $25 million reward for his scalp, which severely limited his mobility, and made a number of his gun-shy followers avoid meeting with him in the flesh, out of fear the Navy SEALs could show up any time with SEAL recon rifles blazing.

It was obvious he needed a big, gruesome hit—as spectacular and bloody as Osama's 9/11 attack. But his operatives in America told him that kind of elaborate operation would be impossible with all the new airport protections in effect, and the militarization of the Secret Service. Plus, trusted advisors warned that most of the soldiers available to him in the United States, for such a mission, were far less than 100 percent reliable.

His decision was that President Biden had to be assassinated, which he knew would horrify the Western world, causing panic and confusion, and galvanizing his position as head of Al Qaeda, and the world terror movement. He was sure his mentor bin Laden—whom he always referred to respectfully as "the Emir," meaning "commander"—would approve.

He was presented with many plans for the killing of Biden, but his favorite was the scheme to plant a poison gas bomb with both ricin and Ebola in the White House. One of his operatives could simply take the public White House tour and plant the device. It would be very small and made of plastic to avoid setting off metal detectors. One idea was that the martyr would be in a wheelchair giving cover, including disguising the bomb as an oxygen tank.

The poisons would do a truly horrific job of killing and would spread around the nation's capital, dealing a devastating blow to the U.S. government, which would effectively grind to a halt. It would turn out to be an atrocity, possibly an outrage and tragedy on the scale of the 9/11 carnage.

He was assured that Washington, D.C. would have to be evacuated and the death toll would be in the thousands and possibly more.

He would become as notorious and feared as bin Laden had been. And he would gain the respect and fear he had craved all his life.

Several of his soldiers had done the White House tour and mapped out places where such a device could be dropped off and likely wouldn't be found until it was too late. Of course, the bomber would be a martyr; it would be set to explode and spread the pathogens while he was still there, and maybe still holding it. But that wasn't a concern.

While the planning for assassinating the new American president was underway, Zawahiri had an uninvited visitor he wasn't yet aware of: a former Army Ranger who had served in the Afghanistan war in special ops, and had been awarded a Bronze Star, with a "V" for valor, for uncovering a Taliban lab dedicated to producing weaponized pathogens designed to kill American and allied soldiers prosecuting the war.

His code name was "Ranger" or "the Captain"—which had been his rank in the Army Rangers—and he was happily married to Army biochem expert "Laredo." Ranger was now a member of the Proactive Response

Team, or Hunters—an elite group of Secret Service agents who worked closely with Hawkeye CAT. It was their job to track down individuals who threatened American presidents and other government officials, before they could carry out their vile plans.

His group was known colloquially as "the Hunters" because that is essentially what they do: pursue bad players who seek to harm the men, women, and children under Secret Service protection; get useful intelligence about their plans; and, if they have bad intentions, see to it they are stopped before they can act—not like in the past when agents acted after the fact, when it was too late, and the fusillade had already flown or the dirty bomb ignited.

Ranger had moved into the apartment next to the Al Qaeda leader. He immediately wired the apartment walls to monitor Zawahiri's every conversation and determine who his current lieutenants in America were, and hopefully the identity of the chosen Biden assassin(s). He did not have orders to execute Zawahiri, which he regretted, because he was convinced the terror chief was going to carry out a plot against America sooner rather than later, but his bosses felt it would be a bad time to upset the Pakistani government again, just after the repercussions from taking out bin Laden in the country.

Once he was in the building, Ranger began planting bugs that it was very unlikely would be found anytime soon. Naturally, the terror chief's telephone calls were "dark," meaning they were encrypted. The good news was the encryption equipment he was using was relatively primitive, and Ranger had the means to easily and quickly decode his conversations.

The equipment Zawahiri was using would be good enough to keep his plans, and the names and locations of his operatives, safe from Pakistani Intelligence, which would be important to blind them to the nefarious schemes he was hatching in their backyard. But Ranger's state-of-the-art decoding was more than capable of reading every word and location.

He was sorry he didn't have orders to terminate, because he felt the terror chief was probably at that moment the most dangerous man in the world, and needed to be dead. But it would have been more complicated in a crowded urban city than it had been for SEAL Team Six to execute Obama in his remote country hideaway.

Also, Ranger didn't have a team with helicopters waiting. His only collaborator was a former special ops man who had served under him in Afghanistan. He was fluent in Urdu, the national language of Pakistan, as well as Arabic and Pashto, so he could provide instant translation of the eavesdropping. He was also a skilled and ruthless fighter, should the worst happen. Ranger had been with him in some intense and bloody battles and knew that he could entrust his life to this man.

Ranger stood six foot two with a body that was all muscle and he was a natural born fighter. He had been in Pakistan many times—not as a tourist who displays a passport, rather as a marauder who led small platoons of Army Rangers on raids at zero dark thirty, to attack Taliban safe houses where high value targets were holed up planning terror operations.

When Ranger and his cadre moved in for the kill, there was always a prop-driven AC-130 Spectre gunship in close support. The plane was incredibly agile and could go in tight circles at low altitude, pouring thousands of rounds of ultra-high-powered ordnance into the target.

The Spectre carries a 105mm cannon and numerous electric Gatling guns to soften up the enemy. It is called, and not in a jocular sense, "the angel of death." By the time it had accomplished its task, the target would be as soft as a feather pillow.

Zawahiri repeatedly said he knew the Americans were determined to get him and probably would, sooner rather than later. In conversations Ranger monitored, Zawahiri seemed to accept that he was going to be killed eventually, like his mentor bin Laden, and was going to be a martyr in Osama's dark world of terror. In fact, rumors of Zawahiri's death were so common and persistent that most knowledgeable reporters in the Arab world sloughed them off. Still Zawahiri realized he had a target on his back. One day rumor would be a fact. His failing health, including severe asthma, would cull him, or a U.S. special ops team would do the deed.

But Zawahiri intended to make the most of the time he had left to bring the organization up to date, by recruiting new young soldiers willing to die for the cause. The start was to update the training and recruiting video. Tapes of 9/11 had been used since the attack. Everyone in the world had seen them, and the images of the falling towers no longer packed the punch they once had.

Ranger later said, "Zawahiri is always dressed in a white turban and sporting his dark grey beard, looking like a harsh and vindictive Ayatollah, but the surprise to me was that he had a sense of humor and even a grasp of irony. That's not to say he isn't a fan of mass death and destruction, because he certainly is, but he is also a big employer of sarcasm."

A valuable resource for Secret Service agents and soldiers comes from reports produced by West Point's Combating Terrorism Center. The center closely monitored online pronouncements of Al Qaeda and other sponsors of terror, particularly al Zawahiri, to find out details of the new leader's strategy and ideology, including important clues as to what he planned for the world-wide network, as well as information on his resources, broken down by country.

When reporters contacted him, he had the temerity to promptly reply, which set him apart from most garden-variety terror merchants. The West Point analysts reported that Zawahiri had once sarcastically criticized an unauthorized biography of him, claiming it was full of errors and misspellings of names and places. He made a video in which he said, "They have enormous budgets, then they have me come along and correct their mistakes for free." He also joked about the writers "copious knowledge and integrity," obviously meaning his critics have neither knowledge nor integrity.

Jarret Brachman, a private scholar and former research director of the Combating Terrorism Center, and now a private security consultant, writes that since Zawahiri was so obviously bothered by criticism and paid close attention to it, the anti-terror people should have taken advantage of his hyper-sensitivity. He gave examples of Al Qaeda's embarrassing failures, and remarked that they are a very "image-conscious enemy" which desperately needs to be seen as competent in order to recruit young men and do fund-raising all over the world. A terror outfit that appears incompetent doesn't scare anyone, and terror is, after all, their only product.

Brachman writes that the U.S. government anti-terror forces should therefore give a lot of publicity to, and mercilessly rub in, the facts that the first attempt at bombing the USS Cole in Yemen failed because the would-be bombers' dingy sank, and the actual bombing wasn't filmed because the camera man overslept—incredibly inept, Keystone Kops terrorists. And the "shoe bomber" and "underwear bomber" were not quite crack assassins either.

He also points out that the super best-selling book *Freakonomics* detailed that a 1940s radio show caused the Ku Klux Klan members to become demoralized, causing membership and often murderous, racist activities to greatly decline. *The Adventures of Superman* comics had the Man of Steel in a satirical battle with the Klan, which made them look stupid and incompetent. A few years later the hate group all but ceased to exist.

Making Al Qaeda look as foolish and inept as they frequently are might prove to be their Kryptonite.

Ranger was up late. While the bustling streets of Karachi were sleeping, he was busy enabling a device that scrambles all electronic devices—including camera monitors, cell phones and listening devices—and would shut down everything in the apartment building. The scrambler, developed by the United States Air Force, is also used to set off improvised explosive devices and is carried on EA-6B airplanes which he learned to love and rely on during his tours in Afghanistan.

The technology has, without a doubt, saved thousands of soldiers from horrific injury or death in the asymmetrical warfare we have fought for over two decades in the Middle East, and has aborted further terror attacks on the American homeland.

But Ranger only needed to blind Zawahiri while he installed hidden cameras to record his visitors, as well as his comings and goings, and for that, a portable version of the electronic intruder did the job nicely.

He was finished just before dawn, satisfied that American intel was going to have real-time knowledge of what the terror chief was up to, even after Ranger had to take his leave from Pakistan, for whatever reason.

For Ranger knew, from hard experience with the volatile Pakistani Intel people, that he might be given the warm welcome and a glass of vodka one day, and rapid, rude expulsion from the country the next.

It was traditional regional politics, as well as standard spy craft.

Ranger was known to the Pakistani intelligence agency. They were aware that he had been leading raids on the Taliban across the Afghan–Pakistani border while they had been, for years, privately assuring the terror group they were safe under Pakistani protection. Pakistani intelligence knew it lacked the power to stop American and allied troops from surreptitiously crossing the border on a whim and leveling out Taliban strongholds at will—a Ranger specialty.

The Captain, as the Pakistanis called Ranger, single-handedly threw a wrench in the works by repeatedly crossing the border—in their view, illegally—to blow up safe houses with Taliban high value targets inside. His men then invaded, taking hard drives, flash drives, and anything else containing information about Taliban tactics and plans, and laid waste to everything that remained. But most aggravating to the Pakistani Inter-Services Intelligence (ISI) was that Ranger turned over to the United States government damning intel evidence that the so-called U.S. ally was, in fact, in bed with the Taliban and Al Qaeda.

The United States government was well aware, moreover, of the Pakistani sympathy toward the jihadis. After all, their Supreme Court had overturned the murder conviction and life sentence of Ahmad Omar Saeed Sheikh, who had brutally murdered and beheaded Wall Street Journal reporter Daniel Pearl.

Pending appeals from the Pearl family and U.S. government, the killer had been released from prison and installed in a government "safe house" where he could have conjugal visits with his wife and visits with his children. It was a source of consternation and anger in Washington.

Ranger had numerous face-to-face encounters with ISI and even drank shots of Pakistani Bolskaya Vodka with his counterparts on occasion. He was convinced they had a grudging respect for him and would expel him from the country if he was caught, but probably wouldn't arrest him. It was a comradeship of chess masters, intelligence rogues, who play by their own rules—frequently rules that are improvised situationally.

Meanwhile, while Ranger was busy installing the spy cams, Zawahiri was awake and cursing that all his devices had gone blank and his big screen satellite television was dark, including the channel that showed *South Park*, which he felt kept him up on American politics and zeitgeist. He couldn't even call his lieutenants to blast them over it. Instead, he whined loudly to himself and his cat, a captive audience.

He knew what was going on. Either the Russians or the Americans were screwing with his head. Zawahiri knew they were the only countries who possessed and regularly used electronic intruders and this set off alarms in his head, for this meant they knew exactly where he was and could come and get him any time they chose. He was going to have to pack up and move, which he loathed doing because he was very at home in the Rabia section of Karachi.

Losing television connection to the world was bad enough, but having his internet down meant being unable to make regular pronouncements and answer queries from the world, which meant there would immediately be rumors he was dead. That was somewhat upsetting, though oddly he found it amusing, because it always caused a nasty scramble to see who was going to come out top terror dog.

His only real comfort in the situation was his hairless Rex cat, which was sitting on his lap purring as usual. He had decided he needed a cat after watching the Ernst Stavro Blofeld villain in the Bond movies, but couldn't have a long-haired Persian like Blofeld, because it would irritate his allergies and might lead to a potentially lethal asthma attack—an ailment which had bedeviled him all his life.

Zawahiri, like his old friend Osama, reveled in being a villain. The wicked but clever characters in his favorite movies were always the bad guys, which didn't diminish for a second his utter conviction that Allah was on his side and that the terror he created was Allah's righteous revenge against the infidels.

A few days later Ranger listened to a conversation the terror chief had with a lieutenant, bemoaning the electronic intrusion—which he called a "high tech rape" for which he swore to "get revenge."

Hearing his anguish and rage was most satisfying to Ranger. But most important was intel pin-pointing the terrorists' locations. Zawahiri had given away the plot with actionable information. Within hours the bad guys and their poison bombs were captured and the terrorists forced to give up handlers and equipment that had been smuggled into the U.S.

Mission accomplished.

But the larger mission of ending the terror chiefs reign would take several years. Ranger's last eavesdrop of the terror chief was Zawahiri calling to his troops for "muscle." Considering that Ranger had gathered enough intel about his safe houses and future plans to sign his death warrant, he packed up and made his way to Lahore, where he caught a commercial Qatar Airlines flight to London.

His report, totaling over one hundred typewritten pages was turned in immediately after he was back in D.C. It was classified as Top Secret and distributed to the CIA and other top intel agencies who had al Zawahiri on their priority hit lists.

Diagnosing himself as suffering from exhaustion, Ranger went to bed and slept for the better part of two days, sleep made restless by vivid dreams of a drone shrieking through an amber-tinged sky and exploding in al Zawahiri's bedroom, leaving only his smoking head intact.

It didn't matter to him that it took almost a solid year for the execution to take place. He was satisfied that he had been one of the agents to silence the key strategist "behind an international campaign of terror that culminated in the September 11 attacks on the U.S."

The kill chain had dispensed its rough justice again.

CHAPTER FOUR

The Reckoning

A series of catastrophic terror attacks, both domestic and foreign, rocked America, leading up to the historically worst of all time on September 11, 2001. The attack on the World Trade Towers that cost more than three thousand deaths immediately and many more from the toxic fallout, changed everything.

The U.S. intelligence agencies realized their counter assault efforts had to be stepped up drastically.

America went to war with radical Islam in the Middle East and quietly reorganized the intelligence operations from top to bottom.

The old model of gentlemanly Secret Service men just waiting for an assassin to "bring it on," waiting for a rifle attack to be launched from a darkened window, would obviously no longer cut it.

The attempted assassination of Ronald Reagan had been a key event in undertaking the transformation, after which Nancy Reagan told top advisor, family friend, and presidential advisor Michael Deaver, "We've got to ramp this organization up. I want the Secret Service to become an organization with such grit and power, no one will ever dare to point another gun at a president of the United States."

The first step in finding a solution was to create and deploy a tactical, combat-ready team of battle-hardened soldiers called a Counter Assault Team (CAT), which would travel with the presidential motorcades in their own vehicle. In the beginning they were lightly armed with .38 caliber revolvers, because there was an understandable early reluctance to arm men with weapons of war. (The compromise was that one of the crew would have instant access to the firepower of an Uzi submachine gun.)

As the group grew dramatically in numbers and budget, they recruited soldiers with backgrounds in Special Forces, including Army Rangers and Navy SEALs. And, as the terror threat became too obvious to deny, Hawkeye CAT's armament improved as well.

That is Nancy Reagan's quiet legacy—o she was publicly mum about it, but very proud to claim it in private company.

Realizing they would inevitably find themselves confronting ruthless and often suicidal terrorists, the Hawkeye CAT pioneers were issued bulletproof Suburban SUVs and armed with fully automatic assault weapons—the Knights Armament SR-16s. The SR-1 machine gun fires a 5.56mm NATO round and is capable of firing 750 rounds per minute. You don't want to be on the business end of such a gun.

The vehicles Hawkeye CAT rides in motorcades are today literally bristling with weapons—they are fortresses on wheels, with a heavy machine gun that pops up out of the specially modified sun roof, with a Hawkeye CAT man wielding it with the ability to swing it around 360 degrees.

That was roughly the kind of harsh blowback that Nancy Reagan had demanded for the protection of all future American presidents. It was the vengeance she wanted against future would-be killers, following the attempted assassination of her "Ronnie," her "room-mate" and "best friend."

Hawkeye CAT is no longer shy about showing its firepower and is prepared to use it if necessary, if and when it gets the order. Its soldiers also carry flash bang grenades and other weapons.

After getting off to a shaky start as a new elite group within an elite organization that plays by rules of military engagement rather than police procedures, it has gained respect. Its soldiers are now highly trained and equipped with state-of-the-art armament, and capable of taking on and defeating the fiercest terror outfit.

In the event of a full-out terror attack, in an attempt to kill or even kidnap the American president, the regular Secret Service Presidential Protective Division would speed away with the president's armored limousine, while the Hawkeye CAT soldiers would lay down suppressive automatic weapons fire and flash bang grenades, allowing the rest of the motorcade and the president to escape, hopefully unscathed.

Their orders are straight forward: attack and destroy any violent threat to the president and others under their protection with awesome and overwhelming fire power. Their orders do not involve taking prisoners and they aren't equipped to do that; there's no space in their vehicle for prisoners and they are not issued hand cuffs. The uniformed Secret Service and local police can mop up after Hawkeye CAT has carried out its duty. They were not designed to be a defensive organization.

Because of their fearsome reputation, many in the gentlemanly and highly traditional Secret Service made no secret that they thought CAT was ruining the image of the Secret Service with their "thuggish, Sgt. Rock, tough soldier look," and lobbied for their abolition in the mid-1980s. Known for physical prowess and backgrounds in special ops, they were sometimes shunned by the button-down, old-fashioned agents who dated back to the JFK and LBJ days—in the eyes of the CAT men: the skinny black-tie fraternity.

Some Secret Service supervisors thought CAT men unseemly, with their brazen displays of firepower and combat uniforms. They thought they were not suited for polite company, whether in the White House or in kings' palaces overseas. It was even strongly suggested they cover up their proudly bulging biceps.

Fortunately for the nascent Hawkeye CAT, the opposition didn't have the bandwidth to publicly make their case, because, after all, they were *Secret* Service and sworn to public silence about their tactics and design, and especially internal squabbles.

It's a fact that Hawkeye CAT's sole mission is not to defend per se, but instead to attack and defeat. It is unlike any other domestically based quasi-police organization. Hence, it has required firm orders from the highest levels of command to ensure Hawkeye has gotten a permanent seat at the table.

But while the debate raged within the Service, some of the larger field offices—including Los Angeles, Miami, Chicago, and New York—had already allied themselves with groups like the crack Anti-Terrorism Unit,

New York City Police Department Counterterrorism Bureau (CT), which had far greater resources and networks of informants in terror fighting, but did not have the funding level of the Secret Service or the legal ability to operate across state borders. The Secret Service field offices, grateful for the assistance, and at home with the terror cop culture, provided them with both. In some cases, the two groups became better friends and colleagues with each other, than with colleagues in their respective agencies.

Hawkeye CAT officers—the "kill team"—do not wear black suits and jog alongside the President's "Beast." They wear black combat uniforms and are protected by thick Kevlar body armor, making them look even more formidable.

The team also deploys with the Vice President, foreign dignitaries on official business in the United States, and the minor children of officials under their protection.

At about the same time, the Service created a Proactive Response Team, charged with hunting down bad players who posed an active threat to the protected, including ex-presidents, their minor children, wives, and senior government officials. The proactive group, which came to be known colloquially as the Hunters, would capture or eliminate dangerous threats *before* the damage was done.

Hawkeye CAT and the Hunters were designed to be the "street fighting" wing of the Secret Service and the combined last line of defense against a terror attack on the top layers of American government, which, of course, seems sadly inevitable today.

The former Navy SEALs, Army Rangers, and other special ops veterans who make up the two forces are the strong sinew that holds the president's shield of protection in place, and the state-of-the-art equipment and weaponry they rely on make the two groups formidable foes for any potential adversary, whether at home or abroad.

The so-called "Beast" limousine that transports the President more closely resembles a tank than a car. It weighs 6.2 tons and the presidential compartment in the rear has multiple glass partitions, five layers of bullet proof glass, and a satellite phone which connects directly and instantly to the vice president and the Pentagon high command. The doors have eight inches of armor, and the fuel tank is likewise armor plated, and guaranteed not to explode even if hit by ricochets or an explosion.

The Beast has multiple tear gas launchers, front and rear, as well as James-Bond-like smoke screens, also front and rear. There is always a refrigerated bag of the President's blood in the car—CAT has trained medics that travel in the motorcade with the team, as well as a doctor on twenty-four-hour call for worst case scenarios—as well as semiautomatic twelve gauge shot guns. For added insurance, there is always an identical Beast following or leading. If the bad guys picked the wrong limo, they would get a nasty "lady or the tiger" type surprise, because its passengers are heavily armed Hawkeye CAT soldiers.

The main conveyance for CAT soldiers is a Command SUV converted for special ops use, called a "Roadrunner." It is equipped with UHF Satellite Communications antennae and encrypted computer systems that can keep secure lines of communication open with FBI, CIA, and the Pentagon in the event of a massive terror attack or other crisis, in order to keep the "continuity of government" functioning through even the worst cataclysmic event.

The Roadrunners have special concealed caches holding extra magazines of high-powered ammunition, and other war materiel that can be accessed by the touch of a button. They are modern urban warfare quasi-tanks, specially designed to combat ambushes and fight in close quarters, while hopefully minimizing unintentional civilian casualties (although they would be hard to avoid in an all-out assault situation).

If the chief executive is on board, the secure communications systems would allow him to order a nuclear retaliatory strike amid international chaos and, God forbid, a mega-death calamity.

Hawkeye CAT, its Roadrunners, and the Beast, were transported across the ocean by a giant Lockheed C-5 Galaxy, to accompany then President Trump on a state visit to London in June of 2019, where over a hundred thousand raucous, raging protestors greeted him.

At the U.S. Embassy in Regent's Park, where Trump stayed, Hawkeye men set up heavy weapons on the roof, fearing armed terrorists might use the huge protest as cover to launch a suicide attack against the president, or that the protestors might, in a frenzy, attack and try to breach the embassy's security to get at him.

The "invasion" of the Hawkeye CAT was greeted with great interest in a country which, until relatively recently, didn't allow police to carry any sidearms. The British newspaper *The Sun* pointed out that President Trump's Hawkeye squad was named Hawkeye Mogul, which was then President Trump's code name. The paper acquired photos of the Hawkeye CAT in full combat uniform, toting their lethal gear, and referred to them as the President's "crack kill team." It was, more or less, a true description, though not considered a good image to project, especially on a visit to a top allies' capital.

The Sun's extensive and accurate coverage of the team raised eyebrows at Secret Service headquarters in Washington, where the organization much prefers anonymity, and to live up to the designation "secret," to the extent that's possible in a democratic society.

A current member of the team said, "The less written about Hawkeye CAT the better we like it. The last thing they want is for the organization to be talked about and written about. The worst-case scenario would be for some anti-law enforcement congressmen to open public hearings about weapons, tactics, and methods. They would doubtless want to pass legislation to severely limit Hawkeye men from doing their job.

"No good would come of Hawkeye CAT having one hand tied behind its collective back at a time when the danger to the nation's leaders, and to America, is at its worst."

The Sun noted that during Trump's previous visit to the U.K. he avoided London altogether when an estimated "250,000 people marched against him." The paper reported Trump would visit then Prime Minister Theresa May for talks at 10 Downing Street, where a contingent of thousands of London's Metropolitan Police would forcibly, if necessary, keep demonstrators several blocks away. During his visit to Westminster Abbey, where he would lay a wreath for the Unknown Warrior, protestors would also be kept a distance away for his protection, and obviously to prevent the Hawkeye Mogul team from springing into action and potentially sending a fusillade of fire in the mostly narrow crowded London streets.

The paper also reported that Trump would, at all times, be in possession of the "football and biscuit," with which he could launch a nuclear attack on any rogue country that launched a nuclear weapon at the United States or one of its allies, including and especially Great Britain, our main nuclear partner.

The forty-five-pound nuclear briefcase is carried by an aide-de-camp and is meant to be just a few feet from the president, whether he's awake, asleep, or in the shower. The biscuit is a credit card sized plastic card with the current nuclear launch codes.

Saving the American president from assassination, and neutralizing the perpetrators of a potentially deadly attempt, is the number one charge of Hawkeye CAT, but equally vital is the charge of ensuring the "continuity of government," including the nation's ability to retaliate and defend herself in the event of thermonuclear attack.

Guaranteeing the chain of communication between the president, vice-president, and military high command at the Pentagon, at all times, is its sacred duty as well. Whenever the president is not in the White House, whether making a speech in Washington or on a state visit to the Far East, Hawkeye CAT must always be aware of the location of the football and its carrier, in case war is threatened.

The football—officially, the Presidential Emergency Satchel—was created in the wake of the October 1962 Cuban Missile Crisis, almost certainly the closest the United States and the then Soviet Union came to a nuclear exchange. It was first brought to the attention of the public, more or less accidentally, in May of 1963, when it was photographed in the hands of an aide to President Kennedy during a vacation trip to the Summer White House on Cape Cod.

The President was less than sanguine about being the man with the power to launch a potential end-of-the-world strike and asked an advisor, if he was not in the command-and-control headquarters of the White House Situation Room, what the launch order protocol would be.

"What would I say to the Joint War Room to launch an immediate nuclear strike? How would the person who received my instructions verify it was actually me and not a rogue imitating me?"

The aide passed the president's query along to the Joint Chiefs of Staff, and they took immediate action to answer the question by building a fail-safe solution. The football would be designed to verify the president's identity and instantly put him in touch with the Pentagon command authority with a secure connection.

In his book *Breaking Cover*, the former head of the White House Military Office, Bill Gulley, wrote: "There are four things in the Football. The Black Book containing the [current] retaliatory options, a book listing classified site locations, a manila folder with eight or ten pages stapled together, giving a description of procedures for the Emergency Broadcast System, and a three-by-five card with authentication codes, which the president usually carries separately from the Football." Once the code is accepted, every nuclear-weapons-equipped system—including missile silos, submarines and bombers—are alerted and given the primary and secondary targets. The mushroom clouds will sprout within thirty minutes of the order, and cannot be recalled—a chilling realization.

According to a report from the Atomic Heritage Foundation, former Vice President Dick Cheney observed, "The president could launch a kind of devastating attack the world's never seen. He doesn't have to call the Congress. He doesn't have to check with the courts. He has that authority because of the nature of the world we live in."

Indeed, according to reports, President Richard Nixon was deeply depressed and drinking heavily during the final days of his presidency in 1974. At a White House meeting with congressional leaders, out of the blue he announced ominously, "I can go in my office and pick up a telephone, and in 25 minutes, millions of people will be dead."

California Senator Alan Cranston admitted years later that he was "shaken and stunned" at the president's incredible pronouncement, especially since he was, at the time, intoxicated and deeply depressed. Immediately after leaving the White House, the senator contacted then Defense Secretary James Schlesinger about the incident and spoke earnestly of "the need for keeping a berserk president from plunging us into a holocaust."

It was said at the time that the defense secretary gave orders to the high command that if the president ordered a nuclear attack, they must first check with him or Secretary of State Henry Kissinger before launching. Legally, the defense secretary and the generals are compelled to comply with the president's orders in such a situation. The window of opportunity for U.S. survival, if the president was not "berserk" and a real nuclear attack was under way, would be so narrow that bickering among the top government officials could mean the complete destruction of the country and the annihilation of the vast majority of the citizens.

Would the Joint Chiefs of Staff take that risk?

One hopes we'll never find out.

Almost fifty years later, House Speaker Nancy Pelosi feigned hysteria and called Chairman of the Joint Chiefs of Staff General Mark Milley to urge him to stop an "unhinged" President Trump, then in his last days in office, from using the nuclear codes to start a holocaust which would prevent or delay him from being removed from office. This was despite the fact that his term was days from ending, and he had clearly not been reelected. General Milley listened attentively to calm the Speaker, but took no action. Unlike Richard Nixon, Trump had said nothing to indicate he was unhinged or that he was speculating madly about the awesome life or death power bestowed upon him by his high office and the constitution.

Pelosi made her extraordinary phone call to America's top military man, telling him to ignore the president's power to defend the country from nuclear annihilation, without a shred of evidence. Her call was propelled by *her* unhinged loathing of the man and his politics/attitude. It also was illegal to attempt to interfere with the President's constitutional authority, for which Pelosi could, theoretically, have been impeached and removed from office.

But the political motive was to leak the fact of the call to ensure the leftist media would run with it, and further the narrative that Trump wasn't competent to hold high office, and that with him in the Oval Office, the world was in danger of apocalyptic peril.

Apparently, the Soviet Union didn't take the threat of nuclear war with as much angst as America, because it took them until the 1980s to develop their own version of the nuclear football. Named the Cheget, after Mount Cheget in the Caucasus, the Soviet version came as a reaction to the increasing speed with which a Nike Zeus missile could deliver a thermonuclear device from a silo in Nebraska to Red Square in Moscow. The Soviet retaliation system and the current Russian rules has more safeguards than the U.S. protocol, where the life-or-death power rests solely with the president. Their system was, and is still, a three-man-consent launch: the president, defense minister, and top general all must agree to pull the trigger.

In the Russian Federation of today, Cheget is a symbol of state power and is ceremonially passed to a new head of government, ceremonially handed on, when there is an incoming administration, like a totem of power.

Cheget and the U.S. nuclear football are otherwise identical systems, securing authentication of the ordering authority or authorities. But the Russians have added another layer to their atomic knife drawer: a Doomsday system, not completely dissimilar to the one envisioned in the Stanley Kubrick 1964 black comedy *Dr. Strangelove*.

It is designed to react without requiring human intervention: If its radar installations ringing the nation detect missiles headed toward Russian air space, a nuclear retaliatory launch is readied to fire at the attacking nation.

Unlike the Doomsday cache of bombs hidden in the Ural Mountains in *Dr. Strangelove*, the device—called "Perimeter" by the Russians, and nicknamed "Dead Hand"—gives a narrow window to abort once it receives radar information deemed to be a nuclear attack. It is programmed to attempt to reach the three Chegets and several bomb shelters deep beneath the earth, scattered around the country, where surviving members of the high command may have ridden out the initial attack, *but if it doesn't get a satisfactory response at once*, it automatically launches.

In the first month of Joe Biden's presidency, over three dozen House Democrats sent a letter to the new commander-in-chief requesting that he voluntarily surrender the sole authority to launch a strike. Instead, the lawmakers suggested he imitate the Russian protocol and share the authority with at least two other top government leaders.

Despite an abundance of caution and restraint on the part of the two atomic superpowers that has spared mankind from a nuclear weapon being fired in anger for over seventy years, there have been numerous flubs on both sides.

Incredibly, over the years, the biscuit—the blueprint for nuclear annihilation—has been lost several times: Jimmy Carter sent his to the dry cleaner once, and Bill Clinton simply misplaced his, making for a screw-up that sent Hillary into a blind rage. According to an old friend from Wellesley College, it was one that caused the First Lady to hurl a priceless antique White House flower vase at Bill, narrowly missing his head.

General Hugh Shelton wrote in his book *Without Hesitation: The Odyssey of an American Warrior*: "At one point during the Clinton Administration the codes were missing for months. That's a big deal, a gargantuan deal."

According to Shelton, President Clinton would have been unable to respond to a nuclear attack on the United States or her allies unless he was in the White House or another secure government facility, and was apparently too embarrassed to ask to be issued a new biscuit for fear it would encourage the newspapers to mock him, making him look like "a person too scatterbrained to be president."

According to the friend, Hillary shot back, "And they would be right."

Ironically, during her 2016 run for the presidency Hillary Clinton accused Donald Trump of being too "thin skinned" to have his finger on the nuclear trigger—although she knew from experience that it was her husband, who essentially *misplaced* the top-secret codes for months.

On another occasion Clinton dashed out of a meeting in downtown Washington and lost his ball carrier all together, apparently completely forgetting the importance of keeping the carrier as close as his shadow.

When Ronald Reagan was shot by John Hinckley Jr. on March 30, 1981 and rushed to George Washington University Hospital for emergency life-saving surgery, doctors found the biscuit in a pocket of the custom-made Italian suit they had to cut off him—which infuriated the sickened and almost dying president—and having no idea what it was, tossed it in the trash. It was later found in a plastic bag of bloody clothes by a stunned Secret Service man.

Another president who nearly fumbled the nuclear football was Lyndon Johnson. When John Kennedy was assassinated in Dallas, it was discovered that Johnson had refused to attend his scheduled nuclear briefing and had no idea how the system worked. On the fraught plane ride back to Washington, carrying the President's body and his widow in her blood-stained pink Chanel suit, Lyndon Johnson had to be given a quick tutorial on the subject, learning that he was then the only person in the country tasked with making about the most serious decision a person can make historically, and in every other way.

The Russians have made their own share of mistakes. The first Soviet leader to have a Cheget, Konstantin Chernenko, lost his, but apparently had the good sense to order a replacement. When the Soviet Union disintegrated in 1991, parts of the Russian nuclear armada that was based in Ukraine and Belarus were lost and fell into the hands of bad players, who tried unsuccessfully to sell them to terrorists, a plan that was thwarted by what was left of the KGB.

CHAPTER FIVE

Dirty Bombs and Deadly Germs

Laredo was hard at work in her lab on an early spring day. During the chopper ride to work she could smell freshly cut grass, but as she entered her lab, located in a secret military installation in the Washington area, she smelled only harsh chemicals.

The lab was miles from Secret Service headquarters on H Street, mainly because the brass didn't want to be anywhere near the pathogens and other nasty biochem and radioactive material she worked with daily. The windowless room's walls, floor, and ceiling were covered in thick lead and the ventilation system is designed to filter the danger away, so that while she might well perish, her experiments wouldn't leak out and lead to mass death.

She was examining a homemade, domestically produced "dirty bomb" cobbled together from the radioactive material contained in smoke detectors and discarded medical equipment, produced by a young man who apparently wanted to prove he could make a radiological weapon, as though he was going to get a Boy Scout merit badge. The radiation count was surprisingly high though, and had it been weaponized with a conventional explosive attached, it would been less a direct threat to human life than a wide dispersal of radiation that would have done economic and psychological damage: terror.

Another dirty bomb case she had done a forensic investigation of was that of James G. Cummings, who had planned to set off his bomb at Barack

Obama's inauguration. Again, it would have had a horrific terroristic impact. Fortunately, Cummings's wife, who had long been abused by him, shot him in the head while he slept, shortly before he was able to make the bomb operational.

The FBI, who were initially called by local authorities, sealed off the scene. They discovered internet literature on building a dirty bomb and a shocking cache of ingredients with which one could manufacture such a weapon.

Cummings was a multi-millionaire. He had a reasonable knowledge of radiology and the money to purchase the ingredients, so he had amassed gallons of hydrogen peroxide, aluminum powder, beryllium, boron, black iron oxide, magnesium ribbon, boron, uranium, thorium, lithium metal and thermite. He also had information about obtaining and using radioactive materials, including cesium-137, strontium-90, and cobalt-60.

Laredo's assessment of her investigation: "He was well on his way to making a dirty bomb that would have had a catastrophic effect on the inauguration and in Washington. The U.S. Capitol would have damn near glowed in the dark."

As if that weren't enough criminality to get him a one-way ticket to hell, he was a white supremacist who idolized Hitler, had Nazi flags and memorabilia displayed around the house, *and* had child pornography on his computer.

His wife, Amber Cummings pled guilty to the killing, but Judge Jeffrey Hjelm suspended sentencing due to "extenuating circumstances."

He should have given her a medal.

Another case was Justin Sheridan of Urbandale, Iowa, who was turned in by an apparent family member claiming he was building "some kind of bomb." Police found twenty smoke detectors minus the radioactive ingredient, and drug paraphernalia, in his basement workshop.

The thing that drove Laredo to distraction was that any nefarious half-wit with access to the internet could potentially build a radioactive device that would cause great harm and have lasting ill effects. It's impossible to stop people from buying smoke detectors and the how-to info is readily available and can't be completely deleted.

And it seemed as though the motive—good or evil—was rarely the cause, instead the driving force was almost always maniacal self-aggrandizement, on top of a childish desire to go down in history.

Weaponized germs are an idea that has had an attraction to the out-gunned and out-manned for centuries.

In 1763, when the British were struggling to keep a toehold in the New World, while fighting their forever foes, the French, germ warfare was tried.

The French were partnering with the Delaware Indian Tribes to secure the land, and odds for the British were grim. They were anxiously awaiting the arrival of a young, dashing lieutenant colonel named George Washington, who had developed a warrior's reputation. But in the meanwhile, desperate times called for desperate measures.

Fur trader and militia captain William Trent resided at Fort Pitt (where the present-day Pittsburgh lies), at the confluence of three mighty rivers—the Ohio, Allegheny, and Monongahela—making it strategically a critical trading and defensive location in North America.

Trent was visited by members of the tribe, who informed him in gravest terms that "a great number of Indians were going to attack the fort" and urged him to abandon it, rather than perish.

The desperate British had another idea. They had a gift for the Delaware tribe's leaders, sort of a biological trojan horse: two blankets, a silk handkerchief, and linens from a smallpox hospital. The hope was that the highly contagious disease would infect tribe members and spread widely.

The germ warfare attempt failed for a reason not understood for many years: while smallpox (the virus's scientific name is *variola*), are indeed highly contagious, it can only be spread by airborne droplets. So, perhaps the first attempt at germ warfare on the North American continent failed.

Two centuries later the Imperial Japanese Army perfected the sick art of infecting Chinese prisoners, including children, during their occupation of Manchuria. According to a report by writer Richard Stockton, the army's Unit 731 was tasked with develop[ing] "horrific weapons of mass destruction for use against the Chinese population.... Inmates...were infected with the most lethal pathogens known to science...which causes bubonic plague and typhus, which the Japanese hoped would spread from person to person...and depopulate disputed areas."

The report states that on "October 4, 1940, Japanese bombers deployed over the Chinese village of Quzhou...casings, each loaded with 30,000 fleas that had each sucked blood from a dying prisoner. Painful flea bites...afflicted nearly everyone."

The Obama Administration, unlike its predecessors, sent an early warning on bioterror and chemical weapons shortly after taking office in 2009. The document promised his administration would "strengthen U.S. intelligence collection overseas to identify and interdict would-be bioterrorists before they strike."

The new administration promised to provide "a well-planned, well-rehearsed, and rapidly executed epidemic response [that] can dramatically diminish the consequences of biological attacks." It promised to accelerate the development of "new medicines, vaccines, drugs and diagnostic tests and to manufacture them more quickly and efficiently." The memo suggested that the U.S. would be a world leader to "diminish impact of major infectious disease epidemics: promote international efforts... to make medicines that will be available and affordable in all parts of the world."

It concluded, explaining "these memos are intended to be of strategic and pragmatic value for the incoming officials of the Obama Administration who have responsibility for biosecurity in the White House and in the federal agencies."

Asked if the memo's guidelines were implemented, Laredo, who had by then been studying biosecurity for almost fifteen years, shook her head.

> I will give them a C minus. It was feel-good talk but was
> largely ignored. A danger looming on the distant horizon

doesn't make for a politically appealing project to spend billions on, when people are clamoring for government to provide better schools, fix the potholes and cure heart disease and cancer, which they can see is killing their loved ones every day.

Plus, it's patently ridiculous to even talk about finding a vaccine for a disease that doesn't currently exist. The Obama Administration couldn't have worked on a vaccine for Covid 19 in 2009 because it didn't exist yet, and nobody could have predicted the viral structure. The most dangerous influenzas and other diseases tend to each be unique; what treats one effectively is useless on another.

You have to go to work on a vaccine when it's actually too late, and many thousands of people are stricken and dying or dead. It seems cold hearted, but it is science and it is the way nature—sadly—works.

A theoretical bioweapon is something ordinary citizens can't wrap their heads around and they probably don't want to. Their eyes glaze over. The Army has funding for my colleagues and I to do research on chemical and bioweapons. The simple reason is because if we aren't prepared for action, the U.S. military could get sick and ineffective and be unable to stop the vulgarians at our gates.

When you put it in terms of our survival as a nation, people are willing to spend some of their tax dollars, in fact a hell of a lot of tax dollars, to save us from being slaughtered and pillaged.

Laredo was working in her biochem lab on a new mystery pathogen that had been discovered in Afghanistan, at the northern Maryland Army research installation, the Aberdeen Proving Ground, when her encrypted cell phone gave its jarring report, signaling it was time to drop everything. A helicopter was ready for transport to a crime scene. The briefing would be aboard the bird.

A Roadrunner zipped toward the helipad at speeds that would merit serious speeding fines in everyday life. It was obvious a major crisis was underway; the signs were written in neon.

A Marine UH-60 Black Hawk, with twin jet engines whining, sounded like it was waiting impatiently. Mounting the steps, she was surprised and happy that her partner was Ranger. She was still dressed in lab clothes, which he had figured on; he handed her a fresh hazmat suit.

The Black Hawk rapidly climbed skyward and followed the I-95, and then pitched west in the direction of the presidential hideaway named after President Eisenhower's grandson. The earth soon disappeared in the clouds as the chopper reached its cruising altitude and speed of nearly two hundred miles an hour.

Ranger said they were going to Camp David, where President Trump was spending the weekend meeting with his defense and intel principals. Maryland State Police had gotten a tip that a Saudi national had somehow gotten past perimeter security and was less than a mile from Camp David, hiding in the woods. His ex-wife had told cops he was armed, and she claimed he had "some kind of poison." She claimed he had said that "inshallah," he was going *to get* the president.

Ranger and Laredo would be joined at Camp David by elements of the Secret Service Hawkeye CAT—Ranger's former organization when he had first joined the Service—which was equipped with heavy weapons, because there was doubt that there was just one lone actor with some form of "poison."

As the Black Hawk sank into the early evening spring mist blanketing Maryland's Catoctin Mountain Park, they, of course, realized the helicopter had entered a highly restricted area—one of America's most restricted. Entering without permission was to ask to be blasted out of the sky without warning by missiles in underground bunkers that dot the surrounding area. Something of a chilling feeling, Laredo mused to herself, knowing that missile batteries were focused on your ship, that could annihilate you in a nano second. Hopefully nobody down there has an itchy trigger finger, she mused.

Security is so tight around Camp David that the five hundred and fifty-acre Catoctin Mountain Park does not even acknowledge its existence on its park maps. On a few occasions in the past, F-16 fighter jets had to scramble to intercept passenger planes that inadvertently violated the no-fly zone over Camp David, but until now no one on foot, or in any conveyance, had ever come close to the perimeter of the president's country home without permission.

Camp David was designed to be the place where presidents could roam freely, without the intrusion of guards constantly watching their every move. It's the place where President Kennedy took a long walk in the woods with his predecessor General Dwight Eisenhower, to discuss a strategy to avoid nuclear holocaust over the misbegotten invasion of Cuba.

The state police, whose job it is to guard the entire area, were alarmed. How was it possible that a gunman, or *gunmen*, had evaded Camp David's elaborate security measures, including satellite imaging, and gotten within a half mile of the president without being detected?

The police had alerted the Secret Service that the would-be assassin was indeed a Saudi national, who had, according to his estranged wife, become radicalized reading propaganda on the internet. According to her, he dreamed of becoming an Islamic martyr, and had often expressed great admiration for the 9/11 terrorists. He wanted to be famous in the Arab world by exchanging his life for that of the president.

The information set off alarms on the bank of jumbo computer screens at the Secret Service ninth floor Joint Operations Center on H Street in Northwest Washington, D.C., a building that is totally unmarked. A visitor notes that there are no trash cans anywhere near the building, to deprive a terrorist of a convenient place to secrete a dirty bomb or a biochem weapon.

The duty officer in charge of the Intelligence and Assessment Division picked up his encrypted phone and alerted the Deputy Director that they had a Level III threat—the most serious category—on their hands. Within minutes the team was formed and was enroute to Camp David, as well as extra boots on the ground protecting the president.

Most would-be assassins shoot at the White House when the president is thousands of miles away because they don't exactly have access to great intel and, fortunately, the vast majority of such people are losers, who couldn't successfully plan a stick up of a 7-Eleven store.

"As soon as we got word a bad guy had penetrated security in the Catoctin Mountains, we moved our team in," said an agency source. The first ferreting was done with a then new electronic device created and supplied by the Air Force Research Laboratory, which reads the signal from any Android device and locates Bluetooth signals and the possessor. That worked, giving them an exact location out of all the possible hiding places in the park.

It goes to show that if you want to hide out don't bring along your cell phone.

They then acquired satellite imagery of precisely where he was hiding, and through infrared imaging discovered he was alone. The potential assassin was quickly surrounded at his improvised campground, and after a brief standoff the intruder was flushed out and arrested.

> Expecting him to have an arsenal, we were surprised to discover he had only a 30.06 hunting rifle, albeit a deadly weapon. We were expecting more like an AK-47. But the prize appeared when we cut his sleeping bag open. In the stuffing was a baggy of white powder with an oily look, which Laredo was pretty sure was anthrax.

> The other, equally disturbing find was that he had a detailed map of Camp David's entire security system. I was surprised and appalled. It had details of the security, barriers, and even locations of surveillance cameras. This was no lone wolf jihadi assassin. So, we got our man,

but we didn't get his backup. This was an inside job. The realization was that it was going to take a joint task force of all the intel agencies to root out the mole, and it had to be done quickly before he or she could do some major damage.

Ali Amin was turned over to the uniformed agents and went without a whimper of protest. He knew his confederates were still at work, and the scheme was still operational. It was like he fully expected to get caught.

Ranger and Laredo raced for the helicopter to get back to the lab to test the "poison" powder.

The FBI later made arrests of two apparently disgruntled ex-employees who had radical Islamist ties.

Stanford University biophysicist Steven Block is very concerned about the surge in interest by rogue nations and terror groups with biological weapons, which he grimly calls "the poor man's atom bomb."

Writing in *American Scientist*, he complained, "Where are the biological scientists willing to go on the record about bioweapons?" He warns that biological weaponry is "a serious threat to peace in the twenty-first century."

There are over two dozen bioagents ranging from Ebola, smallpox, and typhus to several genetically engineered pathogens that can be unleashed as weapons of mass destruction.

Block notes that biological warfare is the only way terror groups and rogue states like Iran and North Korea can match the military might of the U.S. in highly asymmetrical warfare.

Such warfare follows no rules—terrorists don't sign treaties that prohibit the use of poison gas or mandate humane treatment for prisoners of war. All those civilized niceties are tossed out the window in asymmetrical warfare.

In terror war there are few, if any, actual battles that are soldier on soldier. War is waged against soft targets—unarmed women and children, not brawny men with automatic weapons and supersonic bomb-laden jets.

Anthrax is the most popular choice of terror, simply because it is extremely deadly unless treated almost immediately with high doses of penicillin. It is also easy to manufacture and remains stable over a period of years, unless exposed to sunlight.

Professor Block writes that it takes relatively skilled biologists to successfully handle anthrax without infecting themselves. To safely weaponize extremely dangerous pathogens is tricky: "The idea that anybody can brew this stuff in their garage vastly overstates the case, but any technology that can be used to insert genes into DNA [and make a pathogen more powerful and deadly] can be used for either good or bad."

The father of modern chemical warfare was the Polish-born German scientist Fritz Haber. Mustard gas was one of the weaponized chemicals he invented for use in the trench warfare of World War I.

At the Second Battle of Ypres, Belgium, in April and May of 1915, soldiers who were exposed were blinded, incapacitated, and suffered greatly as a result of exposure. They described "a shimmering cloud around their feet and a strange peppery smell in the air." Soon they itched uncontrollably and broke out in blisters and coughed up blood. It turned out to be the most horrific chemical weapon ever deployed, killing over ten thousand in its initial use on one day.

At least 1.3 million were severely injured, and many permanently blinded by the World War I gas attacks.

It was absorbed through the skin; hence, gas masks were useless. The butcher's toll on that first day was shocking, even by the horrors of the bloodbath that was the first World War. Over the course of the war both sides used the weapon extensively, leading to collateral damage when the wind shifted and civilian populations were impacted. The carnage was so dreadful that even monstrous Adolph Hitler, who was a corporal in War I, chose not to deploy it in World War II. (However, that didn't stop him from killing six million civilians, mostly Jewish, with a poison manufactured by the supposedly venerable German firm I.G. Farben.)

Even so, Haber bragged about the efficacy of his concoction as a weapon of war and promoted its use. When questioned about the unfathomable suffering it caused, he remarked "dead is dead."

Herr Haber apparently wasn't a real sensitive kind of guy, though he might have been good to his mom, but then again, maybe not.

Incredibly and ironically, given the unimaginable pain and death it caused, mustard gas was found after the war to be an efficacious lymphoma treatment. Medical records of poison gas victims showed they had a shockingly low white blood cell count. It was theorized that if it could kill normal white blood cells, it could probably also kill cancerous ones, which proved to be true.

It was the discovery of what is now called chemotherapy and has saved millions of lives.

Laredo told the author, "The story of the horror of mustard gas leading to chemotherapy seems incredible, but it's actually not surprising. They, in effect, did drastic experiments on the bodies of tens of thousands of humans, and naturally they collated the results of each 'experiment.'

"War itself is one giant horrific experiment. Fighter pilots who were shot down and floated in freezing ocean water gave a great deal of insight into the human body's reaction to hypothermia, and led to treatments that saved lives in the end—at a cost of unimaginable human suffering."

Laredo and Ranger spoke little on the short flight to the site of her lab. The baggie of white powder, which sure as hell wasn't nose candy, was the eight-hundred-pound gorilla sitting between them.

Halfway through the heavy double lead doors Laredo spun around to face Ranger. "You don't have to come in for this."

He smiled wryly and said, "I'm not afraid."

"Neither am I, but maybe we should be, because anthrax used by terrorists is being genetically engineered to be penicillin-resistant and extremely virulent. There are also stealth viruses designed to infect, but exhibit no symptoms in the victim until they're triggered. And there is no way to know what the trigger is or when it will be activated."

They silently donned hazmat suits and she went to work analyzing the powder: putting a sample into a vial, then inserting a Bioflash Biological Identifier probe tip, connected via a hose, into the powder. The result was, as she fully expected, positive for anthrax.

Later, she compared it to the genetic makeup of pathogens in the Department of Homeland Security database, to determine whether it had been genetically tampered with. That was a positive match as well.

It clearly wasn't a case of a lone wolf. Amin was almost certainly just an errand boy, but this was a professional job, carried out by professionals, hoping to cause massive damage and suffering at the president's country hideaway. It was planned as an event that would cause panic and sap the public's trust and faith in government.

Further lab testing proved Laredo's field assessment had been correct. It was an unusually virulent strain of anthrax and it had been genetically modified to be resistant to treatment with penicillin.

Terrorist Amin admitted under interrogation he was planning to spread the poison around Camp David, in the hope that President Trump and his family would get exposed and succumb. He refused to turn in his mole or moles who had supplied him with maps and other information about Camp David security.

Because he was a foreign combatant deemed a part of an ongoing terror plot, he was assigned to the prison at Guantanamo until the conspiracy was ended. A stint at Gitmo has a way of loosening reluctant lips.

Ricin is another popular poison, even more deadly than anthrax. It is even easier to produce, and it is difficult to limit production. The castor bean that yields ricin is derived from a common house plant that can be grown without any special skill or knowledge.

It's hard to imagine a poison more lethal than ricin, says Michigan State University toxic plant specialist Peter Carrington. "A volume roughly the size of a grain of table salt would be a fatal dose for an adult. It is something like 1,000 times more toxic than cyanide." Its history as a weaponized toxin goes back to at least World War I, when the U.S. military experimented with its application as a coating for bullets and cannon balls. During World War II, it was again considered for use with bombs, but sarin gas was considered more deadly and easier to control.

The Soviet KGB found ricin to be an effective weapon for use in political assassinations. Apparently, mistakenly thinking he was safe from the KGB in London, Bulgarian dissident Georgi Markov took a walk across the Waterloo Bridge on the Thames River on his way to the BBC. In such an exposed position he was a clear target for a sniper. The lethal weapon was an umbrella that used compressed gas to fire a tiny ricin pellet. He was hit in the leg and died two days later.

A special poison branch of the British Ministry of Defense conducted an autopsy and discovered the ricin pellet. It was clearly one of the favored method of permanently eliminating dissidents. Aleksandr Solzhenitsyn suffered ricin poisoning after being threatened by KGB agents back in 1971. He lived to bear witness to the vile deed.

In the U.S., in recent years, ricin was the bio agent used in eleven out of thirty-one attacks. Mostly it is used as an aerosol in a confined space, because that is more effective, and the targets largely tend to be government officials whose decisions angered their constituents for a variety of reasons, most of which make little sense, but obviously were important to the assassin.

Al Qaeda has made extensive use of the poison, simply because it is easier to produce in crude labs than anthrax. It is a favorite of terror groups and rogue nations because there is no antidote or cure once it is inhaled or ingested; although several possible vaccines are being tested, none have yet been tested on humans.

Laredo said, "It takes a special kind of person to attempt to kill with ricin. A bullet is, of course, deadly. But it is a relatively clean kill. Ricin poison causes a slow, painful, excruciating death and there is no cure. It takes a special, twisted personality to want to inflict that kind of a death. Ricin killers are a particularly sick breed who revel in the knowledge that victims are going to die slowly and in terrible pain."

In a strange episode in 2013, ricin-laced letters were mailed to President Barack Obama and New York Mayor Michael Bloomberg. Soon after the letters were intercepted, Shannon Guess Richardson—a thirty-five-year-old woman from New Boston, Texas—traveled to Shreveport, Louisiana and reported to police that her husband Nathan Richardson, an Army veteran, had mailed the toxic letters.

She was a former Dallas beauty queen who had minor roles in *The Walking Dead* and *The Vampire Diaries*.

The two had a bitter divorce in 2013, and she was seeking revenge. To put the cherry on top of the frameup, Richardson also sent a ricin-laced envelope to a man named Mark Glaze, who headed a gun control organization founded by Mayor Bloomberg. Nathan was a marksman and a hunting enthusiast, so his wife apparently hoped investigators would be certain he was the guilty party.

A joint investigation by the FBI, Secret Service, and local authorities revealed that Richardson herself had mail-ordered castor bean seeds and lye, to brew a homemade batch of ricin, which she mailed to the president and the mayor, hoping that her estranged husband would take the fall.

Instead, Richardson was arrested and charged with the crime. She then changed her story, claiming that she did mail the letters, but that her husband made her do it. She was eventually sentenced to eighteen years in federal prison for possession and manufacture of a biological weapon, and ordered to undergo psychological treatment while in prison.

The Discovery Channel Series "Who the (Bleep) Did I Marry?" featured the case, narrated by her ex in an episode titled "Poison Love."

At the sentencing, prosecuting U.S. Attorney John Bates called it "one of our most unusual, even bizarre cases."

On April 16, 2013, at the Secret Service remote screening facility in suburban Virginia, miles distant from the White House, an alarm sounded over a package addressed to President Obama. All mail addressed to the White House naturally goes through the screening process before it is allowed to be delivered.

Examination of the suspect package preliminarily tested positive for ricin poison. Nearly simultaneously, another package addressed to the U.S. Senate, and a third addressed to a Mississippi federal justice, set off warning bells. They too tested positive for ricin.

The letter to Obama said: "To see a wrong and not expose it is to be a silent partner in its continuousness," which sounded like childish doggerel, rather than the raging of a crazed ricin killer.

The Joint Operations Center at Secret Service headquarters was alerted. Ranger was awakened and put on the case, along with Laredo, who brought her bio-warfare detection gear to the party.

Curiously, the presumed mailer signed off on the material, scribbling, "I am K.C. and I approved this message." FBI agents arrived in force at the Corinth, Mississippi home of Paul Kevin Curtis at 5:15 a.m. Central Time, rousted Curtis from bed, and brought him to a secure location for interrogation, although the agents had grave doubts that he was the ricin perp.

A simultaneous biological attack on the three branches of government was considered practically a full-scale attack on the government of the United States. There was general agreement the attack should be considered the possible first wave of a violent assault on the nation.

Enroute to the FBI center at Quantico, Virginia, where Curtis was being held in a sub-basement originally designed as a bomb shelter, six stories underground, Ranger and Laredo were briefed on the evidence the FBI had so far.

Laredo and Ranger's first reaction was agreement with the FBI agents that it sounded like a set up. True, some potential assassins long to be caught, but this seemed too easy, too pat. And the guy had no history of either criminal or irrational behavior.

But there was a ticking ricin bomb out there. Somebody had manufactured it, and so far had gotten away with mailing it to the president of the United States. There was a high probability he would next mail it to a person or persons without benefit of an off-site screening facility.

The briefing included a statement from the brother of the suspect, that piqued Ranger's attention: "My family wants the person or persons responsible for such behavior to be brought to justice. We have no reason to believe Kevin would be involved. We love him and look forward to getting answers to make sense of all this."

It sounded sincere. His first thought was to go to Mississippi to interview the brother and find out about Curtis' life and what enemies he might have. It sounded very similar to the Shannon Richardson ricin case and could be a scorned lover or an aggrieved business partner.

Talking about the case much later, Ranger recalled: "It's rare that relatives lie to you in a convincing way. They tend to give the truth away whether they want to or not. I have frequently gotten actionable intelligence from relatives who were actually trying to cover up and help their kin get out of trouble."

There was a note in the briefing material that Curtis, forty-five, was an Elvis impersonator—not a line of business in which you would expect to make a lot of deadly enemies.

Under intense interrogation by a revolving cast of questioners from the FBI and Secret Service in the dank, windowless subterranean bunker, Curtis showed a rather remarkable lack of panic. He was being charged with a capital crime for which the penalty was life in prison. Yet, he hadn't asked for a lawyer, wasn't sweating, and looked his questioners straight in the eye and calmly answered, without pausing or looking at the ceiling or the floor, which guilty people typically do when they are adlibbing lies.

At one point, Laredo asked point blank, "So, how is ricin made?" His eyes widened and he laughed out loud. "I don't know what the hell it is."

Curtis suggested that his one-time friend Everett Dutschke, a martial arts instructor, might have sent the ricin letters to frame him. He said that he and Dutschke had been in a bitter online feud, and that his former friend had vowed to get him.

★★★

Ranger decided to fly down to Mississippi to have a word with Curtis's brother, Jack. Laredo was going to stay at Quantico and keep him informed of developments.

Jack Curtis agreed without hesitation to an interview. He proved to be as disarmingly honest and forthright as his brother. The only enemy of his brother that he was aware of was the same man Kevin Curtis had named. He said that the two men had known each other for years and had an ongoing feud that went back years. And he repeated the charge that Dutschke had threatened to "get" Kevin.

Ranger filed his report to the Joint Task Force, recommending that Dutschke be arrested immediately and his house combed for evidence of ricin.

The FBI did a lightning-quick arrest that night, to prevent him from destroying evidence.

Laredo flew down to Corinth with the FBI to take part in the search. She found multiple traces of ricin in the house, saying that he had been sloppy, which was a good thing. There was undisputable evidence he had produced the poison.

Dutschke soon pleaded guilty and was sentenced to twenty-five years in federal prison.

CHAPTER SIX

Nuclear Nightmares

Hawkeye CAT soldiers are taught early in their training that their goal, their sacred duty, is to save the president's life, for the all-important reason that in a national emergency he needs to be alive to make decisions that will keep the government functioning and defend the nation with a nuclear response, if need be.

Making certain that the president is within easy reach of the nuclear football is as important as protecting his life.

A veteran former member of Hawkeye told the author, "During initial training my group was lectured by a Stanford University professor—who was a cerebral, skinny, baby-faced guy in a designer T-shirt—on our mission to keep the U.S. government functioning following a cataclysmic event. He said that we could be the difference between the nation surviving a nuclear exchange or not. The enemy would try to decapitate the government by killing or gravely injuring the head of state, and hope the ensuing chaos and shock would leave the government temporarily paralyzed long enough for them to finish us off.

"Our job was to make sure they failed, and that the president would be able to continue serving as Commander-in-Chief, and lead the retaliatory charge with his sword raised high.

"He told us point-blank that we could be the last hope of saving civilization from complete destruction, by keeping the president alive and our democracy safe, during a sudden and brutal attack on the nation."

Former Hawkeye CAT soldier Dan Emmett wrote in his book *Within Arm's Length,* "[The] real mission was to deploy in case of attack, to draw fire away from protectees, and onto ourselves, while the Secret Service shift evacuated POTUS to a safe zone. Their true purpose was to be sacrificed, if necessary, in order to give time and opportunity for the president or vice president to escape from the kill zone. From the beginnings of the program the assignment attracted those with a sense of adventure and with a seeming disregard for danger, and there never has been a shortage of volunteers."

Emmett also notes that the modern Secret Service is a "no more mister nice guy" organization. "There was a saying in the Secret Service that you either played ball with the Secret Service or the Secret Service would ram the bat up your ass, and this was certainly our game."

Former agent and Hawkeye CAT man Emmett, who served in the '80s and '90s, wrote on a return visit to his former brothers-in-arms that the CAT team had progressed "light years" since he had left. "The truly extraordinary agents who make up CAT are a force to be reckoned with and a source of pride for all Americans. When the day comes for CAT to deploy in a live-fire situation to save the life of the president—and that day will come—I have complete faith they will succeed."

He wrote that "with the constant threat of attack on America by radical Islam and other terror organizations…the Counter Assault Team enjoys a reputation in international law enforcement and counterterrorist communities as one of the most elite units of its kind in the world."

Hawkeye CAT has, fortunately, not yet been deployed in a full combat mode, because laying down suppressive fire in an urban area—especially in downtown London, or Washington, D.C., or any congested urban center—would likely cause a great deal of collateral damage, that is, civilian deaths.

For that reason, only the Director of the Secret Service or, in his absence the Deputy Director, are authorized to order a full combat deployment of Hawkeye CAT. It would be a decision that would have to be made in seconds by someone who may be far from the scene at the time. And it would have potentially dire consequences.

On one occasion, when Donald Trump was first president, some anti-Trump protestors threw red paint on his motorcade, presumably to resemble blood. The decision was made not to unlimber Hawkeye Cat's fierce fire power, but to stage a practice deployment. As they had practiced many times in a simulated city at the FBI training facility in Quantico, Virginia, the regular Secret Service contingent peeled off and took the president to a safe, fortified underground bomb shelter with its own secure source of air and water, guided by a police escort, in case the provocative incident signaled a coordinated wave of attacks or even a "dirty bomb" attack.

All appropriate police agencies were automatically notified that a Hawkeye CAT drill was underway, which they had all been briefed on in detail.

The Hawkeye team stayed in place, where, if necessary, they would have held off the bad guys with withering fire. The men climbed out of their Roadrunner quickly, dramatically brandishing their weapons, which must have seemed like a scene from a Hollywood movie to startled citizens passing by.

It went without a hitch in the crowded inner city of Washington, D.C., and was a good demonstration of a real-time, real life practice of handling a terror attack and/or assassination plot. The decision to simulate with a president aboard, with no warning, was a sign the men were, and are, more than ready to leap into action.

Everyone knew their job and they all performed.

The U.S. was finally rising to confront the level of danger that existed because of the heightened jealousy and rage against the American model of democracy.

The shocking incident took the President by surprise, but he said nothing until it was over, and then cheerfully, personally, thanked the Secret Service contingent and Hawkeye CAT for a job well done.

A month later Hawkeye CAT was again challenged when George Floyd's death was caused by the extremely dangerous drug fentanyl, which is one hundred times more powerful than morphine and fifty times stronger than heroin. His autopsy showed other opioids in his system as well.

A mob of outraged protestors threatened to breach the gates of the White House, loudly proclaiming their desire to get the President.

The protocol for Hawkeye is to keep as low a profile as possible with the understanding that their uniforms and weapons are both provocative and make scary news photos. There had been major chagrin when the London *Sun* did their splash of words and photos announcing that Hawkeye was in England to protect the American president.

The paper didn't know, or didn't mention if it did, that Hawkeye accompanies the American president wherever he goes, whether it's to North Korea to make a historical visit with Kim Jong-un, or to chip a few shots at a private golf course.

A few will ride in Marine One, depending on space available, and the contingent will ride on a combat-ready Chinook helicopter with all their weaponry ready for a fight—if necessary.

Hawkeye was created during the administration of Ronald Reagan, with the insistence of Nancy Reagan. Both Reagans were enthusiastic about the creation of a Praetorian Guard to defend the nation's leaders. For Reagan, under whom the guard was called Hawkeye Rawhide, after his code name, there was something comfortingly theatrical about the black clad guardians and their bristling weaponry.

He reflected that if Hawkeye CAT had been in place when John Hinckley Jr. attacked him, there might have been a different outcome, which was precisely the First Lady's goal.

Bill Clinton largely ignored them—he famously "loathed the military"—just as he disregarded the regular Secret Service. Hillary largely saw all Secret Service as manservants and asked them to carry her bags—which they pointedly refused to do. To say the least, it is not their job or duty.

But Bill didn't hesitate to put his own life and the lives of his Hawkeye brigade on the line for a photo op during a trip to Korea, when he insisted upon taking a walk on the "Bridge of No Return" in the still hotly contested, so-called demilitarized zone separating North and South Korea.

While the notoriously reckless president strolled on the bridge, soldiers on both sides—including the Hawkeye brigade—cocked their rifles and stared down their scopes, while Clinton preened and mugged for the cameras. The Hawkeye men were happy afterward to have escaped alive, and without reigniting a war that had killed over thirty thousand Americans in the early 1950s.

George W. Bush, code-named Trailblazer, went out of his way to let the Secret Service know he appreciated their work, and prayed the near apocalyptic response of Hawkeye would never be required on his watch.

Laura Bush made sure the men and their families were invited to a White House Christmas party, where she and the president personally thanked each one and their families for putting up with their embrace of danger, and frequent family separation, during their travels to protect the president.

Barack Obama, code-named Renegade, told a close friend, who often stayed in the Lincoln Bedroom, and was a close friend of the entire Obama family, that they made him nervous and he was uncomfortable in their presence. He said that he would have ordered the group disbanded, but thought it would make too much news and call attention to the fact that such a draconian-tasked group existed so close to the presidency. First Lady Michelle, on the other hand, told the friend she approved because she was frightened by the myriad serious threats and plots against the first black Commander-in-Chief, and she wanted back-up to prevent him being harmed.

Regardless of the president's loathing or love for the Hawkeye Contingent, like most government entities, once established it is rarely, if ever, dismantled or downsized, but instead grows ever bigger, and generally acquires more authority, equipment, manpower, and office space. Also typically, like most other parts of government, it grows exponentially in numbers and purview. Hawkeye operatives are now present on all Marine One helicopter trips, as well as on Air Force One.

In fact, every time Air Force One is carrying the president— or Hawkeye as he is code-named—CAT must be on the runway in a Roadrunner with five heavily armed men. The big, lumbering plane—a military designed version of the Boeing 747-400, fully loaded with eight tanks of fuel, weighing 380,000 pounds or 57,000 gallons of Jet A or Jet B (in cold weather) fuel—sits on the runway like a gigantic terrorist target. With the president aboard, it has to be protected at all times.

The Roadrunner stays with it until the big plane begins taxiing down the runway; then it follows close behind until take off, but not too close, because with nearly 200,000 pounds of thrust, the plane could blow the armored CAT SUV clean off the runway, which wouldn't look professional or very safety-conscious. Although the risk is very real, the mission seems so dangerous the men invariably laugh hysterically as they go about their chores. It is frankly the kind of risk-taking thrill for which they signed on.

Hawkeye CAT has also become a back-up to the Secret Service Uniformed Division, and is an emergency back-up at the White House in the event of an actual armed invasion, a disastrous event that has grown increasingly likely in recent violent and riotous years.

They are only too aware that if the U.S. Capitol can be breached and vandalized, so too can the White House. In 2020, Trump's last full year as president, protests in front of the White House became more violent and Antifa and Black Lives Matter contingents became more daring and aggressive. The integrity of White House security and the safety of the president, vice president, and their families, became more and more problematic.

Fires were set all over the downtown area surrounding the White House. Commercial grade fireworks, capable of inflicting deadly injury, were thrown over the White House fences on a regular basis, endangering Secret Service officers as well as employees of the executive mansion, and possibly even the First Family.

Mob rule, looting and the burning of private and public buildings was regularly encouraged by firebrand Democrat politicians in Seattle, Portland, and other American cities, and the wrathful leftist press— particularly the *Washington Post*, CNN, and MSNBC—gleefully egged the violence on.

As a result, a rarely-engaged protocol became almost commonplace while the assaults raged: bringing the president, vice president, and their families to safe zones in subbasements of the Executive Mansion.

It was a fraught task for the agents, simply because presidents don't like to appear to be hiding, and when word of the precaution leaked, the press and rival politicians leaped to suggest Trump was all but hiding behind his grandma's skirts. They failed to mention that he wasn't asked to go to a secure location, he was *told* to by the Secret Service, who have that right and duty in a dire emergency.

A full motorcade, with a heavily armed Hawkeye CAT contingent was ready to roll on a moment's notice. It was kept at the ready just outside a hidden escape tunnel, and would deploy in the event the president and First Family had to be relocated. The violence and threats of an actual breach of the last defenses led the agency to fear it could happen, and forced it to make contingency plans to defend against a hostile invasion of the White House.

Had that dreadful scenario unfolded, it would have been the first time since the British invasion in 1812 and burning of the White House in 1814, when First Lady Dolley Madison famously ordered the Gilbert Stuart portrait of George Washington removed to a safe location just before British soldiers began looting and torching the mansion.

The fear wasn't that barbarians would successfully get through the gates during the Trump presidency, but that a serious and violent attempt, endangering the life of the president, would force the unleashing of Hawkeye CAT, and the hellish response that would inevitably ensue. There was a terrible sense that the threats, and attempts at a breach, could have forced the hand of the Director to push the go button for the first time.

If a contingent of rioters got through the fences and were entering the building, he would have little choice.

Everyone involved knew that Hawkeye soldiers would do exactly as they had been trained and that would mean reaping the whirlwind.

The executive mansion, office buildings, and all the grounds were closed to the public, and all but essential personnel sent elsewhere, until the threat was over. There was almost a government in exile.

Hawkeye CAT was deployed 24/7, prepared to go into combat mode in a last-ditch fight. There was a grim sense of siege, with all the presidential security on high alert, working eighteen-hour days, and in constant emergency mode.

During the siege, all caution and public relations were tossed to the wind. They felt there were rioters with weapons at the gate, and an apocalyptic battle was in the offing. "It felt like wartime," said a Secret Service agent. "There was an air of being in a hostile foreign country. It built to a crescendo with the January 6th fiasco at the Capitol. Death threats were increased by a factor of four. That mob action unleashed a very dark and frightening force, with serious reverberations regarding the safety of the Chief Executive, who is always the object of wrath in times of turmoil. Who else is there to blame for inexplicable and uncertain times?"

The pandemic was raging at the same time that images on cable news showed many of the nation's major cities in flames.

The men of Hawkeye CAT could only keep alert and prepare for the emergency retaliatory response they had trained to perform.

"Whenever the presidential motorcade traveled through Washington, there were angry, fired up mobs screaming obscenities and even throwing rocks," said Ranger. "Pelosi and the press had ratcheted up waves of hatred, blaming the president for the Antifa and loony-tune-led violence at the Capitol. It was ugly, but there was no reaction on our part.

"It was a very sad time. The president could have handled it better, but at every rally he routinely fired up his people, and the day of the march and subsequent violence at the Capitol was no exception. He had no idea there was a large contingent of Antifa with a plan and the equipment at the ready, to trash the Capitol and to gleefully let Trump bear the brunt of blame.

"It was a huge success for them; a disaster for the country."

Hawkeye CAT normally tries to keep a low profile around the White House, regardless of whether it is a president like Obama, who didn't want to see them at all, or one like Trump, who loved them. It also lies low because the White House is normally a public building regularly visited by school classes and tourists. Its headquarters is in the West Wing, called W-16, where the team stays when the president is at home, and from which it can deploy 24/7 if needed.

"Hawkeye CAT soldiers quickly pick up on which presidents are admirers and which ones loathe them, and act accordingly. Under Reagan they had the run of the White House and were also in full view at his Rancho del Cielo in the California mountains. With Clinton and Obama, and now with Biden, they lay low and were careful not to be photographed anywhere near the president or on the grounds of the White House. It wasn't a happy time. It's hard to do a dangerous job every day and know you not only aren't appreciated, but are scorned." said a retired member of the contingent.

O n a sizzling late August night, when the air is so hot and thick it's like being in a sauna,, in Washington, an alert police patrol officer noticed men dressed in D.C. Water and Sewer Authority uniforms. Because it was after midnight and on the Ellipse in the shadow of the White House, the police notified dispatch and asked them to check with the Authority's emergency repair unit to make sure it was their operation. Quickly they got a response that no late-night emergency repairs were under way.

The cops called for backup and the Secret Service Uniformed Division was notified. The cops formed a perimeter and sealed the entrance. Soon four men with gas masks on emerged and surrendered. They were charged with numerous local infractions and hauled off to jail. Later that night, D.C. detectives paid a visit to the men's house in the Petworth section of D.C. and discovered what appeared to be a sophisticated lab in the basement.

The FBI was notified and sent a forensics team to investigate. The neighborhood was quickly sealed off and evacuated. The Feds reported they believed the lab was set up to produce some sort of a pathogen for biological attack. Because the men were probing tunnels near the White House, the Hunters' chemical and biologic unit alerted.

The go-to agent for pathogens was a thirty-something woman, wiry and athletic, who goes by the nom de guerre Laredo to protect herself and her family from the terror organizations whose plots she regularly thwarts.

Laredo, whose well-manicured fingernails have depictions of symbols from the periodic table of elements, told the author her unique story in detail.

> I studied chemistry and biology and got a biochemistry master's degree. I then joined the Army and was sent to the Army War College to study chemical, biological and radiological warfare protection.

> I was an Army brat and traveled the world with my dad, who was a colonel. My mom died of breast cancer when I was twelve, so I had to take care of myself and help my dad as much as I could. In our grief and need to soldier on, we very much bonded. I suppose the propellant for my career has always been a desire to make my dad proud of me.

> When I became interested in biology during high school, dad suggested I specialize in biological warfare. Probably not the typical career path for a kid, but that was us.

> He said it was the upcoming big field. In the age of terror, there is a great need for people trained in stopping or containing pathogen and chemical attacks. Instructions for making dirty bombs are all over the internet. Plague has been used as a weapon since the 14th century and bioweapons are big on the radar screen of terrorists. Pathogens are relatively easy to assemble; they are cheap, compared to dirty bombs for example, and they are extremely deadly.

> It was a given that I was going to join the army. I had wanted to since I was about five. Other little girls wanted to dress like a princess; I wanted to dress up as a soldier.

Pathogens are far easier to smuggle across borders and are far less detectible than a radioactive device, and can be even more lethal.

Laredo had been assured by numerous experts, including her then army lieutenant general dad, that she would always be in high demand with expertise in chemical and biological warfare because, sadly, it was going to be a big part of future asymmetrical warfare. Of course, it was a far more dangerous career than being a soldier. The average soldier seldom, if ever, engages in combat with the enemy. They are mostly deployed in back up or supporting roles.

A biochemical expert, on the other hand, confronts a wily, nearly invisible, and vicious enemy all of the time, frequently alone and without warning as to what the enemy she is confronting is made of, and whether or how it has been altered to be incurable and hypertoxic.

Laredo learned early in her training that pathogens are relatively easy to manufacture and even easier to deliver. For the most part they are odorless, tasteless and silent, perfectly capable of entering the victim's body unnoticed, then attacking the host from within, ensuring that the game of life and death is over before there is an opportunity to fight back by seeking a cure.

Humans have a visceral reaction of dread to pathogens, similar to but even worse than, for example, arachnophobia. At least spiders are visible, pathogens are not. The psychological effect on soldiers and civilians is both brutal and able to cause drastic psychosomatic impact, even on the lucky ones who are not infected. There are also varied and sundry methods of spreading pathogens; from aerosol spray to polluting water and food supplies to the old KGB trick of using a weaponized umbrella to prick the victim with a lethal poison like ricin.

There are myriad targets for pathogens in terrorist warfare. Numerous attempts have been made to contaminate the White House and the surrounding blocks of the nation's capital. Making the centuries-old presidential mansion uninhabitable would have a psychological impact as devastating as a more cinematically dramatic attack such as 9/11. Terror is about the impact of the attack on the enemy—in this case, the people of the United States—but equally important, it's about cheering on enemies of America who loathe the nation's success and wealth.

Another target would be the nation's food supply. Even the contamination of a few bottles of Tylenol in the 1980s caused widespread panic. Poisoning of a small batch of fruits, vegetables, or meat would have a devastating effect on the population, shattering trust in the government and the food supply. The economy could crash and the country spiral out of control.

"There are few things more terrifying than releasing plague-like, multi-drug resistant pathogens on civilians," Laredo explains:

> It's relatively easy for a trained bio person to alter the code of a pathogen to shift its identity and become all but impossible to treat. The process is called "gain of function." It's often a haphazard operation of mixing up bits of different viruses and seeing what emerges or injecting the viruses in animals to study if they mutate into something more lethal and harder, or even impossible to control. Perhaps the worst part is that it is relatively so easy to do. Just get instructions from the Internet and make a toxin from hell.
>
> It would travel from household to household, city to city. No one could be sure who was infected and who wasn't, people would be afraid to help each other or co-operate with the government in the fight against the unknown enemy who introduced the pathogen. Not knowing for sure who was the enemy would make people point fingers at each other and turn on innocent people.
>
> During my missions to Afghanistan we knew that elements associated with ISIS were experimenting with bio warfare. There was ample evidence they were weaponizing it, particularly into aerosol, and dropping it on isolated villages just to see what would happen. And

interrogated prisoners admitted ISIS was getting help with the manufacture from North Korea and Iran.

Obviously, this threat was kept as quiet as possible out of fear it would cause panic. But it was very real and there was evidence of plans to smuggle pathogens into the U.S. and release them.

Laredo said the Secret Service Hawkeye CAT goal is to prevent protected persons from contracting a disease, and to have facilities in the White House to diagnose and hopefully treat a poisoning and rapidly introduce an antidote if possible. If such a bio attack is made on the nation's leaders, Hawkeye CAT would be able to contain it and prevent any spread. She sees that as her charge and her role in the Secret Service.

Unfortunately, the White House has, in recent years been a regular target for—mostly—hair brained attempts to smuggle in chemical, biological, and even radiologic weapons. It's not the kind of information the Secret Service likes to publicize, and like many, if not most, attempts on their protectives, the reports are filed away and kept from the press to prevent both panic and copycat attempts. However, in recent years there have been attempts to plant weapons during public tours of the building. Little old ladies to school children—sometimes knowingly, most often unwittingly—have attempted to drop off lethal packages.

Sensors have now been installed all over the Executive Mansion to sound alarms and have successfully prevented numerous attempts. Details of the sensors are highly classified and will certainly not be discussed in this book. But they have proved extremely successful.

Medical facilities inside the White House and other government buildings have been quietly upgraded and continue to grow more sophisticated. Most of the people under protection have already been vaccinated against a variety of possible problems. In addition, government buildings have been retrofitted to enable effective sealing from pathogens released in the air.

Laredo is constantly in touch with her colleagues in the FBI and other intelligence agencies on the problem and possible solutions.

But believe me no one in the community is sanguine that there aren't fanatical, determined terrorists planning ever more cunning and diabolical attacks.

I recently attended a briefing at the Bureau about protocols in the event of a full scale bio attack on Washington or New York City. There was consensus that martial law would have to be declared because the infected would have to be completely quarantined, and many would not go easy with that. After all, "shelter in place" in the age of Coronavirus was very unpopular and, in some places, there was open rebellion, even against wearing masks.

There also would have to be mass inoculations, and these days it is not just the snaggle-toothed no-nothings who would resist. Many college-educated professionals, including Robert Kennedy Jr., have embraced the idea that vaccines cause autism and other serious ailments.

They would have to be forced. It would be an event unlike anything the nation has been through. I know it is essential that an emergency—worst case—plan be ready in case the horror scenario unfolds. It will take a lot of planning in advance if we are to have a fighting chance as a nation to survive.

A few hours after the D.C. cop's discovery of the faux sewer workers near the White House, Laredo's encrypted cell phone buzzed. She noticed the time was 4:15 a.m. Her pulse rose as she awoke and realized that this was a serious biochem emergency. In a matter of minutes, she was stepping into her DuPont Encapsulated hazmat suit. Her husband patted her suit, checked that everything was connected correctly, and gave her the thumbs up. (Laredo always refers to him as Ranger, because ever since they met at the University of Texas in Austin, he had made it clear he was going to join the elite Army Rangers. Laredo signed up for the Army the same day.)

When she slowly made her way out of her Capitol Hill townhouse, weighted down by her hazmat suit and breathing tank and regulator, a Secret Service SUV, one version of the Roadrunner, was idling out front. It was a highly modified Ford F-350 Super Duty designed for Special Ops. The super-sophisticated vehicles—of which there were six as of this writing—are built for the Service by Air Force Space Command at Peterson Air Force base in Colorado, and can only be assembled in highly guarded secrecy on that base. The vehicle's satellite system is connected to the Warfighter Information Network Tactical and the Panther Satellite Communications terminal.. They are also said to bristle with weaponry and other highly classified devices.

Laredo carefully hauled herself up into the vehicle and settled in for the drive across town to Spring Road N.W. in Petworth and the newly discovered secret lab. The driver started to engage the Roadrunner's sealed windows, which would put the driver and passenger in separate bubbles, with separate air supplies.

The two greeted each other first, but said nothing for the rest of the drive out of respect for the degree of danger they were both approaching, especially Laredo. Though as she later said with typical swagger, "I was born to do this shit."

As dawn approached, the SUV arrived at a three-story early 20th century rowhouse which seemed (because of the rogue lab she knew was inside) to vibrate evil and terrible danger—the heart of darkness, she thought. She knew the FBI had already been inside, but hadn't touched anything, so there was a huge danger it was booby-trapped.

A D.C. Police car was parked out front, as was a uniformed FBI car. Laredo nodded at the cops, and couldn't help but think, "They are glad I'm going in and not them." The driver followed her up the steps to the entrance, and thoughtfully gave her hazmat suit a last-minute check.

The old house at first just smelled musty, but deeper inside there was an overwhelming bitter chemical odor. The walls were covered in peeling floral paper. The dingy, Victorian interior gave off heavy vibes suggesting that the women from *Arsenic and Old Lace* had once lived there. There were a few old chairs with the stuffing hemorrhaging and broken legs giving them a lopsided, drunken feeling. Arab-language magazines were strewn on the floor. There was a cache of porn in a bathroom; the Ayatollah wouldn't approve, Laredo laughed. It was a house to get the job done and be abandoned.

Opening the door to the basement, she shined her flashlight down the rickety wooden staircase, which ominously had several stairs missing and others dangling by a nail. The railing held little solace because it was barely attached to the wall.

Her first impression of the lab was that it was sloppy and unprofessional, slapped together for one quick purpose, and the architects of this sick project wouldn't give a damn if the people assigned to make it happen lived or died. Examining the equipment, Laredo formed a quick and chilling hypothesis; they were making Marburg Ebola virus in aerosol form. The Soviet Union had experimented with an aerosol version of the virus for use as a bioweapon, and found it had a fatality rate of up to 90 percent; plus, it was stable and had a reasonably long shelf life.

The crude but workable setup had her pulse racing at the simplicity and banality of a plan with such evil potential—a potential to be worse than 9/11 by far. It sent a chill up her spine. A stream of sweat coursed down her brow and she felt embarrassed, even though she was alone. "I've got to snap out of this," she thought.

Laredo took samples, sealed them carefully, and made the trip up the stairs and out of the rowhouse, with a sense of urgency and excitement that the fiendish lab had been discovered before it could be unleashed on the nation's capital.

She said a silent prayer of thanks to the alert D.C. cop who had noticed the bogus sewer repairmen.

CHAPTER EIGHT

Cubs of the Caliphate

The Secret Service has a unit composed of men and women recruited from Silicon Valley and other high-tech centers from around the country, who have offices at the agency's headquarters in Washington. They monitor world-wide internet traffic around the clock, looking for threats of any kind against government officials.

Every hint of a threat, or plan to harm a protected person, is picked up and recorded for analysis and/or action. ISIS and Taliban propaganda videos are given priority, because they often inadvertently—out of braggadocio or for recruitment purposes—disclose future plots, as well as methods and weapons to be deployed in terror attempts.

Radical groups are constantly advertising themselves to recruit preferably young and economically desperate potential cannon fodder, and to solicit contributions from wealthy Islamists around the world.

So, when a cherubic ten-year-old American boy popped up on an ISIS video in 2017, chillingly saying, "My message to Trump, the puppet of the Jews: Allah has promised us victory and he's promised you defeat," with a near snarl, ears perked up and the tape was rushed to the action analysts.

He continued, "The battle is not going to end in Raqqa or Mosul, it's going to end in your lands…. So get ready, for the fighting has just begun."

Ranger was the most experienced Middle East warrior in the agency at the time and was assigned the task of helping the military retrieve the boy, and of terminating whoever was controlling and manipulating him.

His immediate thought on being briefed was that the boy was going to be used as a suicide bomber. ISIS was skilled at the sick art of brainwashing young boys into believing in jihad, and even desiring, and actually looking forward to the glory of sacrificing their lives for the radical Islamic cause.

At that age—ten—they were taught to fight with AK-47s and to assemble and wear their own suicide vests.

In Ranger's opinion, the boy had to be found and extracted from Syria, if he was to survive.

On the second day on the rescue mission, Ranger got a very lucky break. Local police in Elkhart, Indiana got a phone call from a student who had come across the video and recognized his former classmate. He said he had been a sweet boy. But, obviously, suddenly, shockingly he turned into an anti-Semitic, venom-spewing radical with hatred for America, who broadcasted thinly veiled threats against the president.

Police interviews with others who knew the family said they had had abruptly moved to parts unknown, with the boy and his sisters.

It made Ranger wonder aloud "what the hell are school children doing watching jihadi propaganda films online?" But he was happy and grateful for the info.

Local cops had turned their information over to the state police, who called both Army Intelligence and the Secret Service. The lost boy was named Matthew Sally. His mother was identified as Samantha Elhassani.

Stepfather Moussa Elhassani, and mom Samantha, who was apparently in thrall to Elhassani, had taken Matthew and three female siblings first to Turkey, then into ISIS-controlled territory in Syria. Moussa was apparently obsessed with joining ISIS and planned to train with the jihadis, turning the ten-year-old Matthew into a sacrificial lamb.

He knew that he would be rewarded for finding a child who could be made into a martyr. A sacrificial lamb, especially an American, is a most precious gift, and he would be rewarded.

The Indiana schoolteacher who had gone to the police had once met Moussa and Matthew's mother, and thought they were seriously disturbed, almost certainly dangerous people, who shouldn't have children in their charge. She expressed profound concern for the boy and begged the police to do something to save his life from the monsters, especially his stepfather who was obviously using him, planning on sacrificing the child's life for his personal elevation in the twisted world of terrorism.

It was later learned Moussa had already promised the boy as a suicide bomber.

A UN children's agency spokesperson said at the time, "Child recruitment across the region is increasing. Children are taking a much more active role. They are receiving training in the use of heavy weapons, manning check points on the front lines, being used as snipers and worse of all, being trained and used as suicide bombers."

Christian Science Monitor reporter Ben Rosen wrote that security forces had apprehended a sixteen-year-old with two kilograms of explosives under his soccer shirt, in the Iraqi city of Kirkuk. "Earlier that day, a suicide bomber about the same age killed [himself] and six others outside a Shiite Mosque."

At a soccer awards ceremony in the southern Iraq village of Al-Asriya, a suicide bomber of fifteen or sixteen set off his suicide vest, killing forty-three people, mostly children.

As the tide turned against ISIS, increasing its losses in battle and greatly depleting its forces of cannon fodder volunteers and reserves, its situation became critical. The U.S.-led forces were rapidly driving it out of most of the territory it had gained; as a result, the jihadis' tactics became more desperate and despicable, relying on children as suicide bombers and soldiers more and more.

Their sad, tortured army of child soldiers were known as the "cubs of the Caliphate."

At Secret Service Headquarters, Ranger made plans to carry out his mission, calling old friends who were still in special ops out of Bagram Air Base in Afghanistan. He told them he was leaving that night and requested whatever help they could give. After some hasty conferences, he was told to bring his old uniform so he could go into combat, should it come to that.

He told his wife Laredo that he was psyched to be back in his captain's uniform and to fight alongside his former brothers-at-arms.

She could only manage a wan smile at his obvious joy at possibly seeing combat again. But a flood of memory of sleepless nights she had spent while he was six thousand miles away, in almost daily battle over there, brought the pain and fear for his well-being back.

The eighteen-hour flight to Bagram was aboard a giant Lockheed C-5 Galaxy cargo plane, a flying groaning board loaded with heavy weapons and tons of ammunition. There was always fear that the cumbersome weapons and ordnance might have been sloppily secured. All it took was a groggy soldier with a hangover to make a mistake. The work was tedious, repetitive, and usually done in a hurry, because the planes were always under pressure to get in the air and deliver war supplies that soldiers in the field desperately needed.

If a jeep, truck, or tank came loose, a passenger could be hit and killed, or even worse, the thin aluminum skin of the plane could be breached, which would be an unspeakable disaster. People might be sucked out through the hole, or the plane could go out of control and possibly crash.

Those were Ranger's dark thoughts as he attempted to get some sleep.

His fellow passengers were mostly weapons—not great conversationalists. The trip was grueling and didn't have any in-flight entertainment or beverage service, to say the least. As a result, a lot of the passengers brought their own beverages, usually in a flask. As the only officer in the passenger compartment, he knew that, by the book, he should have said something, but he didn't have the desire or the heart.

He thought, "let them have their fun, where they're going there won't be much of that, if at all."

Ranger had made the trip often enough to know it was always miserably cold until the approach to Bagram, then it became brutally hot.

This wasn't his first Afghan rodeo, by a long shot. He had tangled with Taliban and ISIS many times and knew there was no ungodly horror they wouldn't commit to get their way. They were human tarantulas, motivated by a perverse version of the Islamic religion, that had been twisted like a pretzel to convince followers that life in this mortal coil is useless, so it's actually better to fight and die for Allah, then to live and love and achieve art and science for human progress.

On final approach, the blast furnace sweeping over the interior of the plane made Ranger feel oddly comfortable to be back in the hellish land he had grown to tolerate. The irony almost made him laugh, but not quite. The situation was far too serious: almost always, life or death.

As the plane landed, Ranger felt he was ready for the madness of the Bagram base tents. A strip of land near the landing strip housed an alphabet soup of intelligence agencies, all of whom seemed to be fighting their own private war, at times seeming to be at cross-purposes. And it wasn't just Americans—the command-and-control operations of allied nations bivouacked there. It was really a NATO base.

But he had to admit he almost looked forward to the battle he might soon face.

The good news was that Army Intelligence had located the boy in Syria, and all that was left was to move in with a team of Rangers to extract him—without setting off his suicide vest, or his stepfather who might kill him rather than let him escape.

Ranger had often seen the scattered, bloody remains of suicide bombers and their victims. As battle-hardened as he was, it was a sight you never forget, especially when the victim is a young boy.

Fortunately or unfortunately, due to the expansion and savagery of the terror groups, the rules of engagement had changed since he had last served in Afghanistan several years before. Drones were regularly deployed over Syria and Pakistan; special ops raids, like the ones he had specialized in leading, were almost routine. The ISIS and Taliban fighters certainly feared the drones circling menacingly overhead, day and night, but somehow went on with ordinary life. When they heard a drone coming, they often tried to hide behind a tree. But if it was a high-value target, the kill chain controlling the drones from halfway across the world would aim the Hellfire missile right at the tree, blowing it and the fighter to kingdom come.

Ranger had seen a video of Matthew building a suicide vest and putting it on, as well as one showing the then ten-year-old wielding an AK-47, taking it apart and putting it back together like a professional soldier. Incredibly, the video had been shot by the boy's mother Samantha. Great mom. He thought she needed a long prison term, at least, even though she deserved some credit for getting Matthew to safety before it was too late.

Another video, also taken by Mom, showed how Matthew was being trained to kill the Americans coming to rescue him. His twisted mother, who was from a successful family with radical Islamic sympathies, had set up the entire situation, having smuggled thirty thousand dollars in cash and gold into the country. The money and the boy were handed over to the terror group in exchange for accepting Moussa as a member and training him as an ISIS sniper—apparently, his dream job.

The Special Ops Rangers had assigned a Global Hawk drone to circle the house in Raqqa and to record young Matthew's mother's decision to flee her husband. Samantha seemed to given her all for her husband's success, but she had apparently hit her limit when Moussa purchased two young Yazidi women to work as household and sex slaves.

The Army command knew there was zero point in asking the Syrian government for help, because someone in their ranks would doubtless tip off ISIS. Plus, Syrian soldiers sent to rescue them would almost certainly sexually abuse the girls as well, because they would consider them already defiled and beyond rescue.

That was, sadly, how most Syrian authorities typically reacted to the horrors they witnessed, and turned a blind eye toward, day in and day out.

The more savagery they saw, the more they themselves practiced savagery. They were the same people who, following orders from their hopelessly corrupt government, dropped poison sarin gas on their own civilian population, killing scores of men, women, and children.

Matthew and his three sisters were put in the hands of paid professional smugglers who stuffed Matthew in a barrel, because as an adolescent boy he would be classified as a soldier despite his age, and wouldn't be allowed to leave the country, but be conscripted into a militia or terror group—whichever offered the best reward.

They made it to a Kurdish refugee camp and, rather miraculously, eventually back to the U.S. was charged with aiding and abetting terrorists, and sentenced to six and a half years in prison.

Matthew was sent to Florida to live with his biological father, Juan. In an interview with the BBC, he told of his ordeal, showing maturity and a keen sense of observation well beyond his years.

"I was so young. I did not really understand any of it." He said the stepfather forced him to make the threatening video during the two years of his virtual imprisonment. But he recalled the horror of being under the power of a deranged man. "He was starting to lose it, he was mentally unstable, very unstable."

He talked about arriving in Turkey and sneaking into Syria at age ten: "We ran across an area that was very dark. It was at night, there were random spots of barbed wire. There wasn't much going through my head except, 'I need to run.'

"When we were first in Raqqa, we were in the city parts. It was pretty noisy, gunshots normally. Once in a while, there was a random explosion, like far away though."

Speaking of being back in the Unites States, finally safe, getting therapy and leading a normal life again, Mathew said, "It's like being in tight clothes all day and then taking then off and chilling in a hot bath. That's what it felt like. Like sweet relief. It felt good."

Knowing the children were gone, Ranger and his colleagues made the decision to neutralize Moussa Elhassani. He was clearly the one who was threatening President Trump and was a dangerous, sociopath, still on the loose.

A Predator drone was standing by, being monitored by satellite connection from Creech Air Force Base in Nevada. Drone intel was so valuable to Special Forces that the Army was at the time spending over $1 million a day on satellite rental alone.

The sex slave girls were outside, apparently doing chores and were barely out of harm's way. But it was the moment.

As soon as they received the order, a Hellfire missile was launched, and Moussa was no more. The roaring blast left the house nothing but twisted and smoldering rubble and knocked the girls almost ten feet from where they were standing. They were stunned and covered in black soot, but they were free, relatively unscathed, and safe. The only trace left of Moussa was his smoking, decapitated head.

The analysts in Nevada always went over the scenes of destruction carefully after firing a drone-based Hellfire missile, not out of morbid interest, but to see that the intended victim was dispatched, and that there was—one hoped—no collateral damage. Sometimes they found scattered body parts, but most of the time, if it was a direct hit, there was only one identifiable body part, as with Moussa's head.

There was satisfaction that the boy and the two girls were safe, but there was no hi-fiving or celebration anywhere along the kill chain, not in Bagram, Ramstein Army Base in Germany, or in the control room at Creech Air Force Base in Nevada.

Employing weapons that the victim couldn't see or hear coming, controlled by someone on the other side of the world, like a bolt of lightning out of the sky, had an element of playing God, and it made Ranger feel very uneasy, especially since the final go decision had been his.

It was a priority to carefully record the damage to be certain, and to preserve evidence there were no innocents killed. Hundreds of civilians had been killed in Pakistan since George W. Bush initiated the program of taking out high-value targets with drones, and Barack Obama greatly increased the frequency of precision strikes, with the goal of saving American and allied casualties in battle.

In one terrible mistake in March of 2011, forty people who turned out to be civilians attending a tribal meeting were killed. To avoid repeats of that tragedy in 2020, a new helicopter-like drone called an A160 Hummingbird, which resembles a mythical flying saucer, was put into service. It carries an imaging system called ARGUS-IS which provides video streams of ten frames per second in real time, delivering clear imaging to track people and vehicles from altitudes above twenty thousand feet. It has the added advantage that the Taliban and ISIS have no weapons that can reach anywhere near that altitude.

The firm belief, born out by casualty numbers, studied by Special Ops and Hawkeye CAT, is that the drones have saved countless lives of soldiers and operatives, who otherwise would have had to fight fierce battles on ground that favors a guerrilla army like the Taliban/ISIS forces.

In war there are always civilian deaths and a great dislocation of the indigenous population, which is sad but inevitable. The creators and managers of the kill chain point out, in strong terms, that the United States didn't pick a fight with the terrorists. The terrorists picked a fight with America, and a steep price comes with that mistake, and always has historically. Taliban and ISIS apparently labored under the false impression that America was going to fold her cards after 9/11. Even thinking *that* was delusional.

That's the same mistake Imperial Japan made at Pearl Harbor. The terror chiefs should, perhaps, have referenced Japanese Admiral Isoroku Yamamoto who wrote in his diary after the attack on Hawaii, and the ensuing highly premature victory celebrations: "I fear all we have done is to awaken a sleeping giant and filled him with a terrible resolve."

The Secret Service, unlike most law enforcement agencies, casts a wide net and frequently uncovers wrong-doing that is not strictly part of the official charge—which was why the concept of the Hunters was not alien. Simply reacting to an attempt on the president's life was obviously the key mission, but never was it seen as the be-all and end-all.

In August of 1938, during an investigation of a counterfeiting operation, undercover agent Stanley Phillips was offered five hundred dollars to murder a man, so his wife could collect his life insurance policy. Agent Phillips agreed to participate and uncovered a Murder-Inc.-type outfit that regularly obtained arsenic from rogue doctors and morticians to carry out a poison for profit operation.

Over the course of the investigation, seventeen men and women were arrested and charged with over twenty-one murders.

One of the first to threaten President Trump was a Pennsylvania man, Shawn Christy, with a long history of terroristic threats against former vice-presidential candidate Sarah Palin (whom he threatened to rape), as well as a tax clerk in his hometown of Bangor, Pennsylvania, and the mayor of McAdoo, Stephan Holly, whom he had attempted to assault with a four-foot stick. So it was no surprise that Trump's take-no-prisoners approach to politics would catch his combative eye.

A self-described "survivalist," he was considered a Level III danger to the president and other agency protectives.

On August 22, 2018, the Secret Service issued an urgent "Wanted" poster announcing that "Shawn Christy is wanted for threatening to kill law enforcement officers, government officials and President Donald Trump. Christy is considered armed and dangerous."

The Agency offered a twenty-thousand-dollar reward for information leading to his capture. Ranger, who was assigned to the case along with the FBI and U.S. Marshals, joked that the warrant should have said "wanted dead or alive" like in the Wild West. "He's a goddamn mad dog."

Christy made his threats on Facebook, presumably because a post can be viewed by millions, getting these writers the widespread attention and notoriety they crave.

Retired Secret Service agent Jeffrey Bramer, who worked from 1984 to 1990 in the Protective Intelligence Squad during the Reagan and Bush years, recalled that most threats were made in person, with no attempt to hide their identity.

> People would regularly show up in person at the northwest gate of the White House to make threats against the president. If they were armed, or if their threat seemed serious, the uniformed Secret Service would call my office and one of us would go and interview the person, get a picture taken of him or her, and assess the risk. We always carried pictures of the guys we rated as a real risk. I still have some of them.

> Each case had to be judged on an individual basis by the agent. A great deal of money and effort was spent trying to develop a profile to determine who was dangerous and who was not. In the end all the profiles by top psychologists and others proved to be almost worthless.

> We studied the Kennedy assassination and numerous attempts and realized each case was unique. There

were often cases of a guy mouthing off in a bar because he was pissed off at some policy of a president, or a statement he had made. Then there were cases where an individual took action like throwing red paint or even blood at a motorcade.

It is surprising how often that happens. We then had to determine whether to take them in our custody or let the local cops prosecute. It was a judgement call and rested with the instincts of the agents present.

John Hinckley was arrested at the Nashville airport when Jimmy Carter was in town to appear at the Grand Ole Opry. He set off an alarm going through security. He was carrying a weapon and bullets. The FBI interviewed him and determined, according to their profile, that he posed no threat to the president. They missed many clues in evaluating him. It was just months before he shot Reagan.

Shawn Christy was determined by the agency to be a serious threat because he had already attacked government workers, was known to be armed, and—unlike most other potential shooters—he disappeared when the Secret Service came to interview him.

Christy threatened to kill Pennsylvania District Attorney John Morganelli and President Trump, promising to "use lethal force on any law enforcement officer that attempts to detain him." He posted a threat to the district attorney, writing: "Keep it up Morganelli, I promise I'll put a bullet in your head as soon as I put one in the head of Donald J. Trump."

You post a threat like that and guess who's coming to dinner: the Hunters.

The twenty-seven-year-old was described as five feet, ten inches tall and 165 pounds, with a tattoo on his arm and a distinct lisp. Obsessed with famous government officials since he was a teen, Christy first contacted Alaska Governor Sarah Palin, while volunteering to work for the John McCain-Sarah Palin Republican ticket.

A year later he attempted to contact Palin's fourteen-year-old daughter online, apparently without success. Miffed at the rejection, he began sending threats to Palin, John McCain, and President Barack Obama, warning them to "watch your back."

Next, he took a Greyhound bus to Washington, D.C. Knowing he was making threats against government officials, his father contacted the U.S. Capitol Police. Shawn was taken into custody upon arrival in Washington, but released to the custody of his parents.

Concerned about Christy's obsession with her family, the former Alaska governor obtained a restraining order, complaining of constant threats and harassment by phone and online.

A year later he was arrested by a U.S. marshal and charged with illegal possession of a firearm, but was quickly released.

By 2018 he began posting threats against President Trump, warning him to "keep probation officers off my ass."

He then began his dangerous hejira, stealing cars and abandoning them, from the eastern Canadian border to the American Midwest.

In July Christy returned to Pennsylvania and broke into the home of his uncle in Butler Township, and stole a .22 caliber handgun, a 9mm pistol, a .380 handgun, and ammunition. His father, Craig, sent him a Facebook post begging him to come home and turn himself in to authorities. But, apparently emboldened with his stolen weaponry, he traveled to Greensburg, Kentucky and stole a Jeep from the home of Dakota Meyer, the former husband of Sarah Palin's oldest daughter Bristol.

Traveling in a Secret Service Command SUV Roadrunner, Ranger joined the hunt, but unlike the law enforcement officers who relied on psychological profiles, he relied on the tracking lessons he had learned from his dad hunting in Texas Hill Country. He eventually tracked his prey through six states and parts of Canada.

Ranger profiled Shawn Christy as extremely immature for a man in his late twenties. He lived in his parents' basement, couldn't hold a job, and was extremely resentful and frightened of authority figures, although he'd made it his life's work to get close to and communicate with them.

He was compulsive and naïve as well as insecure. Insecurity meant that he would always return home, even when he was being pursued. Stealing cars and abandoning them was like an addiction. He would drive in a big circle with no goal in mind, then return to McAdoo, Pennsylvania. When he felt the need for a gun, he stole one from his uncle, because he knew that if he got caught, he wouldn't be shot—a stronger possibility if he broke into the home of a stranger. He lacked familiarity with weapons because he hadn't ever owned one of his own. He also stole from ex-employers because they were familiar properties and, again, he figured he would get away with it if caught. He threatened people constantly, but had never fulfilled any of the threats—so far.

Christy was clearly a loner, as well as a loser, and didn't appear to have ever had a lover, male or female.

His predictability meant he would never actually travel cross-country or leave the country for long. Ranger concluded all he had to do was wait for him to return to the general area of McAdoo.

Ranger was convinced there was zero chance this Wiley Coyote would get anywhere near President Trump, or that he ever actually intended to menace Trump in person, because he was a coward. But the possibility he would try to leave his mark by killing someone without protection, like Sarah Palin or a tax collector, was a serious possibility.

The Hunter was closing in on Christy, and was right behind him when he broke into the Skitco Iron Works, where he had once worked, stole a shotgun, and used a computer to post on Facebook as a way of talking to his parents, saying he had shattered his knee during his getaway in Maryland a few days earlier. About a mile and a half from his hometown of McAdoo, Pennsylvania, it appeared Christy was running out of steam. But he crossed over into Ohio, about one hundred miles west of Pittsburgh, ditched his latest stolen car, and tried to disappear into the woods, shattered knee and all. Ranger thought this interesting...wounded prey taking to the brush.

Several other federal agents and Ohio Highway Patrol officers were also on his trail and had released police dogs. Finally, he was cornered between a rocky crevice and a dry river stream.

The arrest was made east of Mansfield, Ohio, near Camp Mowana. The fugitive was relived of the .380 pistol and a knife. He would be returned to Pennsylvania to face a federal court in Scranton on charges that would keep him in custody for a long time.

The three-month chase was over.

In the end, Christy was found guilty of eleven felony counts.

Ranger told the author,

> President Trump was always hands-on with the Secret Service. He's the only president I've known who remembers everybody's name and talks to us like family. He's a pleasure to protect.

> And he knows all about the Hunters and has told the higher ups he wants to make sure we are fully funded all the time. Since almost nobody knows we even exist, we don't get much flack, and we aim to keep it that way. Anonymity is essential to our carrying out our mission.

> Trump is the first president to bother to learn who the Hunters and Hawkeye CAT are and what we do, and he appreciates us.

> A lot of what we do is dangerous and there is always the potential for getting in serious legal trouble if we were investigated by people trying to make a political point. The Defund the Police crowd would like nothing better than to destroy us, even though our mission is to aggressively defend the people we are charged with protecting and stopping people who want to use weapons of mass destruction, including chemical and biological warfare to make their twisted, sociopathic points.

People either don't realize we live in the age of terror and the old ways can't contain it any more or, worse, they don't care.

Hunters are unorthodox, but in many ways, we are, along with Hawkeye CAT, the last line of defense for the nation's government.

In late summer of 2020, Hunters got alarming reports from the Protective Division that at least one drone had come dangerously close to President Trump's 757 version of Air Force One. The plane carrying the president, first lady, and their then fourteen-year-old son Baron, had taken off from the Morristown Municipal Airport in New Jersey near the president's golf club, and was about to land at Joint Base Andrews outside Washington.

The small drone appeared to be deliberately navigated to hit the plane. The question was: was it kids pulling a prank, or terrorists trying to fly the drone into one of the plane's engines, possibly with explosives? State police and the Secret Service Uniformed Division were investigating, and Ranger was on his way to Joint Base Andrews.

Even a small drone weighing a few pounds could shatter a cockpit window and, if it was steered into an engine, conceivably take the plane down the way birds have done on rare occasions. In 2017, a civilian drone struck an army helicopter in New York City. The helicopter was seriously damaged but was able to land safely. Two years later, a KABC-TV traffic helicopter was struck in downtown Los Angeles and was also badly damaged. Major airports, including Newark Liberty, have been shut down because of drone activity, causing the FAA to pass regulations requiring civilian drones to be equipped to transmit their identity and location, by the end of 2020. But that wasn't in effect when the drone buzzed Air Force One.

While state and local police seemed to be dithering and not terribly interested in finding the perps, Ranger had them nailed an hour after he arrived, based on old fashioned leg work and the fact that he flashes a federal badge and looks intimidating as hell.

They weren't the kids he expected, but twenty-somethings who should have known better. They admitted they hated Trump and his family, but turned over their drone, which wasn't equipped with explosives or other weaponry. He prepared to turn the idiots over to local cops, when they surprised him by explaining they knew some other drone fans who had told them they intended to actually bring down a plane, and claimed to have weaponized drones to do the job.

"They had gone to Virginia because they had friends who lived near Andrews whose sport was shining laser beams into the cockpits of landing fighter jets. I guess it was their twisted idea of being a peacenik."

Ranger perked up and took off his bad cop hat and donned a good cop smile. "If you lead me to these guys, you've got a get out of jail free card."

"They had been properly frightened by their close encounter with me, so I was sure they would stay out of trouble with drones for the near future. They were idiots, but they had proved to be useful idiots, my favorite kind."

It turned out the bad guys lived in Paterson, New Jersey, and had ties to radical Islam.

Ranger called for reinforcements and headed to New York.

> I didn't want to stumble into an ongoing operation and screw things up, so I called a friend at NYPD Terror Intel Group and told her what I was onto. That got her attention big time and she asked if she could assign a few guys to join in the fun.
>
> I said, "When I'm playing in your backyard, you're always welcome to join my operation." She ran their names while I was on the phone and said it was a hit. There were warrants on both and for over-staying their student visas."
>
> The deal was they would pick the suspects up and I would sit in on the interrogations. That suited me because I

didn't want to get into a fire fight in Paterson, New Jersey, that would take some sticky explaining.

A few hours later Ranger was eyeballing the suspects through a one-way mirror. They were what he expected: Sallow faces, dank eyes, and morose glares of defiance.

"They reminded me of Taliban I had watched through my sniper scope in Afghanistan in the moments before I squeezed the trigger. I saw them as the faces of the creatures who made the Twin Towers fall. I saw the falling man tumble his way to eternity.

"I never have any regrets, but I often ask for God's forbearance."

The NYPD Terror Group got right to business, mentioning the idea of the two men spending the rest of their lives in Cuba at Guantanamo, baking in the searing tropical sun. Waterboarding was also casually mentioned. They exchanged glances, expressing a growing sense of panic, which Ranger caught in the corners of their eyes. That definitely got their attention, and suddenly they knew a lot more about the plots they were involved in, and even remembered who the leaders were.

Ranger later said, "these guys were definitely not the varsity team, but a lot of the time you have to hunt for the weakest link. I knew they were in good hands in NYPD Terror Group custody and wouldn't be menacing air traffic in general, and the president's plane in particular, for a long, long time in the future. The FBI would soon be involved and hopefully a large and sinister organization would be dismantled, and the perps stored in Supermax for a long stretch.

"So, I packed up and headed home to file a report—the least likable part of my job. But I had bagged the bad guys and got a fount of information that would be shared with the Secret Service. It would make the men and women we protect safer."

CHAPTER TEN

The Birth of Hawkeye CAT

March 30, 1981 was a rainy, dreary day—an afternoon with a portent of malice.

President Ronald Reagan was delivering a routine address to a labor union group in the Grand Ballroom of the Washington Hilton Hotel. He was disappointed by the polite applause he received, but left feeling the address had been a mild success and would insure continued AFL-CIO support. He wrote in his diary, "speech not riotously received."

Nancy was lunching at the Georgetown home of Michael Ainslie, the president of the National Trust for Historic Preservation, with the vice president's wife, Barbara Bush. Halfway through lunch the First Lady was stricken by what she later described as a vague feeling of great unease: not feeling ill, but troubled. She reluctantly stopped eating her poached salmon and drinking her Chardonnay, and with sincere apologies excused herself.

She was concerned that her host would think something that was said had upset her. Even Nancy admitted over the years she had been a bit brittle. But subsequent events would erase that concern.

She was relieved that her limousine was at the front door waiting. Secret Service Agent George Opfer was unusually quiet. She later said she wondered if he shared her feeling of general angst. He usually had some interesting behind-the-scenes gossip of the White House that Nancy loved to hear. Knowing that he would never repeat a word she said, the First Lady openly shared the current buzz that she had heard.

The quiet made her sense of dread palpable as she watched the bleak, still, wintery cityscape pass by. She starred at the silent radio, but something stopped her from hitting the on-button and getting the latest news from WTOP. She felt in her heart that something very bad was going to happen, but hadn't happened yet. Instead, she stared out the window and sat in stony silence.

When the black, bulletproof limousine pulled into the south gate of the White House, the First Lady's mood changed from dread to panic. The grounds were alive with police. Men openly wearing their FBI badges and carrying weapons were more numerous than she had ever seen before. There were dozens of uniformed D.C. police surrounding the gates, cars of the federal uniformed Secret Service were parked on the Pennsylvania Avenue sidewalks, and agents were surrounding the mansion, also openly carrying assault rifles.

It was completely obvious there had been an attempt on the President's life. Nancy's blood ran cold. She knew, without benefit of a mirror, that she was ashen.

As the reality sank in, Nancy realized she was having trouble taking a breath. She fought it with every particle of her being; she knew this was a moment when she was going to have to be strong—Ronnie would expect nothing less of her.

The Executive Mansion was in full siege mode.

She struggled to not show the panic that was welling up inside her, and entered the White House with a wan smile. Rather than go to the family quarters, she took the elevator to the White House solarium, where she was greeted by the chief usher of the White House, who brought up the details for an upcoming party. Nancy saw his lips moving, but she couldn't comprehend what he was saying. It did occur to her that in the White House everything was on a "need to know" basis. Nobody idly informed you of anything.

With the chief usher prattling on about party plans to the uncomprehending First Lady, the door opened and Secret Service Agent Opfer entered the room. "There was a shooting. The president is going to the hospital."

A few minutes later she was in a two-car motorcade on her way to George Washington University Hospital. Downtown D.C. was in chaos and the streets were gridlocked. Frustrated and nearly in shock, Nancy threatened to get out and walk the rest of the way to the hospital.

She almost had to be restrained.

Another Secret Service agent got into the front seat and another car pulled into the lead. Six agents were in the car. They hit the flashing lights and gained a D.C. police escort on the way.

Finally, traffic began to move, and the Secret Service was spared from having to put the first lady in a head lock. Traffic melted away as people on the sidewalks sensed who was in the motorcade; some put their hands on the hearts, others saluted. Everybody in the world seemed to know what had happened—just not the First Lady. She was touched by the respectful display.

At the emergency entrance, Deputy Chief of Staff Michael Deaver bounded out and opened the car door before anyone else could, took her petite, manicured hand, and helped her out.

"The president has been shot, but the doctors say he will survive."

Nancy struggled to respond but her words came out garbled at first. Finally, she said emphatically, "I have to be with him right now. Mike, they don't know how it is with us. He has to know I'm here! I need to see my husband!"

It, of course, occurred to her that if somebody had gotten to the president, the Secret Service had failed in their sworn duties. They hadn't done their job. Period. She knew it wasn't fair to point fingers at the people who put their own lives on the line every day for them, but she was sensing that there had been a systemic failure, and it felt like a betrayal. The government of the greatest nation on earth can't keep the chief executive safe. What the hell?

Nancy Reagan was code-named Rainbow by the Secret Service, some said because of her volatile temper that came in numerous bright colors. At that moment she had to struggle to avoid having a flare-up, which she knew would have been wholly inappropriate.

But she felt that surely there had to be a better way to protect the president's life, and she vowed to make it her crusade. She knew it wasn't the kind of thing to do publicly—it wasn't first-lady-like. It wasn't "Just Say No." It would have to be a behind-the-scenes campaign to create a new and improved Secret Service. Later, she noted in her diary that what was needed was a redesigned Secret Service capable of matching the bad guys, bullet for bullet, in the age of terror.

As soon as Ronnie was better, she would talk to him, informally and quietly, about putting her in charge of a task force to reorganize the agency and supercharge their ability to protect the president. She knew there would be kickback because government bureaucracy instinctively abhors change. She had worked for eight years, struggling alongside Ronnie, to try and spur the obdurate bureaucracy of California, and now she would go to work with him on Washington's even more entrenched deep state.

But the fact that he had nearly been assassinated would put a bite in her argument that would put the most intransigent opponent at a disadvantage.

Deaver told her the wound was very serious. The bullet was just an inch from his heart, and he had internal bleeding which the doctors were struggling to contain. What he didn't tell her was that the doctors were far from certain they would be able to save his life.

She later thought that the reply that came out of her lips at the news sounded nearly like a screech or the cry of a wounded animal.

"Mike, tell me what happened, who did it, and why?"

"A crazy kid named Hinckley. He had gone gunning for Jimmy Carter. The cops got him on a concealed weapons charge in Nashville. He had apparently planned to shoot Carter at the Grand Ole Opry. Then he wanted to kill Ted Kennedy, presumably to join the rogue's gallery of Kennedy assassins.

"They missed all the clues and let him go."

Deaver said that the government at the time had a list of twenty-five thousand people who it considered might attempt to kill a president, based on threats, being turned down for a gun purchase, and other suspicious information. There were also about four hundred individuals deemed dangerous enough to be surveilled if the president was to be in the cities where they lived.

Hinckley was on neither list, despite having tried to smuggle guns on a plane in Nashville and being arrested for gun possession. The longtime presidential friend and confidant could only shake his head.

The pronouncement only served to redouble Nancy's desire, that would become a quiet crusade, to "amp up" the Secret Service protection afforded U.S. presidents.

The FBI now maintains a Terrorist Screening Center master list to which numerous government agencies around the world contribute, including the aviation agencies, intelligence, and local and state police, among others. It is now routinely shared throughout all government security entities.

The scene at the hospital was even more chaotic than at The White House. Pennsylvania Avenue was crowded with television trucks and camera crews. Reporters were being held back by police, but in the excitement, they kept surging forward.

Finally, with prodigious police help, the limo managed to get to the emergency room entrance. This time it was Nancy who was bounding inside, nearly hysterical at the thought of what she was going to see. Brushing past security and frantically working medical staff, she entered the trauma bay and nearly collapsed. Ronnie looked like he had aged many years in the few hours since she had last seen him.

According to Bill O'Reilly's excellent account, *The Day the President Was Shot*, Nancy Reagan later recalled, "I saw him lying naked with strangers looking down at his naked body, and watching the life ebb out from him, and as a doctor's daughter I knew that he was dying." A tube was draining internal bleeding caused by a bullet still lodged next to his heart. She later learned he had lost half of his blood supply and barely had enough in his body to survive.

Reagan, then seventy, opened his eyes and tried to smile. Even under the direst circumstances he could muster a good-natured quip.

"Honey, I forgot to duck," he said, quoting what boxer Jack Dempsey said to his wife when he lost the world heavyweight championship in 1926 to Gene Tunney.

She leaned over and kissed his anguished face and said a silent prayer that he would survive, against all odds, as tears flowed down her cheeks. She whispered to her husband, "Ronnie, I'm praying." He smiled again and squeezed her hand, then drifted back off. Doctors and nurses who noticed the incredible tableau averted their gazes, to allow Nancy's prayerful gesture to take place with as much privacy as a frantic trauma bay could allow.

She later reflected on the ordeal in her 1992 autobiography *My Turn*, "When you are as frightened as I was, you reach out for help and comfort in any direction you can. I prayed what seemed like all the time, more than I ever have before."

When they wheeled him toward surgery and past Mike Deaver, Reagan looked up and asked his advisor and friend, "Who's minding the store?"

At that moment his gurney was wheeled into the operating room, and Nancy was told she couldn't come any further and would have to wait until he was out of surgery.

Thus began one of the hardest ordeals of her life, waiting for a life-or-death verdict—God's judgement.

Nancy, who was the daughter of a Chicago neurosurgeon, introduced herself to her husband's chief surgeon, Dr. Benjamin Aaron, and began what would become a nearly daily conversation with him. "She was tough," Dr. Aaron later recalled. "We couldn't throw fluff at her. She asked lots of questions and was prepared. You could tell she was completely devoted to her husband."

Nancy Reagan was not vituperative, she wasn't given to tantrums like Hillary Clinton, and she didn't try to use her pillow-talk advantage to control policy.

Her main legacy—as evidenced at the grand palace that is the Reagan Presidential Library in Simi Valley, California—was the "Just Say No" anti-drug campaign, her good taste, and seemingly unlimited budget for haute couture. The First Lady's clothes, worn at major events during the Reagan presidency, are one of the most popular exhibits at the Library.

But after the assassination attempt, she took up another cause she rarely, if ever, discussed publicly. Mrs. Reagan was determined that the Secret Service would build up its muscle and add a layer of ultimate defense to supplement the brave and heroic men in black suits. What she spent much of her considerable energy and passion to help create came to be known as Hawkeye CAT. Finally, there was a heavily armed cadre of ex-special-ops soldiers who would always travel with the president, equipped with overwhelming firepower to counter any threat.

It was a game changer created by Nancy Reagan's persistence and passion, to help ensure that what happened to her Ronnie would never happen again.

Her tenacious lobbying to the top managers of her husband's cabinet eventually paid off, adding a layer of iron to the agency that had never before existed, in the form of hardened combat veterans from the Army Rangers, Navy SEALs and other special operations fighters, trained to charge into action at lightning speed, like a super-dependable cavalry.

The former First Lady had created a new dynamic for presidential protection through her lobbying in high places, and it was her quiet legacy, that she doubtless would have been cheered to know has only grown stronger, more powerful, and more competent at their warrant to protect the current "Hawkeye" at whatever cost is necessary. The failed assassination attempt on her beloved Ronnie would reveal the hard steel in her character as well, that had led her to navigate a career in the shark-infested waters of Hollywood, and later the equally treacherous alleys of the Washington political landscape.

Nancy was forever grateful to Secret Service Agent Jerry Parr, who had hustled Reagan into the safety of his limousine and out of the line of fire, seconds before John Hinckley Jr. was able to get off a potential kill shot.

Unaware at first that the president had been hit in the chest with a ricochet that pierced his lung, the car was headed for the White House and safety in case there were other assassins, possibly working together. Then Reagan complained of chest pains, and Parr noticed blood on his lips, and immediately redirected the car to George Washington Hospital, where doctors stabilized the critically ill president, eventually saving his life.

At first Parr was sick, thinking the rough push he had given the president into the limo, and his desperate—and well-rehearsed—move to throw his body on top of the president to protect him from gun fire, had broken his rib.

Nancy always referred to Parr as "one of my true heroes" and said "without Jerry looking out for Ronnie on March 30, 1981, I would have certainly lost my best friend and roommate to an assassin's bullet. Jerry was not only one of the finest Secret Service agents to ever serve this country, but one of the most decent human beings I've ever known. He was humble but strong, reserved but confident and blessed with a great sense of humor. It is no wonder my husband got along with him so well." It seems she was describing the perfect Secret Service agent.

The two remained close friends until Parr's death in 2015, at eighty-five.

Nancy and Ron's daughter Patti Davis was in California when the shooting occurred. She recalled that she was in the middle of a therapy session when one of her Secret Service agents burst into the room. At first, she was shocked that he would crash into her doctor's office, but the first words out of his mouth were, "There's been a shooting."

She recalled in a *Washington Post* article years later that she and her brother Michael and sister Maureen were put on an Air Force transport plane to Washington, still not knowing if their dad would live or die.

"Shock is a strange thing," she wrote. "It crystalizes some memories and blurs others. I can still see my mother sitting up in bed clutching a shirt of my father's—she'd held onto it all night, breathing in his scent.

"I don't remember the drive to the hospital, but I remember coming into the room and seeing my father. His face was so pale it was almost translucent, and I had the sudden feeling that he might have died and come back."

Davis reflected on the shock of those first days and weeks, and compared the state of the nation's collective grief to today's harsh and brutal political landscape.

"Politics suddenly became incidental, almost irrelevant…people were stunned, grieving, softened by sadness…strangers opened their arms to me, and I gratefully accepted their embraces. I don't know whether we will ever experience that shared sympathy again in the United States. The lines have cut too deep, the distances are too great, and cruelty has become mainstream.

"We have put down roots in soil that doesn't nourish us, but rather poisons us."

Anyone who imagines "taking a bullet for the president" is a myth should consult the historical record on the date March 30, 1981, when a sick loner named John Hinckley shattered the thin membrane of civilization outside the Washington Hilton Hotel.

The would-be assassin slipped in with the gaggle of press, taking photographs and writing about President Reagan's appearance—a mistake that would be corrected immediately, making sure the legitimate members of the press were clearly holding prominent identification so the Secret Service would be aware of any pretenders.

Hinckley, alternatively suicidal and homicidal, obsessed with the actress Jody Foster, planned to assassinate Ronald Reagan to win her favor—as demented a plan as any ever hatched by a lunatic. Armed with a .22 caliber revolver loaded with Devastator bullets (which, with their lacquer-sealed aluminum tips with a lead azide center, are designed to explode on impact), he slipped out of the shadows as President Reagan emerged from the hotel ballroom where he had spoken to a labor group. He fired six rounds: one hit White House Press Secretary James Brady in the head, inflicting a critical wound, and D.C. police officer Thomas Delahanty was shot in the neck.

But at a critical moment when Hinckley had the President in his cross hairs and was going for the kill, Secret Service agent Timothy McCarthy stepped in front of the president. Taking a wide stance to make himself the target, he pivoted to the right to cover Reagan and took a bullet in his lower abdomen, which pierced his lung and liver.

Agent McCarthy clearly took a bullet for the president, probably saving his life.

The president survived.

In his book *In The President's Secret Service*, Ronald Kessler quotes a veteran agent saying "It's just basically you're going to try to get the man out of the way, and if you take some rounds, so be it."

As of this writing, twenty-nine agents have lost their lives bravely protecting the United States's leaders.

The assassination attempt profoundly changed both Reagans and Ron's Presidency. After regaining his strength and wellness, Ronald Reagan came to believe that God had spared him for a higher purpose, and he dedicated himself to proving he was worthy of divine intervention.

He credited the horror of that day with reinvigorating his presidency and changing the trajectory of his life and legacy.

Nancy later wrote that Ronnie threw himself into his work, and refused to surrender to the pain that would dog him for the rest of his life, as well as the mental trauma they both suffered.

The First Lady, on the other hand, never fully recovered from the psychological trauma and horrors of that day. At one point she asked him to consider not running for a second term, but relented because she knew he had important work to do for the country and the world. It haunted her days and often kept her awake late into the night. She didn't like letting him out of her sight, and insisted on accompanying him whenever and wherever possible.

"How was I ever going to live through eight years of this? Night after night I lay beside my husband and tried to drive these gruesome thoughts from my mind. Ronnie slept, but I could not...."

As soon as their life returned to a normal routine, she began her plan to remake the president's security apparatus—with his approval and complete cooperation—often to the annoyance of White House staffers, who traditionally jealously guard their prerogatives when it comes to presidential travel, security, and scheduling.

The good news was that Nancy reported that her new role strengthened their already symbiotic partnership and loving marriage.

Years later, when President Reagan had been out of office for a year and a half, and sadly stricken with Alzheimer's, everyone, including Nancy, thought they were safe. After all, nobody tries to kill an ex-president.

But the many decisions he had made during eight years in office had made some Americans very happy and others very angry. Tax cuts were popular with many, while his AIDS policy infuriated advocates who thought he hadn't done enough to find a cure.

A horrifying home invasion and attempt to murder former President Reagan *and* Nancy Reagan, in late June of 1990, left the Secret Service shaken and demoralized. Top brass down to rookies were convinced they had to change the rules and become proactive: hunting down and neutralizing threats to the people they are charged with protecting.

The conventional wisdom that ex-presidents needed only minimal protection, because they no longer had power and no longer had enemies, was forever erased from the Secret Service rule book.

Twenty-year Secret Service veteran Scott Alswang told the author that the man who had nearly killed the Reagans had slipped through the agencies' hands because they weren't equipped to track down and neutralize potential assassins before they struck. Instead, they were trained and ordered to watch their subjects—despite serious threats—and wait for the bad guys to make their move.

"The closest to tragedy that I recall during my career was the case of Gregory Stewart Gordon. He was an African American man from New

Brunswick, New Jersey. A huge man, six foot five and maybe 300 pounds, strong as an ox and filled with rage.

"He also happened to be gay and a religious fanatic."

Gordon had a brother who had died of AIDS and he was convinced that it was entirely Reagan's fault. Regular internet posts came to the attention of the Secret Service, in which Gordon claimed Reagan was the devil, and made much of the fact that the address of the former president's retirement home in Bel Air, California, was 666 St. Cloud Road. His internet postings were signed "King of Kings" and "Lord of Lords."

"Gordon made repeated vows to kill Reagan in retaliation for his brother's death and was quite open about it, posting regular threats. He was assessed as being emotionally disturbed and a Level III risk, which is the highest, but at the time not sufficient grounds for taking action to neutralize him. The Secret Service didn't have the authority, because he hadn't yet carried out a criminal assault.

Hawkeye CAT was fully operational at the time, but only charged with protecting the current leaders.

"I interviewed him repeatedly, and reported that he was well-educated, lucid, and determined to kill the former president."

Gordon was put under surveillance and information about the case was shared with the FBI and local police in New Jersey. When a person under Secret Service protection was near where he lived, surveillance was 24/7.

As months passed without any evidence that he was preparing an attack—by purchasing weapons or attempting to stalk the ex-president— the Service assumed he was just another unhinged person who had moved onto another obsession, as people like Gordon tend to do.

"Then, one day when I went to pay him a routine visit, he had disappeared. A few days later he was spotted at Los Angeles International Airport, and apparently made his way to Bel Air. It turned out he was hiding in the underbrush, keeping a hunter's eye on the president's home. But everyone assumed he had just disappeared."

The Reagans had a five-member Secret Service team, and seldom ventured out because of his ill heath, so at H Street N.W. headquarters no serious alarms went off that Gordon had apparently vanished. That proved to be a serious mistake and nearly a fatal one.

Apparently, Gordon decided the time was right to make his move. He easily scaled the tall rear fence of the estate, made his way across the lawn undetected, and kicked the kitchen door off its hinges. The frail former first lady screamed in surprise. She was alone in the relatively modest kitchen with a black cast-iron table and chairs, where the Reagans frequently had morning coffee and sweets.

Gordon shoved her out of the way, almost knocking her down, when he saw agent Jimmy Yarish, who raced to help. The two men crashed into each other and grappled with life-or-death desperation and ferocity. The lone agent on the scene understood that if he failed, the president and possibly the former first lady would die. The fight was fierce, smashing up furniture in the kitchen and dining room; at one point there was a struggle for a butcher knife which Gordon had grabbed off a counter.

Incredibly, the other four agents in the home at the time were in a break room watching *The Price is Right* with the volume turned up loud, and didn't hear the fierce two-man battle at the other end of the sprawling mansion.

Then, to Yarish's shock and horror, the president walked into the room. With the other agents locked away in the break room, watching a game show, there was no one to whisk the president and first lady to safety. They put their arms around each other and stared at the bizarre scene, mouths agape.

Reagan had heard the noise and wandered into the dining room, oblivious to the terrible danger he was in, too disoriented to understand the horrific drama unfolding.

Former Agent Alswang said, "For most of his life Ronald Reagan had carried a firearm, often barely concealed in a valise he carried, but in his dotage, it was obviously kept in a safe out of his reach. The former president had a terrible haircut at the time and was almost unrecognizable. He had taken to cutting his own hair with kitchen shears and looked sadly frightful."

Gordon, of course, recognized him, causing his rage to flare, ratcheting up his strength and determination for revenge. With the Reagans only feet away, paralyzed with fear, the agent and the assassin continued their struggle. Yarish slammed Gordon's head against the hardwood floor, but the intruder reared right back up and threw Yarish clear across the banquet size dining room, where his head hit a window and shattered the glass. Dripping blood from his head wound, Yarish feared for the first time he was going to lose the battle. Gordon assumed the fighting position and literally growled, sending Ron and Nancy on their heels, embracing each other, but still too stunned to run for their lives.

Suddenly, there were heavy footsteps and the four TV-watchers finally made their entrance. The former first family were escorted to a safe room, and Gordon was handcuffed—arms and legs.

The house was soon filled with cops. Gordon was eventually sentenced to nine years in federal prison—a remarkably light sentence, considering he confessed his intention had been to strangle the Reagans to death with his bare hands.

The shock of the home invasion of the former president's home was on a par with the British torching James Madison's White House on August 24, 1814, which had sent Dolley Madison scurrying to save the famous Gilbert Stuart painting of George Washington for posterity.

The incident was downplayed in the Los Angeles press, which suggested that this had been a simple case of trespassing on the Bel Air grounds and that the Reagans were never actually in jeopardy.

But the Secret Service and the entire intelligence community felt a seismic quake. After barely surviving the John Hinckley shooting, the Reagans had suffered another emotional trauma. They had learned they weren't even safe in their own home.

A new ruling was made that at least two agents would always be on duty with former presidents at all times. Among other fixes the Secret Service proactive agents made were transitioning to more modern, flexible weaponry. The highly effective, but big and unconcealable .45 caliber Thompson submachine gun was replaced, for instance, by the Israeli-made automatic 9mm Uzi submachine pistol, which could be carried under an agents' overcoat. It became the standard arm for decades.

Ranger and Laredo met at the University of Texas at Austin in 2004. They took a chemistry class together and she was smitten immediately. He was well over six feet tall, had a muscular physique which was plain to see in his tight polo shirts, a chiseled face, and—rather surprisingly for a college boy at the time—short cropped hair that was almost military-looking.

They didn't speak in class, but they clearly had eyes for each other. Laredo liked to study in the grass near the 307-foot-tall Beaux Arts University of Texas Tower. Built in 1937, it was for years the tallest building in the state.

Early in their freshman year, Ranger—Laredo's pet name for him after he told her of his intention to join the Army Rangers—surprised her by asking if she minded if he sat with her and studied. She just patted her towel and he plopped down next to her. At first, they said nothing, just stared into each other's eyes: his ocean blue, hers deep brown.

He thought that he could get lost in her eyes and never want to find the way out. They reminded him of a warm lake he and his friends went skinny dipping in on hot summer days in the Texas Hill Country.

Some years later, he heard a song by the indie rock group Warpaint with the line "your brown eyes are my blue skies," which became a greeting he sent in texts whenever they were separated.

It suddenly occurred to the boy that he was getting bedazzled and was already too deep in this girl that he had just talked to for the first time. He broke off his stare, and noticed with joy that she blinked several times. He had succeeded in getting inside her head, as she was inside his.

Laredo had dated several boys in high school and had clumsily played around in back seats, but had preserved her virginity for no particular reason, other than the fact she had never been set on fire yet.

This was different. She hated to admit it even to herself, but this guy reminded her of her father. He had the same confident bearing and military posture, which clearly wasn't a pose, but obviously came naturally to him. Though he was just eighteen like Laredo, he seemed ages older than the boys she had dated.

Over the next hour the two spilled out much of their brief, so far, life stories. Both were army brats who had attended more schools on army bases around the world than they could remember, and both were determined to be career military like their dads. Ranger (it would become his nickname and code name in the Hawkeye CAT, and later the Hunters) told her he had signed with ROTC and was determined to become an Army Ranger. He said she should join as well, and she nodded assent.

After a while he offered to give her a tour of the tower and its vast collection of drawings, blueprints, and designs of the creation of the U.T. campus. He stood up and took her hand to help her up—the first time they had touched—and when she was on her feet, he continued holding her hand as they walked toward the tower, which over the next several years would be their special place.

The building's twenty-seven floors contained the library's stacks of books, which were delivered to readers by librarians on roller skates, as well as offices of the university administration. It is framed by Indiana limestone Doric columns atop the UT Tower clock whose hands and rim are gilded with gold leaf.

Ranger showed her the secrets of the tower, which he had visited often while in high school, and took her to the twenty-eighth floor observation deck, with its striking views of the campus.

Hesitating at first to tell her the horrifying story of the massacre carried out on the campus from the deck, he decided she needed to know the tragic story: On August 1, 1966, twenty-five-year-old former Marine sharpshooter Charles Whitman, who had earlier in the day murdered his wife and mother, climbed to the observation deck armed with three rifles, two pistols, and a sawed-off shotgun. By the time the Austin police finally killed him, he had shot forty-three people, killing thirteen, including an unborn child. The mass murder spurred the creation of SWAT teams in cities all over the country—an ignominious legacy.

Far from being put off by the story, Laredo peppered him with questions and was genuinely interested in all the horrific details.

"This girl is Army Ranger material," he thought, and later told Laredo as much, asking her to apply to ROTC training with him. Laredo did and was accepted.

Laredo respected his strength, sincerity, and sense of mission—unusual in someone so young. She also noticed he kept a tiny Army-issued King James Bible in his shirt pocket during his every waking hour. It had been his grandfather's, who had it in his shirt pocket the day he landed at Utah Beach on D-Day with the Army's 4th Infantry Division. Ranger felt honor bound to carry the Bible into combat as well.

When Ranger proposed a month later, she cried with joy.

But pioneering a role in the Army Rangers wasn't her destiny. Her dad advised her that her skills in chemistry and biology were what the army needed, more than combat prowess. He told her, "I know you could do it. You could be the first woman to graduate from Ranger School. But what the army needs from you is to get your degrees, and go with the Army Chemical Biological Center to fight to protect your comrades-at-arms and your nation from terror, and that is increasingly biochem-related. That's where you're needed."

The dealbreaker for Laredo came when she learned that even if she made it through Ranger School—described as "the 62-day gauntlet of hunger, fatigue, and exhausting tests of physical endurance"—she still wouldn't be allowed to serve in special operations or infantry, and worst of all, couldn't be a member of the elite 75th Ranger Regiment and serve alongside her fiancé.

Never the rebel, Laredo had to agree and tilted her career to work in the equally dangerous field of biochem. And Ranger also agreed, reluctantly. He wasn't a man to disagree with the judgement of an army colonel and his future father-in-law.

Laredo and Ranger told the author they had decided, without mentioning it to each other, that they would marry the day they shared her beach blanket in the shadow of the tower. Both knew and it didn't need to be said. They were later told by Laredo's dad to hold off until after they served in Afghanistan, which also didn't need to be said. They were both determined to serve in combat against terror—he in the Rangers and she in biochem prevention—because that seemed to them, their destiny.

Shortly after graduating from the University of Texas—Ranger with a history degree, Laredo with a double major in chemistry and biology—they were commissioned as Army officers per the U.S. Congress. Ranger took a break before beginning Ranger School, while Laredo went to graduate school to get further degrees.

Right after graduation she reported to the Edgewood Area of the Aberdeen Proving Ground in Maryland, headquarters of the U.S. Army Combat Capabilities Development Command (DEVCOM) Chemical Biological Center. With a Master's degree in Biochemistry from Johns Hopkins University, Laredo's resume was impressive. She explained she wanted to help with the development and testing of vaccines and therapeutics against biochem/radiologic attack, and unearth terrorist plans to use biological and chemical warfare against the U.S.

Her dad, who by then had earned a General's star, had already spoken with the command, and frankly she already had the job, for which she was clearly qualified, but because it was her dream job, she was nervous. Probably nobody in the world had the facilities and the advanced programs anywhere close to the DEVCOM CDC.

She would have a small personal lab at Fort Belvoir in Virginia to study and conduct experiments with relatively benign material, but her main work with dangerous pathogens, chemical, and radioactive substances, would be at Aberdeen Proving Ground in Northern Maryland, to which she would commute in a Huey helicopter.

She was taken on a tour of the "upper floor," containing pedestrian labs, more complex and advanced than any she had ever seen. But the prize was the invitation to don a biohazard suit—which would eventually became as familiar and comfortable as a pair of old worn jeans—and go down to the Level 4 facilities many floors below ground, where the world's most toxic materials were stored.

Some of the toxins under cautious study had been altered by terror labs and rogue governments to make their lethal effects all but impossible to cure, or to make their toxicity a thousand times more virulent than normal.

Each floor the ironclad elevator visited was adorned with dire warnings that would have alarmed most people—with good reason.

She was practically breathless explaining what she had seen to Ranger. "I felt like a little girl on Christmas morning. I want to make that place, and the two others like it around the country, my world, my workshop. I knew the government had sophisticated labs, but I didn't have any idea it was as elaborate and well-manned as it is."

He wanted to know if she was at least a little bit scared. She looked at him like he was speaking Aramaic or some other long dead language.

The truth was she had found her calling and her dream world, a super high-tech playland, where she would be well paid to do what she had long dreamed of doing, and to have the satisfaction of knowing she was keeping people, particularly her fellow soldiers, safe.

The mission of the Chemical Biological Center is quite straightforward: to be the premiere provider of innovative chemical and biological *solutions*.

She later said she was walking on air when she left, knowing that she was going to achieve her long-wished-for goal. She would be one of ten thousand engineers and scientists tasked with neutralizing the biochem threat that was becoming one of the gravest threats to the U.S., the military, and the nation.

And importantly to Laredo, her father would be proud.

The Army Rangers predate the American Revolutionary War, having fought in the French and Indian War on the British side. Frances Marion, the legendary Swamp Fox, was a founder of the first American Army Rangers.

The legacy of the Rangers from the beginning was that they were trained "to kill with a twist of rope, a knife, or their boots or bare hands."

When the barbarians are at the gates, the Rangers are America's first line of defense.

Army Ranger School began at Fort Benning, Georgia, which is where Ranger first reported for duty. It is billed as "one of the toughest training courses for which a soldier can volunteer." It is designed to make its graduates experts at leading difficult missions. It entails two months of training to "exhaustion, pushing the limits of minds and bodies."

The first phase is "Crawl," which lasts twenty days. Volunteers must do forty-nine pushups in "perfect form," fifty-nine sit-ups in two minutes, six chin-ups from a dead hang with no lower body movement, and finally, a five-mile individual run "over gently rolling terrain." Candidates are warned in advance that if they are not in excellent physical condition when they report to Fort Benning, they aren't going to make it, and most—even fit candidates—don't succeed.

Next are rope climbs and plunging into deep water from a great height. They must demonstrate no fear of water whatsoever. Candidates tumble into water with a rifle and load-bearing equipment, from which they must separate and ditch while submerged.

Next up is a twelve mile "ruck" with full gear, to be completed in under three hours.

The ruck is followed by a navigation test conducted both night and day, equipped with only a map and compass. A flashlight with a red-light filter can only be used to consult the map.

The second is the Mountain Phase, held at remote Camp Merrill near Dahlonega, Georgia. "Students receive instruction on military mountaineering tasks, mobility training...and techniques for employing a platoon for continuous combat patrol operations in a mountainous environment." There is also a requirement to conduct air assault missions in high altitude, extremely rugged territory, including the Tennessee Valley Divide, followed by a ten-mile march.

Students are then driven to a small airport for an airborne mission, parachuting into Florida's Eglin Air Force Base to begin the Swamp Phase.

Ranger dashed off a quick postcard to Laredo, telling her it was hard, but he was completely up to everything. He remembers thinking to himself how glad he was that she had taken a different course. He told the author he was sure she could have made it but, like her father said, she had other skills the army needed more than her direct participation in combat.

He proudly told her that the philosophy of the 75th Rangers was to start every day as though a great battle was ahead, and, importantly, not to have any doubts—just accomplish the mission and worry about details when the fighting ends with total victory, if then.

Laredo remembers that she was well aware of the rigors he faced in the training/elimination programs and was worried about him, but snapped out of it when she realized how much higher her consternation was going to be when he went to Afghanistan and was facing a real-life enemy.

In Florida, Ranger students were required to receive instruction on waterborne operations in a coastal swamp and "operate under conditions of extreme mental and physical stress, learning how to determine the difference between venomous and non-venomous snakes." Confronting deadly, hypervenomous serpents—like water moccasins that grow to be up to four feet long—in the field could be challenging for a first-timer. Candidates were also taught emergency field first-aid treatment, including using a suction pump device to remove venom, which could mean the difference between life and death in a very narrow window.

"Students are evaluated on their ability to apply small unit tactics and techniques during the execution of raids, ambushes and urban assaults to accomplish their mission," according to official Ranger literature.

He didn't know it at the time, but that training would come in handy in Afghanistan and again several years later in Hawkeye CAT and the Hunters. They were generally all about "small unit tactics" and "urban assaults," but learning to identify and avoid poisonous snakes would also be useful.

The final lesson was the Desert Phase, with the Utah desert as a training ground. This included learning about water procurement and preservation, and ambush techniques including "how to breach barbed and concertina wire and how to assault a fortified bunker."

With that accomplished, the class returned to Fort Benning and graduation, where a black and gold Ranger Tab was pinned to their left shoulder to be worn permanently above the soldier's unit patch, and they were fitted with the distinctive tan beret of the Army Rangers.

In the first days of the trial-by-fire at Fort Benning, Ranger met Army Ranger Chaplain Major Jon Knoedler. He had humped his way through Ranger School at age thirty-six and passed the sixty-two-day course the first time, which stunned many of the much younger soldiers, who felt it was the toughest challenge of their lives and couldn't believe an "old" man could do it on his first try.

The Chaplain had then deployed to Iraq during the surge, when George W. Bush ordered a major new attack on the enemy. He then did several tours in Afghanistan with the 75th Ranger Regiment, where he admitted he had frequently experienced "many low moments" during

Ranger School and in Afghanistan's Nangarhar province during the bitter cold winters.

But the U.S. Army special ops changed history and drove the terrorists back into their holes or into their graves.

He told Ranger he had been freezing and feeling sorry for himself until he had a conversation with God, who gave him the strength to face up to the challenge and survive. During the days Ranger struggled through the course, despite being in excellent physical condition, having been preparing since he was a teenager, he took inspiration from the Chaplain's example and prayed daily for strength and inspiration.

Knoedler also recorded videos that he hoped would give soldiers succor in the battlefield, which Ranger took along when he later deployed to Afghanistan. Some of the chaplain's preaching to the troops was done with a live snake wrapped around his arm, which got everyone's attention.

Ranger later said, "During low moments the Chaplain's tapes comforted me and encouraged me to fight on. He's a great man."

Knoedler was a constant presence at the Fort Benning field trials. He often walked across a narrow thirty-five-foot-long log suspended high above Victory Pond, encouraging the Ranger School students struggling below.

Many soldiers—with good reason—look with dread and fear at deployment into any war zone, particularly one with the surreal strangeness and harsh beauty, to most Westerners eyes, of Afghanistan.

Lt. Col. Anthony Shaffer, an excellent chronicler of war and spycraft, describes a graveyard of ruined Soviet tanks in his book *Operation Dark Heart*—equipment that speaks volumes about the Soviet empire's disastrous attempt to conquer the ancient Afghan world.

"Faded green Soviet vehicles…tanks, personnel carriers, armored cars, and more were stretched out on a tan, flat plain as far as the eye could see," Shaffer wrote. "The numbers were in the thousands. It looked like a vision from hell. Many of the tanks had golf-ball-sized bullet holes with telltale melting marks around them…that burned through the ten-inch steel and turned the interior of the tank into hot gas and shrapnel. It would have been an ugly way to die.

"The Soviets were just one of many empires...to occupy Afghanistan and all left in defeat. The huge amount of waste...was dizzying."

He points out that the Soviets lost fourteen thousand men, and all that was left of the effort and bloodshed was rotting in the fury of the desert sun. It was a lesson for America's invasion of the ancient kingdom. Fortunately, the mistakes made in the Russian attempt were carefully studied and acted upon by the U.S. expeditionary force.

Little did Ranger or his fellow soldiers imagine that the United States would one day also retreat in chaos, leaving their equipment and Afghan allies to the tender mercies of the savage Taliban.

Ranger did not share the trepidation of most young soldiers. He burned with conviction and felt war was his destiny. He believed in his heart and soul that whatever happened, Jesus was going to take the wheel.

Ranger's first daylight view of Afghanistan was through the open door of a CH-47 Chinook helicopter, where his seatmate was a container of C-4 plastic explosives.

He had on bulky body armor because the helicopters that flew in a ring around Afghanistan, ferrying soldiers and equipment, were a regular target of Taliban AK-47s; rounds regularly buzzed past the ships and often made contact, despite the best efforts of pilots to cling to the landscape, making a harder target.

He was equipped with an M4 A3 assault rifle and a Sig Sauer M11 semiautomatic pistol, and felt hard and ready to get to work.

The landscape of savagely rugged mountains soaring over ten thousand feet, which the helicopter barely skirted, made an immediate impression. Every trip in Afghanistan was fraught with danger and a rush for adrenalin junkies, which describes most of those who volunteer for the Rangers.

He thought the switchback highways looked like a malignant, almost magnificent desolation, but not the unexplored desolation of the moon that had so impressed Buzz Aldrin. Instead it struck him as a Godforsaken hell on earth. It was, after all, the lair of the vicious Taliban and ISIS. The nation had seen nothing but suffering, cruelty, and deprivation for years. He had been briefed on the mass killing of civilians that had been ordered and directed in large measure by Osama bin Laden. The terror chief armed his shock troops with long razor-sharp knives for slitting throats and skinning bodies, as a lesson to anyone who dared to resist them.

As was later said, quite succinctly, if unsympathetically, by Donald Trump: "It's a region of sand and death."

The Taliban had enslaved women, destroyed millennia-old art, and banned door-to-door vaccinations against polio in Afghanistan, deliberately causing the first major recurrence of the disease in any part of the world in almost a half century.

When things got hot and the anti-Taliban International Security Assistance Force, led by the Army Rangers, was closing in, the terrorists would hide behind women and children, losing their black uniforms of death and torture and attempting to blend in with the civilian population, which was so terrified that people dared not point a finger at them.

Ranger learned quickly that the Taliban was an army seldom matched in ferocity and ruthlessness, and that to beat them he was going to have to be ferocious and ruthless as well. Over the course of the battle against the Taliban, over a million civilians had fled to Pakistan to the south and Turkmenistan to the north, where they were unwelcome, and perceived as a strange and hostile tribe, often vilified, and sometimes violently attacked.

The Taliban had effectively destroyed an ancient nation of over 37 million people, that will likely never be the same again.

The eighteen-hour flight on April 23, 2010, from Fort Benning to Bagram, with multiple aerial refuelings, had been anything but pleasant. To be jammed into a C-130 Hercules with almost three hundred other soldiers is a nightmare flight, but all Army flights were overflowing with soldiers as the war ramped up. The American force would soon stand at one hundred thousand as part of the surge to turn the tide of the war.

Ranger was aware it was going to be a tough, bitter fight and his tour was going to be a long twenty-four months in the combat zone. The Rangers were always leading into combat and bearing the brunt of battles—that is their assignment and destiny. It was what he had volunteered to do.

He had no fear of the coming savage battles and wanted to teach the Taliban how the Army Rangers deal with people who pick a fight with America.

But worst of all, he knew how intense his pain and longing would be over missing Laredo.

Despite wearing a camo Gore-Tex parka and thick long johns (which Laredo had insisted he wear), Ranger was shivering with cold the entire trip. The plane was foremost a cargo carrier and was flown like its passengers were machines and war materiel, not men and women. Turbulence was extreme; the constant shuddering and the roar of the engines made sleep all but impossible, no matter how tired you were. The seats that seemed deliberately designed for discomfort didn't help either.

When the turbo prop made a hard landing at Bagram in the dark, Ranger woke with a start, surprised that he had managed to fall asleep.

As of this writing, Al Qaeda and the Taliban (the name comes from the fact they had been recruited from a fanatical Islamic religious group called "Talib") combined had lost over seventy-five thousand terrorists. The U.S. had lost over twenty-four hundred men, the U.K. over five hundred each, Canada, France, and Germany over three hundred.

Surveying the land from the helicopter, he said a prayer that the 75th Ranger Regiment could help to bring a measure of civility and mercy back to the tortured people of Afghanistan and bring the troops back to their home and hearth safely. In the murky dawn light, he made out a long convoy of U.S. troops halted along a one-lane blacktop that he later learned had been built by the Russians during their disastrous invasion of the ancient country back in the 1970s.

Suddenly a small clumsy looking jet with three pods mounted on its wings and a bright gold canopy—which protects the pilot and crew from the super high frequency radio signals the plane uses—swooped out of the sky and descended to a very low altitude following the road ahead of the stalled convoy. It was like nothing Ranger had seen before, but the plane would become a familiar and very welcome sight in the months ahead.

The Chinook took a hard port turn and swung out of the way. Suddenly, IEDs (Improvised Explosive Devices) exploded, one after the other, on both sides of the road. Seeing Ranger's look of amazement, a veteran seated next to him explained:

The plane was an EA-6B Electronic Prowler that, among many other things, flew over roads in Taliban territory and emitted radio signals that detonated the IEDs ahead of convoys. The Taliban used radio signals to ignite the bombs, and the plane mimicked the signals to clear the field of explosives. As several miles of buried IEDs exploded, the road glowed an angry red and a thick, eerie cloud of cordite-laced smoke rose over the area. The smell that thousands of near simultaneous explosions produced was almost medicinal and chemical. There was a hint of urine and sulphur. But every detonation struck him as one less dangerous IED that wouldn't seriously injure an American soldier or a farmer clearing his field. The electronic Prowler effectively eliminated the IED weapon from the Taliban quiver, and saved countless U.S. and Allied soldier's lives.

While the battle unfolded, a Predator drone about two thousand feet aloft was monitoring every detail of the fight and giving real-time images of the enemy's every move to the American commander.

The Predator's big brother, the MQ-9 Reaper can fly up to fifty thousand feet to avoid enemy fire (even radar, if the enemy has that capacity—which fortunately it didn't).

Early in the twenty-year war, the Taliban—used to the oft-cowering Afghan National Army—directly attacked the Army forces, including the crack 10th Mountain Division, Rangers, and other special forces. But they consistently suffered casualty rates in the 90 percent zone and were then blocked from escape, to their surprise, shock, and horror. The scenario usually ended with a smart bomb dropped from a distant B-1, which they couldn't see or hear, literally evaporating the Talibs who had thought they were survivors.

When the battle was done, the drone assessed the damage (called BDA or Battle Assessment Damage) for commanders to study and perfect their future battle planning.

The drones were considered so essential to carrying out warfare that the Pentagon invested billions in 2020 alone, with plans to spend more on research and development.

The outcome of the Taliban spring offensive in Zabul province on the Pakistan border—from which they often attacked and then escaped safely across the border into the arms of sympathetic Pakistanis and their allies in the Pakistan Inter-Services Intelligence (ISI) (who have an official policy of support for the Taliban)—was a disaster.

Commanders in the field gave full credit to the courage and skill of the U.S. and allied troops, but credited real-time intelligence on Taliban movements, strengths, and weaknesses, to the drones for the good battlefield alignment and decision making.

Ranger, who was a history major and had assiduously studied warfare over the centuries, later said, "If drones had existed during some of the most significant battles, there would have been different outcomes that might well have changed world history."

Ranger quickly discovered the Afghan National Army were mostly less than useless. The fact that they dropped their arms and ran when the U.S. decided to abandon the fight in late summer of 2021 came as no surprise to him. Far from defending their own nation and their families, they did almost everything to hinder the allied efforts.

He found the Afghan civilians grateful to have the allied soldiers there to protect them from the depredations of the savage Taliban, but the Afghan Army soldiers frequently used opium and stole guns, trucks, clothes, and equipment from the U.S. Army. Some openly collaborated with the Taliban, and the Rangers sometimes forcefully confiscated their cell phones because they were often used to give intelligence to the Taliban about U.S. Army strategy. Even worse, they had sometimes been used to detonate IEDs killing G.I.s.

The Taliban got financing from sympathetic Islamists in the Middle East, but their main source of income came from cultivating poppy and turning it into heroin to be sold in Europe and Russia. Their drug trade was estimated to have created almost 15 million addicts and killed one hundred thousand each year, according to a BBC News report.

By the time Ranger was in country in the spring of 2010, the Taliban had reversed course and turned to classic asymmetrical warfare. IEDs had been rendered almost useless by the electronic Prowlers, so their remaining weapons were suicide bombers—most often women and children—and snipers. In desperation they were also turning to their rogue allies in Iran and North Korea, as well as Al Qaeda, for help in developing chemical and bacteriological weapons that would level the playing field and likely cause a regional holocaust—an outcome that didn't concern them in the least.

Intelligence showed that development of those weapons of mass death was in process as of 2010.

A year later, on May Day 2011, the electronic Prowler would serve another good purpose when it jammed Pakistani radar to allow Navy SEAL Team Six to stealthily enter the country to dispatch the monstrous Osama bin Laden.

"Growing up with a burning desire to be a combat officer, I envisioned leading men storming beaches like on D-Day," recalled Ranger. "But it turned out I was assigned to lead small squads on ambushes of high value targets, with the goal of eliminating them with 'extreme prejudice.' Mostly they were terrorists and/or heroin dealers on a massive scale. But that was the job and I have to say I got very good at it, thanks to having skilled, dedicated, tough soldiers behind me."

On September 26 2010, Linda Norgrove, a thirty-six-year-old British aid worker, was kidnapped by Taliban and held in exchange for terrorist Aafia Siddiqui, who was known as Lady Al Qaeda and had been sentenced in absentia, by a U.S. court, to eighty-six years in prison for her jihadi crimes and killings. There was no way she was going to be traded for anybody.

A rescue team of twenty-four SEALs from Team Six and twenty Rangers descended on the fortified compound surrounded by a sixteen-foot fence, at 3:30 a.m., in Chinook helicopters, with close fire support from an AC-130 Spectre gunship. Marksmen immediately killed guards with sniper rifles equipped with sound suppressors. The compound was located seven thousand feet up a steep mountain, near the remote village of Dineshgal in Kunar province. The soldiers fast roped into the Taliban compound.

Mullah Basir and Mullah Keftan, designated high value targets, were killed, as were all six Taliban gunmen, who were designated bodyguards. Norgrove appeared to break away from her captors during the fire fight and made a run for it. Reports vary about what happened next, but one thing is sure: Norgrove was killed just seconds from being rescued.

"It breaks your heart to get that close to a rescue and have something go wrong at the last minute," Ranger said later. "But the solace was that band of demons wouldn't be kidnapping again, ever."

Ranger's next mission was to attack and eliminate a Taliban heroin operation. For years, the method of eradication was dropping precision bombs on the heroin labs, using F-22 Raptor stealth fighters. The bombs were most often right on target, and successfully destroyed the tiny factories and usually killed the unfortunate peasants who were manning them.

But the amount of heroin manufactured by the Taliban kept growing exponentially. As soon as one lab was destroyed, two others would pop up in its place. In a country as dirt poor as Afghanistan there was no paucity of people willing to risk everything, including their lives, to learn the relatively simple formula to manufacture heroin and morphine.

In 2001, an estimated, three hundred square miles were devoted to drug production. Ten years later, the figure was around thirteen-hundred square miles. With all its firepower and state-of-the-art technology, the U.S. was clearly losing the war on drugs in Afghanistan, despite the fact that the penalty for heroin production was officially death. Desperate people do desperate things to feed themselves and their families.

A new U.S. Central Command General was appointed in the region, Lt. Gen. Jeffrey Harrigian, who decided the way to stop the drug trade wasn't to bomb the tiny outdoor factories, but to kill the Taliban. The Rangers were tasked with the assignment of attacking Taliban safe houses and eliminating high value targets, who were the command and control.

Often the targets were across the Pakistani border; for years the Americans had been forbidden passage because Pakistan pretended to be American an ally, even though it was openly working with the Taliban.

The intel was that high level Talibs rarely ventured near the crude and often dangerous labs, but operated them from afar. Ranger was soon leading midnight raids across the border, using rocket propelled grenades and C-4 plastic explosives to surprise the Taliban, who had grown more and more confident that the US was prohibited from crossing the border.

A new commander, General Stanley McChrystal, changed that at once. McChrystal—called by former Secretary of Defense Robert Gates "perhaps the finest warrior and leader of men in combat I ever met"—was the commander of the 2nd Battalion of the 75th Ranger Regiment, and became commander of all U.S. Forces in Afghanistan, where he turned the tide toward victory over the Taliban and Al Qaeda. In June of 2006, his team was responsible for locating and killing Abu Musab al-Zarqawi with an airstrike, and he accompanied his men to the site of his death in Baqubah, Iraq where he personally identified the body. He was anything but a desk top commander.

Ranger came in country when McChrystal was leaving (having been relieved of command by Barack Obama for criticizing Joe Biden for his ineptitude); he had studied the general's tactics and leadership and considered him a role model. As commander of the Joint Special Operations Command, McChrystal was credited by a CNN national security analyst for transforming and modernizing the troops under his command in Afghanistan into a "force of unprecedented agility and lethality."

General McChrystal's motto was simply: "We are going to win."

He was Ranger's hero, and Ranger he prayed that he, with God's help, would help make the Commander's motto a reality.

Before crossing the border, EA-6 Electronic Prowlers were dispatched to blind Pakistani radar, as well as to black out the Taliban chief's communication equipment, including cell phone and satellite communications. Power generators were also deadened, putting the Taliban back in a technological sixth century, where they would presumably feel most at home.

Ranger was in constant touch with Creech Air Force Base in the Nevada Desert, where long-distance pilots were monitoring a twenty-seven-foot long Predator drone, two miles above the safe house. Able to stay aloft for up to twelve hours, two Predators took shifts. The drone sent back reasonably clear images of who was in the house, even information based on body heat, that determined how many human beings were in the house, whether they were male or female, adults or children, and what weapons they possessed.

Never in previous wars had a combat officer had the kind of knowledge of an enemy about to be attacked as Ranger was receiving from eight thousand miles away in the Nevada desert. It was the essence of asymmetrical warfare, and the reason the Taliban were turning to chemical and biological weapons that had been banned by most of the world's civilized (and not so civilized) nations for decades.

Unfortunately, the intel couldn't be delivered in real time, though every effort was made to get the images to the field commanders as quickly as possible. The signal and the photos were sent from the drone to a satellite over twenty thousand miles in the sky, then transferred to Ramstein Air Force Base in Germany and switched to fiber optic cable, for the all-important clarity of images. They were then sent by cable under the Atlantic Ocean and across the United States to the Nevada desert, where they were interpreted, and then relayed to Ranger's team on the other side of the planet.

(Andrew Cockburn has published a very good book on the subject called *Kill Chain: The Rise of the High-Tech Assassins*.)

The Prowlers had also set off any booby traps or IEDs left behind. Then the Rangers prepared to burst through the doors, to mop up any Taliban who were wounded, to be helicoptered back to Bagram for interrogation and possible transfer to Guantanamo.

But first the AC-130 Spectre gunship unleashed a Hellfire missile and the fireworks show started. The roof blew off, as well as two outer walls. Terrorists who made a run for it (rather unsympathetically called squirters by the Rangers) were mowed down by the gunship that was waiting in close support, slowly circling low and ominously. After the raiding party had succeeded, Ranger's team cautiously entered what was left of the former safe house and thoroughly searched for computer hard drives, zip drives, and any other intelligence that could lead to locating other high value targets.

After the successful raid in Pakistan, Ranger lit a Cuban cigar, readily available in Afghanistan, and said, "Now we're getting somewhere."

He hated to admit—even to himself—that combat gave him a rush that compared to very few things in life. He was a big man and had been a tall, muscular boy, but he had never been a violent boy or man, never picked fights. But war in Afghanistan was different. First of all, a Taliban terrorist got rewarded, not punished, for the most savage and barbaric of acts. He felt, and his men felt, that the Taliban and Al Qaeda were bitter enemies of America, that they had started the war and seemed to take pleasure in killing innocent civilians.

Every MAM or (military aged man) was considered a combatant, because the Taliban forced every male to fight and would instantly cut off body parts, including arms and legs, if they refused.

Ranger felt proud to be bringing the war to them. Blowing up their so called safehouses, surprising them out of sweet dreams and the comfort of their several wives. It became Ranger's almost daily vocation. He planned most attacks to commence at zero dark thirty, which was his favorite time to strike, in homage to the SEAL's attack and the double tap on bin Laden.

The only person in whom he confided about the heady electric charge that flowed through his body, and the rush of energy and dopamine acceleration he felt, was Laredo. She was never even a trifle judgmental, and shared his joy at inflicting the maximum damage possible, turning the Taliban territory into a killing field and liberating the long-suffering peasants whose lives were hard enough without being tortured by savages.

During the initial assault a 7.62mm AK-47 round had grazed his helmet, "damn near spinning my head around," he later laughed. Ranger wondered, thinking about the incident several years later, "How many lives have been saved by those damn helmets...probably the population of Cleveland."

As proud as Ranger was of the success he was having as a field commander, he had concerns—he later told the author—about the technology that made it possible to make life or death decisions in seconds. He knew there was a sickening number of civilian casualties, most caused by human error—young soldiers with little combat experience trying their best, but some were caused by incredibly complex machinery: computers talking to each other and essentially giving orders, which the commanders had to decide to act on or not, in nanoseconds.

Cockburn quotes an officer tasked to advise Predator, Reaper and Global Hawk drone crews when a strike is imminent, saying, "Well to be honest, sir, everyone around here, it's like *Top Gun* where everyone has the desire to do our job, employ weapons against the enemy." A lot of times they employ their weapons even when they know there are civilians in the danger zone.

There was even a computer game based on computer-controlled warfare, called *Remember Kill Chain*. Ranger had been playing computer and X-Box games since he was a child and was completely comfortable with the technology, but the fact that it was a game based on killing human beings made him more than a bit queasy.

He had studied an investigation into the accidental killing of women and children in an attack back in Urzgan Province in 2010, by a special ops group (not the Rangers fortunately, he thought). In the transcripts of conversations between the pilots and commanders on the scene there seemed to be a palpable desire to hurry up and start shooting:

The pilot of a OH-58 Kiowas gun ship circling the suspected bad guys says, "Can't wait till this really happens with all this coordination and s***."

Another pilot spots a group of suspicious Afghanis, "They're praying, preparing for a battle."

Sensor: "This is definitely it. This is their force. Praying? I mean seriously, that's what they do before an attack."

Mission Coordinator: "They're going to do something nefarious."

Just before the attack begins with Hellfire missiles launched from the gunships, a mission controller warns a pilot that at least once child is in the images he is studying, but it is decided he is a probably a male adolescent, indicating he is a probable combatant, and the attack is begun.

Ranger later said he wouldn't have been able to live with himself if he was responsible for ordering an attack that killed a child, even an adolescent. He said, "Real Taliban hide when they hear drones or helicopters; only kids are naïve enough to stand out in the open."

★★★

During his frequent raids across the border into deep Taliban territory—where the Talibs had long assumed they were safe—Ranger always carried a stash of money, a fairly common practice for special ops leaders, usually ten thousand dollars, which was a fortune to the Pakistanis and Afghans who lived in the region. The money was for gifts, even patronage, to locals, particularly the elders, who were the influencers. He also carried a bag of candy to distribute to the children, many of whom had never eaten sweets.

The bribes were for good will, so they wouldn't consider the Rangers enemies like the Taliban, who were generally feared and despised for their imposition of strict Sharia law, as well as for raping the women and the brutal torture of almost everyone they encountered. The brutality seemed to be just a matter of course, out of habit; nothing personal.

The local people quickly recognized that, because of their huge technological advantage, the Rangers were operating in Pakistan with impunity and dispatching the Taliban without consequence or hesitation. Even the much-feared Pakistani Inter-Services Intelligence (ISI), allies of the Taliban, melted into the background when a Rangers Raid was under way.

On one of his raids, which had become legendary and feared in the region, Ranger discovered something that made the hair on his arms stand on end. In the targeted safe house, there was a sophisticated lab. It definitely wasn't a heroin lab, because they were always outdoors, due to the toxic fumes emitted when poppy was turned into morphine or heroin. This looked remarkably like an on-the-cheap biochem type lab. Cautiously he took pictures, knowing he should just run out the door, and hearing Laredo's voice telling him to do just that immediately.

Back in Bagram he called Laredo on his Iridium phone and told her of his find, almost casually suggesting she should come over and have a look.

Both had been desperately pining for each other over the lonely months of worried, anguished separation, and prayed this might be a ticket to a reunion. She knew it wasn't going to be easy, and in fact would be a hard, dangerous mission, but was electrified by the possibility they might soon be together again.

The bummer was that it was June in Afghanistan and the weather would be hellish, around 125 degrees Fahrenheit for a typical daytime high.

Laredo took the pictures and information from Ranger to her DEVCOM Chemical Biological Center supervisor—trying to hide her glee, considering it was clearly a horribly frightening discovery—knowing it was going to go up the ladder as quickly as a fireman at a four-alarm blaze. The news and photo evidence that the Taliban had a possible safe house biochem lab in Pakistan was earth-shaking news, and had to be acted upon quickly.

She just hoped she would be the scientist to go. There was no doubt in her mind they would send someone, but would it be someone more senior? Would it be a man? That would really piss her off.

And there was no question that taking on—volunteering—for a dangerous mission in a hot war zone, behind enemy lines would look very good on her Curriculum Vitae.

Laredo had been going through a "dark night of the soul" without Ranger. She was going through a period of depression and feeling sorry for herself. She had friends she could confide in and did. But no pleasant company or kind words could assuage the emptiness she felt when, at the end of the day, she returned to her empty bed.

There was also the agony at him being in a hot war zone, working in a killing field, battling a particularly vicious enemy. And she knew her man. When he was leading his soldiers in combat, he did just that: he led, with his sword held high.

She also knew that seeking help officially would have consequences; she would be transferred to less risky and less important duties, which was the last thing she wanted. Laredo intended to get over it with the help of her faith in God.

An hour after presenting the evidence to her bosses, she was on her way home to pack a bag and headed back to Aberdeen Proving Ground, where a C-17 Globemaster was waiting.

She was going to a land that was a place of suffering and death, but she was going to be with her man the following day, and she was glowing with happiness for the first time in what seemed like forever.

The eighteen-hour flight to Bagram was worse than grueling. It was a non-stop with two in-flight refuelings and no bathrooms. She later told Ranger they actually have cans in the event of an emergency.

Upon landing in Afghanistan, the eat radiated through the thin aluminum skin of the C-17, but when the door was open, she felt a blast of heat like nothing she had ever experienced. It reminded her of opening an oven on broil and looking directly inside.

A soldier noticed her discomfort and quipped, "Welcome to Hell, Lieutenant." But he was smiling. If this seventeen or eighteen-year-old kid could tolerate the heat and discomfort of this horrific place, she was convinced she could too. She returned his salute and smiled back.

Once the C-17 had rolled to a halt on the tarmac, Laredo squinted into a near scorching sun and saw Ranger waiting. Her powerful wish and inclination was to run to him, leap off the ground and wrap her legs around his waist, but she knew that would be not in keeping with officer- and gentlemen-like behavior, so she restrained herself. There would hopefully be time for love in the land of death.

But she was so happy she cried.

She was totally prepared for the fact they had to make it to the safe house immediately, with no time to shower or to change. The safe house was in a very active hot zone and the Taliban hierarchy would do everything in its power to prevent the contents of the lab from falling into U.S. Army hands. Time was of the essence on both sides of good versus evil.

One of the things that caught her attention about her minutes at Bagram was the sight of huge army tents, with air conditioners blasting, erected on the base that temporarily housed the FBI, CIA, and a myriad of government agencies, each with a role in the collection of intelligence and the prosecution of the war effort. The huge base was a typical example of asymmetrical warfare battling an intractable and unrelenting enemy, but having air-conditioned tents in a land where most citizens had never had a fresh, clean glass of water seemed awfully ironic.

Bagram was the eyes and ears, as well as the beating heart, of the American war against evil. Years later, when it was surrendered to the Taliban without a fight, she, like most veterans, was sickened and bitter.

Snapped out of dark thoughts at the shock at being plopped down in an unfathomably alien world, Laredo realized her horse was ready and it was time to charge into combat. A Chinook helicopter was warming up, clearly under orders to take off without delay to cross the Pakistan border. Soldiers inside the chopper were busy preparing for combat. After the mind-numbing trip halfway around the world, this was a splash over the head with ice water.

It was her first combat mission.

Ranger tenderly embraced her on the flight, unconcerned about the amused glimpses they were getting, and briefed her on the situation they were facing.

The Army Corp of Engineers had landed at the site at zero dark thirty and thrown up a sixteen-foot fence covered in concertina wire. Two AC-130 Spectre gunships bristling with weapons were patrolling the area and had fired on every Taliban attempt to get close to the mostly ruined former safe house. There had been numerous attempts to storm the building to retrieve their secrets, but after suffering heavy loses each time they appeared to have given up. EA-6 Prowlers were keeping Pakistani radar in the area dead and unable to set off any newly planted IEDs.

The expedition had a window, though a narrow one, to get in, take samples, blow the remains of the building with C-4, and flee back to Bagram and relative safety. Ranger's feeling was that Taliban and Al Qaeda chiefs would immediately realize the importance of what he had found and the U.S. government's extremely strong defensive reaction to it, and do desperate damage control, including trying to kill him and his troops to keep them silent. But what they wouldn't have realized was that the cat was out of the bag. It was too late. The U.S. government and her allies knew they were desperate and had turned to long outlawed weapons, to try to stem the tide of U.S. victory in Afghanistan.

Ranger hated conducting what amounted to a raid into Pakistan in broad daylight, but he knew there was no choice. And knew he had awesome back-up from the rest of the forces in place, including Navy SEALs and the might of the Air Force.

While the Chinook skirted the region's ten-thousand-feet-tall mountain peaks and narrowly avoided the occasional AK-47 burst, Laredo, who was already slick with sweat, stepped into her Level A hazmat suit, and prepared for much worse heat inside the airtight outfit. She carefully double gloved and had Ranger use a generous amount of duct tape to seal her boots and gloves. Ranger handed her a M-11 Sig Sauer semiautomatic pistol to strap around her svelte waist, just in case. She was also equipped with a FLIR IBAC smart air sampling system and a bio-capture device—pretty much the state of the art for biochem ferrets like her.

Laredo was convinced the lab was manufacturing biological rather than chemical agents as soon as Ranger told her of his find. Desperate terrorists who are losing turn to pathogens because they are extremely effective in very small quantities. A dose of biological agents the size of a paper clip can infect thousands and can be up to 14 billion times more deadly than a chemical weapon. (The comparison between chemical and biological agents was contained in a then-classified report—classified for fear it could cause panic, which was certainly a realistic assessment.)

Bio agents are also very quick acting and, unlike chemical agents, are inevitably passed from human to human—and sometimes animals to humans, claiming exponentially more incapacitation and death in the targeted population. Of course, it will also jump to populations that may not have been the intended target, but to terror groups like Taliban, casualties of their own troops and civilian suffering are totally inconsequential. They will all end up in the arms of Allah, feasting on a harem of virgins. Those were Laredo's dark thoughts as they approached the ruined safehouse she had been sent halfway around the world to inspect.

Landing in the makeshift landing zone that had been set up around the ruins, Ranger and his ten men set up a perimeter with heavy weapons. One of the men, Larry, who was familiar with the house and the lab, donned a hazmat suit and showed Laredo through the house to her target room. Larry said he was very sure no one had penetrated the gunships' perimeter because he had set a series of trip wires that would have been almost impossible to avoid, and none of them had been tripped—low tech but effective. He had also set several lasers in place that would have sent a signal to him if there had been a breach.

The ruins of the building had a stench of evil to Laredo, not just from the disease-creating and possibly intentional pandemic-causing lab, but also from the vibe of the Taliban chiefs who had terrorized the region for years from the cursed piece of land.

In the background was the constant soundtrack of war; from somewhere in the distance came the steady thump of artillery exploding—a reminder, if anyone needed one, that they were in the middle of a hot war zone.

She had been around lethal substances at Aberdeen Proving Ground on a daily basis, but this was her first time working in a hot war zone, and she hoped to keep her head and efficiently operate the complicated equipment she was carrying. She also well knew the dangers of encountering something sharp and tearing the hazmat suit, which would likely be fatal. The possibility of booby traps was very real; their only hope was the Taliban had been taken by surprise and didn't have time to build a surprise of their own. But when she saw the make-shift lab, she felt the familiar rush and the high she got from danger.

Larry called Ranger to say, "all appears clear." Ranger said, "10-4 you have fifteen minutes starting now." Larry set the timer on his watch and nodded to Laredo who mumbled through her layers of protective gear, "No pressure."

The lab was as she expected: slip shod, assembled by amateurs who shouldn't have had access to high school equipment, let alone one in the desert producing aerosolized spreading of deadly pathogens. There were clear potentials for leaks that would likely kill the people tasked with distilling the weapon, as well as anyone else in the safehouse, including Taliban leaders—which she thought would have actually been a good thing, if not for the fact they would doubtless spread it to innocents.

The adrenalin rush served to clarify the job in her mind and she swung into action instantly. She quickly took samples, and was sure the pathogen was glanders, a rare but highly effective killer. It lent itself to the Taliban's desperate and evil situation: readily aerosolized, highly transmissible between humans, a three-day incubation period, 50 to 70 percent lethality, no effective drug therapy, and no vaccine.

On her way out she felt a strange lessening of pressure within her hazmat suit, a sign there was a rent in the material, which could mean she was getting contaminated. What the hell had she rubbed against? The lab was a junk shop and it was hard to navigate, with numerous blind spots.

On their way out, Larry, who was Ranger's trusted lieutenant, told her she wasn't to discuss her findings until they got to a safe room—the SCIF (Sensitive Compartmented Information Facility). She nodded agreement, then stripped off her hazmat suit, and without hesitating took off her uniform and underwear. The soldiers did an abrupt and simultaneous about face. Larry also stripped.

She remembered reflecting that the Rangers are tough asses, but they are gentlemen.

Ranger was already on his way with a portable decontamination outfit and sprayed thoroughly and handed them robes.

Out of ear shot, Laredo whispered to Ranger, "that lab has numerous leaks; whoever was working it is contaminated and probably spreading glanders disease, which is quick to spread and virtually incurable."

"Let's talk about it in a secure setting."

One of the soldiers came over with a gas mask on and a flame thrower. He quickly turned the discarded clothes and hazmat material into cinders.

The flight back to Bagram was mostly bathed in silence. Even though Laredo hadn't said anything about her discovery, there was a pall in the air. It was obvious to all the men that there was a grave situation that could spell an appalling disaster, worse than the desperate fighting they had seen and the deaths from IEDs, mortars, and AK-47s. The potential was apocalyptic and almost medieval in dimensions of horror.

Laredo said somberly to Ranger, "So now I know where you've been for the past year. Fun."

Ranger had warned his superiors that they were coming back with bad news, so a SCIF was being readied. He noted that when you return from a hot zone you are regarded with extreme wariness. Nobody was going to want to shake hands, to say the least.

As soon as they arrived at Bagram, they were told the entire mission was classified. Laredo, Ranger, and Larry were whisked away to the

SCIF. A soldier in a hazmat suit relieved her of the sealed evidence bag, depositing it in a metal box and locking it with a code.

In the SCIF there was a secure Iridium phone that was already connected to high command at Aberdeen. The tension in the room and through the phone was palpable. The three were fully aware that the debriefers were in hazmat suits.

Laredo took on the briefing. The mention of the word "glanders" caused an instant buzz from nearly seven thousand miles away at Aberdeen, Maryland, and not a happy buzz. She calmly said the lab was super sloppy and her BioCapture Air Sampler showed there was leakage in the room—serious leakage. Anyone who had been exposed and who wasn't in a Hazmat suit would be dead or dying.

She noted the lab equipment was Iranian in origin. It was well known the Taliban and Iran were allies, but helping the Talib wage biological warfare in Pakistan, aimed at Afghanistan, was an incredible incitement—an act of war. Not that the Taliban gave a damn about an international incitement. After all they committed unspeakable atrocities daily, against both friend and foe.

"I strongly recommend having a team go back to the safehouse to take water and soil samples to see how widespread it is. Glanders can survive very high temperatures and has a pretty long shelf life. The people who worked that lab were reckless; they didn't care about collateral damage. The place has to be decontaminated. The consequences of leaving it be could be catastrophic. The effective dose is extremely low and up to 70 percent lethal. I think there is a time bomb about to go off just across the Pakistan border.

"Person to person transmission of Glanders is high, in fact almost a certainty. The only bright side is that the incubation period is three days, and like Bubonic plague or Ebola, it has such rapid lethality it often burns out before it can infect too many people. Its lethality is what makes it a bioweapon of choice for terrorists; it gets the results they seek—death—quickly."

There was a brief silence. They were put on hold. When Laredo's superior at Aberdeen came back, they were told that all three, plus the other nine Rangers on the mission, had to be quarantined and tested.

Secure quarters were going to be quickly made ready, and bioweapon-trained medical personnel were on the way. Laredo assumed they would all be given doses of streptomycin and sulfadiazine, which were considered at least helpful in combating the effects of the bacterial agent.

Laredo and Ranger shared a weak smile. They were both thinking that at least they would be quarantined together.

Being the two officers in the quarantine group, they were assigned private quarters next to each other. The first thing they wanted to do was notify their parents, because their fathers had high antennae in the army, and as classified as the mission was, they would still get word that their son and daughter could well be in grave danger.

After reassuring their fathers, they welcomed the hazmat-clad doctors, who examined them and Larry first, because they had the most dangerous exposure. After a series of tests and doses of the (somewhat and maybe) effective therapeutics, they closed their doors tightly and fell together for the first time in many months.

Then they got what passes for good news. There was intel that the Taliban had recognized symptoms of glanders in the men who had worked in or around the lab, and that they had ordered them all shot and their bodies burned. So the young couple spent the next days blissfully, on the wings of their renewed love, with the hubris of youth convinced they will never die.

At one point in their joyful reunion Ranger told Laredo he had met an FBI agent who was doing investigations for the Army in Afghanistan, who had told him about a very interesting new career possibility. The U.S. Secret Service was in the process of creating a new, proactive group that would actually go after possible assassins before they acted. He had said their nickname was going to be the Hunters and that a former Ranger would be a great fit.

"And they are interested in developing some assets who are familiar with chemical, biological, and radiological weapons, which are increasingly the tools of would-be assassins," Ranger told Laredo. "I think we should investigate it when we get home."

After three days they were given the all-clear, generating high-fiving all around. Ranger said, "Thank God you weren't too shy to take off your contaminated clothes in front of a pack of soldiers."

"Never been shy, guy. Just wanted to live long enough to marry you."

A few days later Ranger and Laredo were notified they were being recommended for Bronze Stars and promotion to Captain. It was an honor, and they were both pleased that their fathers would be proud. But it was also a major boost to their chances of getting their dream jobs with the Hunter Elite of the Secret Service.

Out of quarantine, Ranger showed Laredo around the heavily fortified Fort Apache that was Bagram Airfield, where the sound of mortar fire was like maddened pterodactyls screeching angrily every morning before dawn. (Fortunately, the Taliban tended to be very bad shots with mortars, apparently a problem with windage.)

He gave her a brief rundown on how the situation had deteriorated for the people of the region. The Northern Alliance, led by Ahmad Shah Massoud, had driven the Soviet Union out of the country at a great price and with very limited help from the United States.

The U.S. wisely took the position that you don't stop your enemy when they are heading off a cliff, which was exactly what the Soviets were doing in Afghanistan.

Several years later, under the stewardship of Bill Clinton, there was no aid or assistance, despite desperate pleas about the depredations of Taliban savagery. Incredibly, Clinton's State Department official in charge of policy for the region told Massoud he should surrender to the Taliban fanatics and leave the people of Afghanistan to a horrible fate of slaughter and medieval rule.

Over twenty years later another Democrat president, Joe Biden, would, in fact, turn the country over to the Taliban.

The Afghan chief also warned the Clinton administration that an Al Qaeda attack on the U.S. was planned and imminent, a warning that was ignored by President Clinton.

Massoud didn't know the exact details of the planned attack, but it became obvious, when it was too late, that he was trying to warn about 9/11. Of course, the attack had been planned in Afghanistan.

Over one million Afghanis fled their homes in desperation while the Clinton administration looked on without concern. The U.S. started supporting Massoud when George W. Bush took office in 2001, in large measure because he supported democracy and women's rights. Because of his human rights policies, Massoud was murdered by the Taliban and Al Qaeda.

Laredo was fascinated by the harshness of the land and the horror of its history. And she respected her man's dedication and bravery, but most of all she was praying that he made it home safely.

The idea of a relatively safe career with the Secret Service was starting to look more appealing.

During his second year in country, Ranger held a captain's rank and was a decorated hero. Clearly feeling his oats, he increased the frequency and the ferocity of his cross-border midnight raids, terrorizing the terrorists, and building a reputation among friend and foe.

During a briefing at the CIA's tent at Bagram he was shown a map indicating the Talib were moving their quarters deeper into Pakistan. The agency believed Ranger was driving them with his raids. He was told by the analysts they had intel that the Taliban leadership was extremely concerned he was compromising their control and command, had destroyed their most valuable weapons, and had stolen top secret information.

Ranger lit up. "Well I guess it's time to double down. That's exactly what I am going to do," he said with satisfaction.

Every day was filled with time-sensitive raids on high-value Talib targets. To Ranger and his brothers there was no time for rest, or even a break. There were pitched and bloody battles in places like Khost, Paktika, and Nangarhar, which on a smaller scale were their generation's Guadalcanal, and—as at the Siege of Hue in Vietnam—the Taliban, like the Viet Cong, literally had two ways home: in a body bag or in victory. The Delta Force and the 75th Rangers were equally determined to return only draped in the garlands of victory, or not at all.

At the battle for the strategically vital mountainous Paktika Province, Delta Force, supported by Army Rangers, engaged Taliban heavily armed with Iranian-supplied ordnance, including rocket-propelled grenades and DShK heavy infantry machine guns. On the first day of intense combat at least thirty Taliban were killed, though when night fell many survivors hid in caves.

At first light, army gunships swarmed through the air firing anti-structure grenades to flush out the enemy, then cleaning the battlefield with rapid fire machine guns. At least one hundred Talib were killed at first light of dawn. But soon after, a Chinook helicopter—carrying thirty-eight American and Afghan special forces on a mission to capture a high value enemy leader—was fired upon and brought down, resulting in the greatest loss of American soldiers in a single incident during the conflict.

Ranger had been scheduled to be aboard the Chinook, but, despite the fact it was his kind of mission, he had declined to leave his men in the killing field without leadership, and apparently God had decided he had other work to do.

At separate ceremonies to award the Bronze Star—he in Bagram, Laredo in Aberdeen—they were both honored for valor in combat and preventing a "catastrophic scourge" that could have been devastating to the troops, as well as the civilian population of Afghanistan. Laredo's dad showed up for the ceremony and presented her with the medal.

President-elect Joe Biden was in a funk. He was slouched in a comfortable overstuffed chair at his $2.9 million house in Rehoboth Beach, Delaware, overlooking Cape Henlopen State Park—a short walk from the ocean. When the wind was blowing on shore, he could hear the soothing pounding of the waves, and loved to deeply inhale the clean salty smell of the sea.

It eased his mind and took him away from the harsh reality of having to make hard decisions, that at least half of the country often strongly disagreed with and many pundits would harshly critique. He reluctantly admitted to a few close friends and his wife Jill that he sometimes felt like he had caught a tiger by the tail, and was thinking, "Now what the hell do I do?"

His house in Wilmington, Delaware is also impressive. But it was acquired, not by having millions to spend, because he didn't (unlike his son Hunter and his brother "serial entrepreneur" James). Instead, it was a result of Biden's love of buying smart when the market was down. In fact, when Obama's election team vetted Biden for the job of vice president, they discovered that, after thirty-six years in the Senate, Biden hadn't become a wealthy man—unlike many of his colleagues, who turned their powerful positions into multi-millions.

After the 2008 vetting, which includes tax returns and all financial information, Obama said, "All these years and you still have no money!" It was a tease, but completely true.

The president-elect Biden closed his eyes and drifted away from the weight that had lately been causing his shoulders to sag when he wasn't in the spotlight, or when he wasn't charged with political passion and melodrama, menacingly predicting "a very, very, very dark winter."

It was certainly the polar opposite of Ronald Reagan's vision of America from a paraphrase of Matthew 5:14: "a bright city on a hill whose beacon light guides freedom-loving people everywhere."

He had gotten an immediate response to his plaint to the head of the Secret Service, about the Hawkeye CAT being both scary looking and intrusive. But it wasn't the response he had expected. He thought the agents would have been rebuked and told to be less intrusive. It made him think back to a remark Jack Kennedy had made when first elected, to the effect that he was shocked at how many things the president "could *not* do."

Biden had gotten a conference call from the Secret Service high command, which they called a briefing on the new Secret Service protocols. They droned on about the new terrorism and how it impacted the office of the president. They told him about all the new chemical and biological threats that were being used by would-be assassins: the constant attempts to introduce poisons like ricin and other pathogens he had never heard of.

At several points, he later said, he had had to bite his tongue to not say, "C'mon, man."

Less than halfway through his eyes had glazed over, and he was praying this lecture would end. It made him feel like a schoolboy being scolded.

The Agency's legal team weighed in with a legalism-saturated explanation of how the Secret Service is compelled by statue to provide protection that it deems necessary to keep the men, women, and children in its protection safe from harm.

The bottom line, which he grasped immediately, was that it was up to them to decide what was "necessary to keep him safe." The argument was that they were aware of constantly growing sophistication and savagery of the bad guys, and he was not.

The message he received, loud and clear, was that these big brawny Sergeant Rock types were going to move into his life and occasionally tramp through his garden and break a teacup in the process. The unspoken rebuke was that all the other recent presidents of both parties had managed to put up with the intrusion into their lives, so who was he to pretend he was above it all?

Suffering from boredom and pique, he had muttered that he had an important incoming call, and thanked them, as he hung up.

Socialist Bernie Sanders, whom Joe didn't trust as far as he could throw him, preached with his usual over-the-top urgency and frenetic passion, that the new administration *must* roll out a super-progressive agenda of tax raising, open immigration, and dismantling of the police and military. Bernie wagged his finger in Joe's face, assuring him that if he swung far left immediately after taking office, he would overwhelm other problems. It would fire up the base with its incendiary passion, making the streets of America roil with self-righteous—mostly peaceful—riots, and Seattle style "Summer of Love" looting, arson, and murder.

Sensing Joe's sense of consternation and confusion, Sanders smiled like a Cheshire cat, certain that he had the incoming president cornered like a rat looking through a rake, and that Biden would not have the backbone to resist pressure from the hard left.

Sighing deeply, Biden realized he had always been jealous of Obama, and felt he had been chosen to be his VP because Barack knew Biden would never eclipse him in popularity or charisma. During the lead-up to the election, he had been worried and depressed that Barack hadn't endorsed him, but his former boss had finally come out swinging during the campaign and more than made up for it. Joe considered he owed his election to Barack as much as to Trump's bluster and sometimes bullying personality, and to the social earthquake of the Covid pandemic and its shocks to the economy—which were of course blamed on the incumbent. It was a political ploy, a talking point that Joe and his TV talking heads, as well as his paid mouthpieces, were going to continue to thump relentlessly to prevent the virus they had dubbed the Trump virus from becoming the Biden virus.

Some of his more cautious advisers, including Barack, whom Biden worshipped and thought the savviest politician ever, had warned that continuing to assault the dead political horse that was Trump was akin to teasing a wounded rattlesnake.

Obama said that Trump was vindictive and held grudges forever. He had been rumored to have contributed to his business rival's ruination, even allegedly contributing to a suicide or two. Being publicly humiliated and defeated for the presidency was going to make him extremely dangerous, and was leaving him with nothing to do in his dotage, save for exacting revenge against the man he almost certainly hated most in the world: Joe Biden.

Joe paced the floor, thinking how much he loved the blood sport of taunting Trump, who reminded Biden of a schoolyard bully who had humiliated boys in elementary school. It warmed the cockles of his heart to lash out at him, after depriving him of a second electoral victory.

The bitterness between the men was more than brutal politics; it was war.

Biden had plans to deprive Trump of many of the perks of being a former president. He was never going to get another intelligence briefing as long as Joe was president, and Biden even hoped to deny him Secret Service protection, although that would require changing the law which guarantees it for ex-presidents. He knew he couldn't help but to keep it up even when it was pointless, and despite the advice of his advisers, and even of Jill and Obama.

When he was a candidate to be Barack Obama's vice president in 2008, he took his ten-year-old granddaughter for a respite in a northern Virginia park far from the pressure and reporters' gotcha questions.

Sometimes the pressure overwhelmed Joe, driving him to seek solace away from the madding crowd. On a crisp fall day, he pitched a tent beside a pond in Claude Moore Park. His Secret Service agents were a bit perplexed, but spread out into the woods forming a perimeter, deliberately staying just out of sight of the candidate.

His motorcade included a Suburban crowded with a complement of six Hawkeye CAT men, armed for battle-to-the-death, who—according to a Reuters description—"have heavy artillery on speed dial."

One later said: "We are used to the whims of the protected, but this was unusual. He even brought his own portable toilet, which was planted in the woods, just in case. We know our presence upsets Biden, so we parked far enough away that he couldn't see us, but close enough that we could keep an eye on him with binoculars. All things considered it was a pleasant afternoon."

New Yorker writer Ryan Lizza was along for the ride, doing a friendly profile for the magazine on the V.P. candidate and then thirty-six-year veteran senator. Lizza wrote, "The image of Biden relaxing at a picnic table in the tent, with his ten-year-old granddaughter Finnegan, who was cheerfully drawing on a napkin, gave the impression of a man not at the center of combat, but off on a distant mission."

Even before Biden was sworn in as president in 2021, he began sniping at the Secret Service, with the majority of the press, who are usually in Biden's corner, cheering him on, even to intervene in personnel matters of the agency, no matter how asinine his pronouncements and accusations. *The Washington Post* reported that Biden's inner circle had concerns about agents having "worrisome ties to Donald Trump, and even questioned their ability to be loyal to the new president."

As a result, some agents who had protected Biden when he was Vice President and went on to other assignments, were called back to the White House.

The then President-elect's aides claimed that one agent assigned to Trump took a leave of absence, to accept a blatantly political job in the Trump White House. The liberal-leaning newspaper claimed in a histrionic diatribe—falsely presented as a legitimate news story—that Anthony Ornato had helped arrange a photo opportunity of Trump daring to brandish a bible, while making a point about riotous George Floyd protesters who tried to burn down Saint John's Church, across Lafayette Park from the White House. (Built in 1816, Saint John's has long been called the church of presidents because many worshipped there.)

The *Post* asserted that federal officers and National Guard troops assigned to protect the White House, the president, and the historic church were out of line, by stopping the torching of the church amid the repeated violent assaults on the White House.

The paper also claimed, without evidence, that Secret Service agents tried to persuade their colleagues to no longer wear masks, because Trump was displeased by mask-wearing. Numerous agents interviewed by the author called the charge "ridiculous," "fantasy," and "insulting."

"We wear masks because we've got each other's backs. We are soldiers and we protect each other from harm. If our brothers fall on the battlefield, we carry them to safety," said one. "Obviously *Washington Post* scribblers, who almost certainly never wore the uniform of our country, wouldn't understand that."

Forcing the Secret Service to drastically reassign their agents was excused by the Bidenistas as the president wanting the "comfort of the familiar."

"You want him to be with people he knows and trusts."

It was as though the Secret Service men who protected Donald Trump were not trustworthy. The Biden camp got off to a very shaky start with the men assigned to sacrifice their lives for the Hawkeye.

The Biden people claimed swapping out the Trump veterans with the old Obama people was just seeking "comfort." In fact, it infuriated both groups. The agents know that all their brothers take their charge with heart and soul as a sacred pledge.

★★★

Biden's dislike of the Secret Service was apparently conveyed to Major, his German Shepherd. Tipped that Major had a penchant for biting agents, the watchdog group Judicial Watch filed a Freedom of Information Act request and eventually received thirty-six pages of "records communications that show the Biden's dog was responsible for numerous biting incidents of Secret Service personnel."

One document notes "that at the current rate an agent or officer has been bitten every day this week [in March 2021] and that agents were advised to protect their hands/fingers by placing their hands in their pockets."

Secret Service photos of the wounds were redacted from the released pages of the official report.

One report stated, "On March 6, 2021, Major attempted to bite [an agent] this evening. He didn't make contact with agent's skin, but he did bite a hole through his overcoat. This marks the third day in a row someone has been bitten by Major.

"Major on Monday afternoon bit another employee, who then required medical attention...."

President Biden's friends agree that he is not a party guy and likes to keep his own company a great deal of the time. Like a lot of almost-famous-for-life-famous people, Joe craves alone time: peace and quiet from the mewling mob, especially political favor seekers, who have been the bane of his existence since entering politics over a half century ago.

He dearly loves his son Hunter, but Hunter had been a needy child and was a high-maintenance adult, who siphoned up every ounce of favors and treasure possible, using his father's name and political power, seemingly oblivious to the potential for blowback.

Also, Hunter's bouts with drug addiction and sometimes poor choices of female company have added to his problems.

Hunter seemed to think that his father—"the big man," as he may refer to Joe in notes to his monkey-business cronies—is impervious to suffering consequences for even the most egregious transgressions.

Jill Biden entered the den with a maid in tow, wheeling an old-fashioned English-style tea service. She closed the door tightly, pretty much in the face of a Secret Service agent. Jill resented their intrusive presence as much or more than Joe did.

The sight of Jill instantly changed his troubled countenance from a frown to a beaming smile.

Neither of them was comfortable with the constant presence of help, let alone people they saw as literally armed intruders.

It was clear to all, but especially to Hawkeye CAT, who read loud and clear the antipathy the Bidens felt for them, that it was going to be a "long dark" four years for them, as well as for the American people.

Jill cozied up, sitting on an ottoman in front of his chair and handed him a cup of tea. She later told a girlfriend, whom she had taught school with, that she thought Joe's hand tremor seemed to have increased, but she attributed that to the pressure and excitement of realizing he had done it: the job he had aspired to was finally his, against all odds.

She also knew that larger challenges and threats to her husband were yet to come.

With the maid gone and the door closed to the Secret Service, Jill said she was convinced they were all taking mental notes of everything they overheard for their post-retirement tell-all books.

Biden gave Jill a brief rundown of what the Secret Service honchos had told him.

She said, "Well you could always have Congress alter the law a bit."

He rubbed his head, as if trying to erase a nasty headache.

"Once we're in office I think I will instruct my White House council to look into it and produce a memo as to what the possibilities are about making them less intrusive. As long as we don't make it appear that we are making the presidency less safe, my voters will agree with it.

"Most of the high tech and poisons, and the rest, sounded like mumbo-jumbo fear-mongering to me. They even said somebody had a plan to beam radiation at the White house, and another group tried to tunnel under the place and plant some kind of poison. I think these guys make this stuff up to make sure their funding doesn't get cut. I've been around forever and I know all their damn tricks. Anybody who thinks I'm a rookie is in for a nasty surprise."

Joe had, coolly at best, finally accepted the full force of the Secret Service in his world, much as his former boss Barack Obama had; obviously, Obama had lived with their constant but distanced presence for years. But Biden was just discovering how magnified their omnipresence was when you have the big job.

When the heavily armed, brawny men of Hawkeye CAT dressed in combat black, making no pretense of being the black-tie-wearing gentlemen who had protected President Ike Eisenhower in a slightly more civilized world, Biden visibly blanched, and the feeling was mutual. But they were going to do their job, which is to keep the new president alive, with or without his cooperation or approval.

Biden received his first actionable threat about a month before he was elected, in September 2020.

It came in the form of a childish, crudely handwritten letter with a "WARNING" intro at the top in red ink. It was left on the doorstep of a family in Frederick, Maryland, who happened to have a Biden/Harris sign on their lawn. The presumed author, James Dale Reed, had left it there in the early hours of the morning and was caught on a door camera video, the bane of midnight creepers.

He was interviewed by local police the following day, after the Secret Service ran a check of people on their watch list and identified him as being a low-level potential danger. Reed naturally denied he had written and delivered the threat, although the images of him dropping off the note were very clear and the handwriting was a match, according to agency experts.

Finally, he confessed and was arrested. Local authorities notified the Secret Service he was in custody, and an agent was dispatched to Frederick to determine if there were additional participants, and possibly a conspiracy.

An agent who participated later said, "It was obvious he was unhinged; the question was whether or not he and his possible collaborators were dangerous, and planning to actually act on their madness."

The threatening letter was unusually graphic and filled with delusionary vitriol. It read: "This is a warning to anyone reading this letter if you are a Biden/Harris supporter you will be targeted. We have a list of homes and addresses by your election signs. We are the ones with those scary guns. We are the ones your children have nightmares about. When we capture Grandpa Biden, we will severely beat him to the point of death. As for Mrs. Harris she will be [sexually violated] with a rifle barrel. Then for the grand end they will be executed on national television."

Hawkeye CAT was notified to step up security for Biden and Harris, assigning ten combat-ready soldiers to Biden and five to Harris. A group of Hunters was assigned to follow up in Frederick, in case Reed had collaborators.

Reed was on the Secret Service watch list because he had made threats against government officials not under agency protection, including Arizona Congresswoman Gabby Giffords. She was the member of Congress who had been shot at a constituent meeting, along with eighteen voters, in 2011. She survived, but her subsequent gun control crusade made her a target of Reed's venom.

A team of local police and agents searched the home of forty-two-year-old Reed, interviewed relatives and neighbors, most of whom said Reed was a blowhard who had a habit of picking fights, insulting people, and making threats, then always backing down.

He did have some legal and registered guns, but not the kind of assault-rifle-type arsenal he had hinted at owning. Most of his hard drives, Facebook posts, and notebooks, contained slightly off-kilter religion-infused sentiments, but nothing that suggested he was part of a conspiracy to kidnap and kill people under agency protection.

In the end the Secret Service backed off and let the U.S. Attorney's Office in Maryland handle the prosecution, which carried a maximum sentence of five years in federal prison.

Joe Biden spent the weeks before his inauguration as America's 46th president riding in a motorcade between his million-dollar Delaware mansion with a swimming pool (that he rarely uses, although he has been known to enjoy moonlight swims in his birthday suit) and his house near the ocean in Rehoboth, Delaware with three fireplaces (that he uses and throws logs on by himself).

On one trip from D.C. to Rehoboth, traversing the long, vertiginous Chesapeake Bay Bridge, the President-elect glanced over his shoulder, through the rear window, at the Hawkeye CAT armored Suburban close on his tail. He noticed something that struck him as strange. There were rifle barrels out the windows, pointing at the sky. He asked an assistant if his eyes were playing tricks on him or if they were gun barrels. She was as speechless as he was. "Yessss, they are," she said.

He muttered, "Damn," and speed-dialed the Director of the Secret Service, James Murray. He told Murray he was very angry. "It makes it look like I'm president-elect of some goddamn banana republic."

Seconds later, the rifles disappeared from view. Apparently, no one had told Joe that CAT men are soldiers, that they are six big beefy guys pretty much sardined into the SUV, which is smaller than a stock Suburban because it is fitted with armor plating and thick bulletproof glass. They don't want to accidentally shoot each other, so they stick their assault rifles out the windows, pointing toward the sky. No previous president the CAT men had protected had ever complained, so they assumed it was alright. They are paid to wield those weapons by the U.S. government, after all. They had been toting weapons for most of their lives, since grandad gave them their first .22 at age sixteen.

They didn't feel they had to hide them like dirty magazines.

Joe turned to his assistant and said, "Please make a note. When we're in the White House I want to get rid of those guys. I don't want to ever see those damn guns again. We're going to take away their assault rifles. They set a bad example with those guns sticking out of the car."

There was a collective sigh, as the Hawkeye CAT men quickly realized there had been a tectonic shift with the 2020 election. But they had no way of knowing the new president was planning to attempt to completely end the Hawkeye CAT program.

The president-elect puttered around in the beach house, often carrying the Primatene mist asthma inhaler he has occasionally had to use since, as a young man, he was given a pass by the draft on service in Vietnam, because he suffered severe asthma.

A Biden friend, who visited that week, said that Joe was strutting around, beaming a toothy smile from ear to ear, clearly proud of winning the prize he had always craved and had been repeatedly denied during fifty years in Washington: The top job.

The friend said, "He doesn't seem to be in the frenzy you would expect of a president-elect. He isn't having tons of meetings and isn't talking on his phone that much. He's oddly, almost preternaturally, calm. I think he has played out this scenario in his head a thousand times, so he's been living his dream of being king for many years. The scary part will come when it strikes him like a lightning bolt that from now on the buck stops with him, and he can't look to Barack Obama for an answer. Even Joe is aware that if it had been up to him, Osama bin Laden would still be alive and plotting attacks on America. He avoids talking about it, but he certainly remembers he gave 'don't go' advice on the decision to take out the terror chief."

Everyone agrees the (slightly) more interesting Biden is Doctor (of Education) Jill.

Writing in the *Wall Street Journal*, Joseph Epstein asked the First Lady, rather harshly,

> Any chance you might drop the "Dr." before your name? "Dr. Jill Biden" sounds and feels fraudulent, not to say a touch comic. Your degree is, I believe, an Ed.D., a Doctor of Education, earned at the University of Delaware through a dissertation with the unpromising title "Student Retention at the Community College Level: Meeting Student's Needs."

> A wise man once said that no one should call themselves "Dr." unless they have delivered a child.

> The Ph.D. may once have held prestige, but that has been diminished by the erosion of seriousness and the relaxation of standards in university education generally, at any rate outside the sciences. Getting a doctorate was then an arduous proceeding: One had to pass examinations in two foreign languages, in Greek or Latin, defend one's thesis, and take an oral examination on general knowledge in one's field.

> As for your Ed.D., Madame First Lady, hard-earned though it may have been, please consider stowing it, at least in public, at least for now. Forget the small thrill of

being Dr. Jill and settle for the larger thrill of living for the next four years in the best public housing in the world as First Lady Jill Biden.

The *National Review* take was even harsher. They scolded: "Her doctorate is garbage because her dissertation is garbage."

It turns out, according to President Biden, Jill's desire to be addressed as doctor, despite never having delivered a baby, stemmed from a pique with her husband over his title of "Senator."

Los Angeles Times reporter Robin Abcarian wrote, "Joe Biden on the campaign trail explained that his wife's desire for the highest degree was in response to what she perceived as her second-class status on their mail. 'She said, I was so sick of the mail coming to Senator and Mrs. Biden. I wanted to get mail addressed to Dr. and Senator Biden.'"

"That's the real reason she got her doctorate," he said.

She is actually something of a ball of fire, while he is kind of groggy and often befuddled, according to people who spend time in their presence.

Jill had been married to a former college football player, had run a successful college bar where Bruce Springsteen had performed before the success of *Born to Run* and Chubby Checker had done the Twist and sung. She had modeled for a time and still runs five miles a day, even successfully competing in the grueling Marine Corp Marathon.

They met after her divorce and the death of Joe's first wife, and he proposed and was turned down several times before Jill finally relented.

Visitors say she is seldom around, keeping her own very busy schedule. In the White House, she is in attendance at the important ceremonial occasions over which first ladies are expected to preside, but has had her own agenda during their White House years, devoting herself to education issues, which is one of her main passions—digging into the issue and making a long-term mark on education, proving she truly earned her degree and to get back at her harsh critics (said a Biden insider).

The four tumultuous years of the Trump presidency were probably the most politically contentious in U.S. history since 1860 and the advent of the Civil War. It was no longer a case of two political parties sparring over issues, but regular clashes in dining rooms, barrooms and on television talk shows, that came close to or even surpassed actual felonious threats against the president or presidential candidates.

The casual way in which charges of treason were made, and thinly veiled death threats were muttered publicly, was deeply troubling to the people charged with protection. Other times, out-and-out suggestions of assassination were bantered about, which were often clearly technical violations of federal criminal laws.

For the professionals at the Secret Service and other government police agencies it was a confusing and frustrating time. They couldn't arrest every tipsy nut in a bar who rails against a political candidate and talks big and nasty.

Nor could they arrest every Hollywood actor or comedian who went on television wishing the president a gruesome end. They couldn't even take action when unhinged actress Kathy Griffin posed holding a fake, bloody, decapitated Trump head.

Griffin was censored mildly, being promptly dropped from her annual New Year's Eve CNN appearance. But there were no legal consequences; the law doesn't allow it because this kind of expression is free speech, no matter how tasteless.

Faded ex-boxer and actor Mickey Rourke declared in a TMZ video that he would love "30 seconds in a room to give [Trump] a Louisville slugger."

Robert De Niro declared, "Of course, I want to punch him."

Madonna told a crowd at the 2017 Women's March on Washington that she had "thought an awful lot about blowing up the White House."

New York City's non-profit Public Theater staged a version of *Julius Caesar* in which a Trump-like character is stabbed to death on stage.

Johnny Depp, who has a well-documented history of domestic craziness, channeled his inner John Wilkes Booth. "When was the last time an actor assassinated a president?"

President Biden even took a swipe saying he would have liked "to take Trump behind the bleachers and beat the hell out of him" if they had attended school together.

So who are the Secret Service supposed to take seriously and who should they ignore? The choice of enforcing the laws as written could make them look like zealots, but a mistake in ignoring a threat could result in a tragedy that would be remembered centuries later.

At Crosby High School in Houston, Texas, on November 9, 2020, a student recorded a thirty-second video in which he brandished two guns and wondered "where the other Trump supporters at" and suggested they should get together and "assassinate Joe Biden."

He then looked at the camera and wound up his bizarre and disturbing performance by saying "Where you at Joe Biden? I'm coming for you."

The Crosby School District decided to err on the side of political correctness, stating that the threatening tape wasn't recorded on school property and didn't mention any students or school employees. No, it just mentioned killing the U.S. president. It added that the decision not to act had been "investigated and cleared by federal authorities," without giving specifics as to what federal authorities were involved or specifically how they had "cleared" the video.

The punishment? The pistol-wielding video maker was kept home several days for "an added safety precaution."

The question is: Who is going to be safe while he is "kept home" and free with his pistols? In addition, are there sinister forces backing this crazy kid, or is he crazy enough to do something to President Biden on his own? Those were the concerns of Hawkeye CAT and the Hunters.

A retired Secret Service agent said,

> The kid waving pistols, threatening the president, and asking for back up from like-minded people, I would definitely interview him, his parents and teachers. I would have found out if the guns were legally registered.
>
> I would want to find out if he talked about killing President Biden regularly, or was it the one-time act of a poseur. Kids often like to act out, it's part of being immature.
>
> If he was in high school, he probably wasn't old enough to legally possess a handgun, and that would be an issue for local police.
>
> As for the celebrities; they are actors and they often act out like children. That's what they do for a living, pretend to be somebody they are not. But that doesn't necessarily mean they're not nutty and dangerous.

CHAPTER SEVENTEEN

Too Little Too Late

The United States Secret Service was originally designed as an elite *reactive* police agency. It was formed on July 5, 1865 as a law enforcement wing of the Treasury Department, largely to combat the then-widespread counterfeiting of currency, which threatened to destroy world confidence in the U.S. dollar.

The first aggressive defender of presidential life was a chief executive himself: Andrew Jackson, the seventh holder of the office. On January 30, 1835, "Old Hickory," as he was fondly called by his friends and supporters, was leaving the U.S. Capitol building heading for his waiting horse and buggy, when he was approached by unemployed house painter Richard Lawrence.

Normally and naturally gregarious, Tennessee southern gentleman Jackson extended his hand in friendship when he saw the man approaching. Lawrence drew two pistols from his haversack and attempted to be the first presidential assassin. Both pistols misfired.

Rightfully enraged, Jackson beat the man senseless with his cane. He became his own first Hawkeye CAT Secret Service man.

In 1867 the agency's duties were expanded to cover all fraud against the government, rum runners, the Ku Klux Klan, train robbers, and other miscreants who broke federal laws.

In 1894 the Secret Service dipped its feet into murky water, providing grudging guardianship of President Grover Cleveland's life. It marked the first time an American president had formally been assigned as armed protectors.

But it would be over thirty-five years before American presidents were fully afforded around-the-clock armed protection. In the years the Service has been tasked with protecting presidents, it has been obvious that presidents, their families, and the others in the protection category are magnets for attacks—ranging from bullets, poisons, anthrax, to ricin. But they have also needed the help and alertness of the presidents. George W. Bush deftly and athletically dodged shoes hurled at him during a speech in the Middle East, while Donald Trump was nearly beaned with a cell phone during a rally.

Abraham Lincoln gave a speech in Washington on April 11, 1865, promising that freed slaves and Black Union Army soldiers would be granted the right to vote in Louisiana. A member of the audience was a pro-Confederate white supremacist from Bel Air, Maryland, who also happened to be a handsome and successful actor from a famous theatrical family.

(In fact, the Booth family still has a Broadway theater named after one of its actor relatives.)

John Wilkes Booth made an oath that day that he would avenge the Southern defeat and the enfranchisement of African Americans, by ending Lincoln's life.

Three days later the actor, furious with the president's promises and driven to madness by constant Union celebrations of the South's defeat, learned that the President would be attending a performance at Ford's Theater, just a few blocks from the White House.

Being a frequent performer at the theater, Booth had no trouble entering the box where the Lincolns were watching the comedy *Our American Cousin*. He discovered, to his delight, that there was no protection at all for the head of state. The one D.C. police guard who regularly accompanied Lincoln when he left the White House, had apparently grown bored with the play and gone to a local bar for a drink, believing his thirst more important than the president's life.

Knowing every line of the play, Booth waited to make his move until Act 3 Scene 2, when the biggest laugh line was delivered, presumably to drown out the gun shot. He managed to come within inches of Lincoln and fired his .44-caliber single-shot Derringer into Lincoln's head.

Described in one account as looking like a "demon," Booth leaped out of the box down to the stage, breaking his leg. But in triumph the actor managed to stand and face the shocked audience, infamously proclaiming, "Sic semper tyrannis! ("Thus always to tyrants!")," and to triumphantly scream, "The South is avenged!"

The fifteen hundred or so theater goers present watched in horror. It was later called the actor's greatest and final performance.

Lincoln was taken across the street to the Petersen House, where he was examined by doctors who confirmed there was no hope. He never regained consciousness, staying in a coma for eight hours. In the morning his breathing grew shallow, his face calm. A witness said the dying president smiled broadly at the end. His secretary John Hay later wrote that "a look of unspeakable peace came upon his worn features."

Author and historian Lee Davis wrote, "It was the first time in four years, probably, that a peaceful expression crossed his face."

He died at 7:22 a.m. on April 15, 1865.

There being no police agency charged with presidential protection, the war-weary 16th New York Calvary was enlisted to lead the manhunt for the assassin. They were men skilled in battle, but ill-equipped as an investigative force. But the epic twelve-day manhunt was directed by an experienced and dogged military detective named Lafayette Baker, who eventually found and trapped the assassin.

Stopped by none of the hysterical and frightened audience at Ford's Theater, one of whom he slashed with a knife, Booth escaped through a back alley, as per his carefully planned getaway. He mounted a borrowed bay mare with a white star on her forehead and galloped through nighttime Washington. The city was guarded by thousands of troops, though none had yet been alerted to the murder. The assassin rode at a normal gait past the Capitol grounds and to the Navy Yard Bridge, which would lead him to southern Maryland and relative safety. Using his finely-honed dramatic skills, Booth charmed his way past a soldier named Sgt. Silas Cobb, who was charged with guarding the bridge mostly to keep defeated and vengeful Rebels from coming into Washington, rather than keeping people in the Capital.

Together with several other unreconstructed rebels, Booth managed to cross the Potomac River into still-Confederate friendly territory. Tipped off by a fisherman, the forty horsemen of the Union Calvary thundered south in pursuit of the assassin and his Johnny Reb cohort.

Booth's last act unwound at a tobacco barn on Garrett Farm in Northern Virginia. Surrounded by twenty-four well-armed soldiers led by Detective Baker, Booth refused to surrender, vowing theatrically, "I have too great a soul to die like a common criminal."

Baker was unwilling to let his men, who had survived the depredations of the Civil War, die in peacetime. He refused to allow a suicidal frontal attack, instead ordering the wooden barn torched. Realizing he was going to be consumed by the fire, Booth offered to come out and fight a duel with the cavalry, opting for the dramatic "death by cop" way out of his hopeless situation.

The detective had been ordered to take the assassin alive, because the government was convinced the killing of Lincoln was part of a broad conspiracy that might have started with former Confederate President Jefferson Davis, and it was hoped Booth would testify against the hated Davis, finally bringing the architect of secession to justice.

Suddenly, a shot rang out and Booth fell. A soldier named Boston Corbett quickly stepped forward and confessed he had fired the shot, which had proved fatal. "Providence directed me," he confessed. (He later amended his statement to say he believed the assassin was about to open fire on his fellow soldiers, and that he had only aimed to disable Booth.)

When newspapers carried the account of Corbett's deed, he briefly became famous and a hero to many of his Union countrymen.

The wound was to the head, and it was said to be approximately in the same place as Lincoln's fatal injury. As the sun rose over the Garrett Farm, John Wilkes Booth was dead, and the great manhunt over.

★★★

Ironically Abraham Lincoln had approved the formation of the Secret Service on the day he was assassinated.

The Secret Service wasn't created in time to save Lincoln's life, but in a bizarre turn was able to save his body from grave robbers.

In 1875, over ten years after Lincoln's assassination, a skilled counterfeiter and plate engraver named Ben Boyd was arrested by the Secret Service, and subsequently sentenced to ten years in federal prison. Boyd's partner and brother-in-law Pete McCartney was suddenly deprived of a lucrative income, and decided on a plan to free him from prison and extort the then-unfathomable sum of two hundred thousand dollars in the process.

The scheme was to go to Oak Ridge Cemetery in Springfield, Illinois, snatch the body of the late martyred president Abraham Lincoln, and hold the body hostage.

Tipped off, the Secret Service launched an operation to catch the would-be grave robbers red-handed. The Feds, with back-up from local police, waited in the darkness surrounding the tomb.

Several hours later, two men showed up with crowbars and the clear intent to carry out the mad plan. They were the professional counterfeiters and desperados Jack Hughes and Terrence Mullen. They entered the tomb and were able, with Herculean effort, to remove the great stone that guarded the president's coffin.

Unfortunately, the gun of an over-anxious local cop accidentally fired, launching a barrage of fire into the dark from both soldiers and police, allowing Hughes and Mullen to escape in the ensuing chaos—but without their grizzly prize.

Ten days later they were both caught and sentenced to a year in state prison for attempted grave robbery, and Lincoln was able to again rest in peace.

★★★

Thirty-five years after Lincoln's death, on September 6, 1901, President William McKinley was shot twice in the abdomen with a .32 caliber revolver by anarchist Leon Czolgosz at the Pan-American Exposition in Buffalo, New York. McKinley perished on September 14th of gangrene caused by his wounds, and the ineptness of the doctors who tended to him.

The government apparently decided, belatedly, that the third presidential assassination was one too many and tasked the Secret Service with protecting the lives of our presidents. The mandate would later grow to include presidential families, other officials, and visiting world dignitaries.

But, almost bizarrely, the U.S. Congress didn't bother to pass a law making it a felony to threaten the life of a president until 1917.

Theodore Roosevelt ran for re-election to the presidency on the Bull Moose ticket, three and a half years after leaving office. Campaigning in Milwaukee, Wisconsin, he was confronted by John Schrank, a delusional saloon keeper, who claimed the assassinated President William McKinley had told him from the grave to kill Roosevelt. He had no explanation for why McKinley wanted Roosevelt to join him in the afterlife.

Schrank brandished a .38-caliber Colt and shot Teddy square in the chest. Luckily for the old Rough Rider, the bullet was deflected by a metal spectacles case and caused only a deep flesh wound. Remaining characteristically unruffled, he coughed into his hand; seeing no blood— meaning he wasn't bleeding internally—he decided to go ahead with his full fifty-minute speech.

Halfway through, alarmed that the crowd was seizing the shooter, Roosevelt ordered police to take him into custody. He told his audience he had been shot and wounded, but barked, "It takes more than that to kill a Bull Moose."

Only after the rousing speech was delivered did he consent to be taken to a hospital, where it was determined the bullet had lodged in a chest muscle, and that it would be more dangerous to try to remove it, given the state of surgical skills and equipment in that antediluvian era, than to leave it in place.

Teddy carried the bullet in his chest until his death.

A brazen home invasion of Ronald Reagan's Bel Air, California estate was committed by an obsessed man, who held the former president responsible for his brother's death from AIDS, and was determined to strangle to death Reagan and his wife Nancy. The horrific episode convinced the Secret Service that it needed a stronger proactive approach, even for ex-presidents, if it was going to ensure the lives of all presidents—former, current, and future for that matter (once the candidate had announced a serious run for the office).

Agents needed to go after would-be assassins before they had a chance to even formulate a plan of attack. In other words, they needed to almost become mind readers who could anticipate an attack by building a hard psychological profile, allowing them to recognize who was a potential killer and who was just blowing smoke.

Ranger and Laredo studied the actions and psychological profiles of assassins and would-be assassins. They wanted very much to learn as much as possible about their likely adversaries. In modern times, the profiles often stretch into thousands of pages, accumulated over years by profilers, agents, and psychologists, who in many cases have spent years in an attempt to get inside potential assassins' heads.

The two agents were both very interested in Lynette "Squeaky" Fromme and Sara Jane Moore, who had both tried to kill Gerald Ford. They later expressed their belief and fear that soon women would become more willing to have and to express extreme views, vent rage, and commit acts of political violence.

Laredo said,

> There was a paucity of profiling information about women assassins. And what there was tended to express

the view that women assassins were poor abused souls, who became unhinged and were acting on hormonally induced rage and senseless anger. That kind of dismissive profiling doesn't help us to figure out what kind of woman commits such a crime and how we can predict patterns of behavior leading to their apprehension before they act.

Sara Jane Moore was fingered by the FBI for whom she informed on radicals, including the Symbionese Liberation Army, but the Service wasn't able to discern what was going on in her head. She was enraged about the Vietnam War, believed it would take an apocalyptic event like a presidential assassination to spark the citizenry to launch a full-scale rebellion and take over the country.

They both admired Charlie Manson, who ordered the Tate La Bianca killings, disguised as being the wicked deeds of a radical Black group like the Panthers. Manson fantasized it would launch a race war and bring chaos and massive bloodletting across the continent, leading to anarchy, he hoped. His demented fantasy was to be cult leader of a dystopian Mad Max world that he would preside over from the Spahn Ranch.

At a violent juncture in American history, with assassinations of Bobby Kennedy and Martin Luther King, bloody riots in many American cities and an ongoing unpopular war in Vietnam with body bags coming home daily, it resonated with susceptible, sick minds.

But it was often taken as the meaningless rantings of fools, who would never actually act on it. Moore was given the all clear by the FBI diagnosing her to be harmless, just days before she nearly killed Ford in a busy park on the grounds of the California State Capitol, in view of the Governor's office.

Women are more likely these days to have guns and often know how to use them, which was not common several years ago. There were few real-life Annie Oakleys.

Of course, my fear is also that with more women studying chemical and biological sciences, it makes it important to keep an eye on women with those skills, who may also express violent and radical views. Most especially those who post—even though it may come off like delusional fantasy—to make weapons to kill a president or to cause mass casualties, and get revenge against what they perceive a cruel, heartless world.

But a person with minimal knowledge can go to the internet and find simple step-by-step instructions to make certain biochemical weapons. That genie is, sadly, out of the lamp and can't be coaxed back in.

We already had *The Walking Dead* TV actress Shannon Richardson manufacturing ricin and sending it through the mail to President Obama and former New York Mayor Michel Bloomberg, in a feeble attempt to frame her husband. Richardson thought that everybody would think women are too "ladylike" to unleash such a horrible poison and she was largely right. But women have been poisoning people for the millennium. *Arsenic and Old Lace* is a fiction, but it's also an exemplar.

I intend to create an actionable, meaningful profile of women who would be prone to using biochem weapons for targeted killing or to spread as an act of mass terror.

The agency has, in recent years, worked hard to convince law enforcement, including local and state police as well as employers and even school personnel, to err on the side of caution in alerting the Service to possible plotters—even seemingly unlikely people, like former Manson girl Lynette "Squeaky" Fromme, who attempted to shoot Gerald Ford in 1975. Fromme was a singer as a child, who appeared on the Lawrence Welk Show and even entertained at the White House, until she ran away from her upper-middle-class suburban home. With that resume, no one would finger her a presidential assassin. But then she was taken in by the Manson family and indoctrinated into the warped ways of Charlie.

★★★

President Ford was in Sacramento, California, speechifying in the lead up to the 1976 election. He walked from the Senator Hotel across L Street onto the Capitol grounds, where he was going to meet with recently elected Governor Jerry Brown.

A friendly crowd gathered as he made his way toward the Capitol Building, and he did the politician thing—stopping to exchange pleasantries and shake hands. He noticed a young woman dressed all in red with a flowing robe, assumed she also wanted to shake hands or ask a question, and turned to face her.

Fromme reached into her robe and pulled out a shining, metallic black Colt 1911 .45, a semiautomatic handgun that had been the standard army-issue sidearm through World Wars I and II, The Korean War, and Vietnam—a highly reliable weapon with great lethality.

Fromme made history at that moment, becoming the first woman to attempt to assassinate a U.S. President.

She swung the gun, aimed between his knees and waist, and pulled the trigger. Fortunately, for Ford and history, she had failed to pull the slide back to chamber a round and there was only a hollow metallic click, heard by many in the stunned, dense crowd.

Fromme shouted in consternation, "It didn't go off. Can you believe it!" It was just blind luck that she hadn't bothered to learn how to use a semiautomatic handgun.

By the way, her motive, later stated during her trial—during which she threw an apple at the prosecutor—was that she wanted to kill President Ford to send a message about pollution and global cooling, which in that zeitgeist was the early version of "climate change." Indeed *Time, Newsweek*, and numerous other magazines in the early '70s, had been predicting a new ice age and *Newsweek* even ran a cover drawing of the Earth sheathed in ice. That got Fromme's hackles up and convinced her Gerald Ford was responsible and had to be stopped.

Protective Services officer Larry Buendorf grabbed the gun, loaded with eight .45 rounds, and knocked Fromme to the ground. Secret Service agents literally lifted Ford off his feet and carried him to safety. The President was offended at being made to look very unpresidential, yelling, "Put me down! Put me down!" Once released, he shook himself off, restored his chief executive dignity, and walked the rest of the way to the governor's office. He calmly shook hands with Governor Brown and had a thirty-minute meeting, during which he made no mention of his close brush with death, until the meeting had ended.

The lesson, nearly fifty years later, is that Squeaky Fromme had been a longtime—really a charter member—of the Manson Family, and should have at least been on a watch list and taken into custody, or at least put under surveillance, when it was known the U.S. President would be visiting Sacramento. But no such list existed at the time, and she was perfectly free to walk the few blocks from her attic apartment to menace the President with a military weapon.

The coda to the incident is that the gun has been on display ever since, at the Gerald R. Ford Presidential Library in Grand Rapids, Michigan.

Seventeen days later, on September 22, 1975, the second female in U.S. history to attempt to assassinate a U.S. president tried to kill Ford in San Francisco, just eighty-seven miles west of Sacramento. Clearly, Moore was influenced by Fromme's failed attempt. So—from a profiling point of view—once there is an attempt, the Agency must double down on caution. It gets sick minds spinning like a lathe.

Sara Jane Moore, then forty-six years old, the granddaughter of German immigrants, grew up in Charleston, West Virginia, and led an "interesting" life (in the proverbial Chinese sense of the word). She was a nursing student in West Virginia as a young woman, then a Women's Army Corp soldier. Bored and constricted by the army, and made angry by people in ill health, she switched careers and became an accountant.

Sara Jane had four children and five husbands. She switched from ardent Christianity to Orthodox Judaism, and—like Belushi and Ackroyd in the Blues Brothers movie—came to believe she was on a mission from God.

Moving to San Francisco because she felt it was a hotbed of revolutionary and intriguingly unhinged thinking, she joined several movements. Predictably, Moore was drawn to the totally off-the-rails Symbionese Liberation Army, and became a bookkeeper for People in Need, a charitable organization the SLA had created with William Randolph Hearst Jr.'s fortune, which they had received in exchange for not killing his daughter Patty Hearst, whom they had kidnapped and held for ransom.

Moore was admittedly obsessed with Patty, then twenty-years-old, who appeared to have suffered from Stockholm Syndrome: joining the SLA, helping them rob a bank while wielding a military-style rifle, looking like a sultry desperado. It was quite a startling metamorphosis from scion of one of the most famous families in America to an outlaw on the run.

When Moore arrived for work at People in Need, she announced she was being directed by God, a proclamation which caused no one in the batty organization to bat an eye.

In every way eclectic, Moore somehow managed to become an FBI informant, simultaneously admiring the SLA's embrace of violence and savage methods, while also secretly informing on them.

Assessing that Moore was mentally unsound, the FBI tipped off the Secret Service that she should be evaluated as a potential assassination suspect. They did, and determined she was not a threat to the president— another near-disastrous misdiagnosis.

The day before her assassination attempt, Moore was arrested by police and charged with illegal handgun possession. A .44-caliber revolver and a cache of ammunition were confiscated, but she was released on her own recognizance.

Again bored with her life, she decided the SLA was correct in its theory that the way to revolution was through extreme, shocking public violence that would awaken the masses. She remembered how the world had seemed to stop after the JFK assassination, and craved the world-wide infamy Lee Harvey Oswald had attained in death.

Moore had been excited by Fromme's attempt on President Ford's life and vowed to finish the job and do it right.

When she read in the *San Francisco Chronicle* that Ford was attending an event at the St. Francis Hotel, she stationed herself across Powell Street, about forty feet from the entrance, armed with a .38 she had purchased in a hurry that morning to replace the confiscated .44.

When Ford emerged, waving in his jovial politician's way to a cheering, friendly crowd, she fired a single shot, missing the President, then raised her arm taking aim again, prompting a brave former Marine named Oliver Sipple to lunge and grab her arm, possibly saving Ford's life. The gun fired again, missing the intended target but wounding a cab driver waiting for a fare in front of the Saint Francis.

Wrestled to the ground by agents, Moore was dragged off to prison, soon pled guilty to attempted assassination, and was sentenced to life in prison. During her trial Moore expressed no remorse and little regret. "Am I sorry I tried? Yes and no. Yes, because it accomplished very little and I threw my life away. And, no, I'm not sorry I tried, because at the time it seemed a correct expression of my anger. I had become immersed in the Vietnam War. I was saying the country had to change. The only way was violent revolution and I genuinely thought that shooting Ford could trigger revolution in this country."

During her trial even her own defense team described her as "bizarre and mysterious."

She served her term at the federal women's prison in Dublin, California working as an accountant, for which she was paid a relatively generous $1.25 an hour.

After serving thirty years, and finally expressing remorse—certainly only because she was told the parole board wouldn't free her if she refused—she was released from federal custody on December 31, 2007, at age seventy-seven. She had indeed thrown her life away.

But she became an instant celebrity appearing on NBC's *Today Show*, where she bragged of her 1979 escape from prison by leaping over a barbed wire fence and running away. She told the audience that if she had known she would be captured within a few hours, she "would have stopped in a bar for a burger and a beer."

Her next taste of infamy came when she appeared as a character in Stephen Sondheim's Broadway musical *Assassins* alongside nine other assassins, including John Wilkes Booth and her fellow breaker of the assassination glass ceiling, Squeaky Fromme.

With Hawkeye CAT and the Hunters on the job it would have been a different story, and Fromme and Moore might not have survived and lived on taxpayer money for decades in prison.

Surprisingly, the Service also solicits tips from mothers of potential assassins who wish to save their sons from carrying out plans which would leave them dead or in prison for life; school teachers with concerns for their wayward students; army personnel; and sundry alert citizens. There has been an attempt on the part of a special group within the agency to get the word out that any information, however speculative or flimsy, will be listened to, treated with sensitivity and discretion, and will be held confidential, and that they are not in the business of knocking down doors in the middle of the night just because someone makes an inappropriate remark, but will discreetly and politely request an interview with the subject and only act upon solid evidence.

The agency needed more money, and more men and women, if they were going to do the job that they were charged with carrying out in 1917. But Congress, which holds the purse strings, and the Secret Service brass, who apparently wanted to prove they were frugal guardians of taxpayer dollars, hit the brakes over the years, severely cutting the budget for things like profiling to determine likely assassins. Some of the staider members of the leadership seemed to feel that profiling was hocus-pocus and would never yield the outcomes that old fashioned gumshoe work would.

It wasn't until after the tectonic shocks of the 9/11 attacks—that were intended by the terror mongers to end with the destruction of the U.S. Capitol and the Pentagon, in order to decapitate the American government—that it was determined the Secret Service had to closely coordinate with the FBI, the intelligence community, and local law enforcement to prevent future plots in advance. The Secret Service was transferred from Treasury to Homeland Security and became an important arm of the national defense against terror and assassination. The agents were no longer going to be waiting for a potential assassin to suddenly emerge from a lair like the Texas School Book Depository, and change history. Agents were going to track them down.

The Intelligence and Assessment Division of the Secret Service worked with the Proactive Crisis Response Group, a private organization which was designed to ferreting out and neutralizing Lee Harvey Oswald wannabes, and other individuals whose threats and behavior indicated they may be planning school shootings.

The Secret Service began using some of its assets and techniques to shed light on such individuals and prevent they could acted on their disturbed plans.

The concept was that these men and women would have discovered the identities of the 9/11 terrorists, whose behavior was extremely suspicious, hunted them down, and eliminated them, because they wouldn't have surrendered peacefully—they were, in fact, suicide bombers.

A twenty-five-year veteran agent told the author that when he began his career, the Secret Service recruited and hired mostly lawyers, but now they recruit soldiers, including veterans of elite special forces groups like Navy SEALs and Army Rangers. The Hunters and Hawkeye CAT are seldom recruited from the ranks of the protective presidential force, but are generally recruited soldiers who have served in combat zones like Afghanistan, with men and women they admired and trusted.

Some are recruited for special skills or areas of expertise they have in dealing with the threat of modern terror. Some groups specialize in preventing nuclear or germ warfare that could be employed to take out a president and his entire cabinet, plus untold numbers of civilians who might be in the vicinity of an attack, or even in the same region.

Unlike the pre-9/11 past when police and intelligence agencies kept their investigations close to the chest, and were extremely reluctant to share their intel and sources with other wings of the government, the Hunters and Hawkeye CAT hold regular meetings with their peers in other intelligence and law enforcement agencies, routinely forming committees to deal jointly with threats and crises.

The heroic work they do in constantly staving off plots against the people they are charged with protecting is seldom heralded in the press, and they generally prefer to keep it that way. They are painfully aware of the old saw that they have to be right 100 percent of the time, while the bad players only have to get lucky once, to change the course of history and gain the infamous roles they wish to play in the history books.

In recent years, the role of the Secret Service has expanded hugely to keep up with cyber threats and terror attacks. The official mission statement of the agency says: "The Secret Service has adopted a proactive approach, using advanced technologies, and capitalizing on the power of task force partnerships. [It] has a pivotal role in securing the nation's critical infrastructure...and the need to combat transnational organized crime that targets the citizens and financial institutions of the United States. The Secret Service's investigative mission abroad is growing as well, creating the need for a heightened overseas liaison presence. Multi-disciplined forensics experts, investigative experts and intelligence analysts provide rapid response and critical information in support of financial analysis, infrastructure protection and criminal investigations."

The Secret Service has developed cyber strategy to monitor threats, including pinpointing the location of an anonymous sender of threats. On February 26, 2019, a Seattle man sent threats using his Gmail account, threatening to "execute" President Trump's senior adviser and son-in-law Jared Kushner "for his countless treasonous crimes," but mostly for his Jewish faith.

In addition to posting the threats, he sent anti-Semitic screeds to at least four newspapers, then openly gloated that he hadn't been arrested yet. But just as he was typing his taunting boasts, an elite group of Secret Service Hunters was closing in, accompanied by local police. They busted twenty-seven-year-old Chase Bliss Colasurdo's door down and quickly subdued him. In a search of his suburban home they found a gas mask, a Nazi flag, a framed portrait of Adolph Hitler, a bulletproof vest, other combat equipment, and hundreds of rounds of 9mm ammunition.

He was sentenced to five years in state prison and ordered to undergo psychiatric treatment.

The newly constituted Secret Service has divisions that specialize in combatting the threats created by the age of terror. They include: experts in chemical, biological, radiological, and nuclear materials, an airspace security branch, hazardous material control, a medical emergency response team, a counter-assault team, a counter-sniper team, a counter-surveillance unit, and a magnetometer operations unit.

As the forerunner of the FBI, the Secret Service was originally charged with enforcing almost all federal laws. On July 26, 1908, with just thirty-four agents, the Service represented the genesis of a federal law enforcement agency responsible for the capture of criminals who crossed state lines to elude local law enforcement. Bonnie and Clyde, as well as numerous other outlaws, regularly fled across state borders with police hot on their trails, knowing the lawmen's authority ended at the state line. Racing for the border became a deadly and often successful game for outlaws. Then the tables turned, with Feds shocking the bad guys by crossing state lines like they didn't exist and busting them in any U.S. jurisdiction.

The Secret Service, and eventually the FBI, closed that loophole forever.

In 1935, the Federal Bureau of Investigation became an independent entity with J. Edgar Hoover as assistant director. It would be charged with defeating espionage, and would take on the new deadly class of gangsters who had become rich and powerful thanks to the enactment of Prohibition.

Notorious outlaws like John Dillinger, Al (Scarface) Capone, Machine Gun Kelly, and many others were soon in the crosshairs of agents toting Thompson submachine guns, including Hoover himself (at least in posed press shots).

Even as an independent agency, the FBI would work hand-in-glove with the Secret Service, sharing intelligence and often engaging in joint operations—with the exception of periods of professional jealousy which occasionally drove each agency to covet all the glory.

The Hunters were formed when it became clear that organized international and domestic terror groups were determined to attack the leaders of the U.S. government, with the aim of killing or kidnapping those who fell under the protection of the Secret Service. The agency urgently needed to protect these leaders from a future 9/11 mass attack.

You won't find the Hunters or Hawkeye CAT mentioned on the Secret Service's website, nor in most of the books that have been written about the Secret Service. In fact, the unit is so secret that most of the Secret Service's own employees have never heard of the Hunters. *Their* identity is the Secret Service's most highly guarded secret.

"We're a small, very tight-knit group," said one of the Hunters, who spoke to me on condition of anonymity. "Everyone is on a first name basis. We know each other's families and we socialize. In other words, we have each other's backs and work together seamlessly."

"We're our own recruiting agency," continued the Hunter, a strapping six foot four former Army Ranger.

> We go to the guys who served fearlessly and with honor
> in the desert. Trust is as important as skill. We're aware

that there are people in law enforcement and government who have their own political agendas and can't be relied on one hundred percent. There is no room for people like that in the Hunters.

Like the rest of the Secret Service we would take a bullet for a president we very much disagree with, as well as one we personally support. There is no room for politics when it comes to life-or-death matters. It's a question of sacred honor and trust, not politics.

Beyond our duties, we have an obligation to keep ourselves and our families safe, which means guarding our identities. Only a handful of people know of our existence, but some of the bad actors do. There have been references to us in recent years on jihadi websites.

The Hunters don't fit the stereotype of the Secret Service agent: a lanky Clint-Eastwood-looking figure loping alongside the president's bulletproof "Beast," dressed in a dark suit, white shirt, and Ray-Ban sunglasses, a bud in his ear, and a microphone up his sleeve. Most of the men and women on the president's protective detail are former cops and state troopers. Their identity is no secret.

The Hunters are an entirely different breed. They are battle-hardened special forces warriors—former Navy SEALS, Army Rangers and Marines—who have served in Afghanistan, Iraq, and other hot spots around the world.

The Hunters and Hawkeye CAT are the shock troops of the Secret Service. Their job is to hunt down, and if necessary kill, would-be assassins and terrorists before they can carry out their plots against the nation and the nation's highest elected officers: the president, the vice president, their wives and children, former presidents, and candidates for top office—plus foreign dignitaries visiting the U.S. on state business.

In addition, the Secret Service has teams of undercover plain clothes agents who are incredibly adept at finding groups with malevolent intentions who happen to be clever and cunning. These bad actors, unfortunately tend to give themselves and their intentions away give themselves up by making threats that are nothing more than braggadocio.

They subscribe to a code of *omerta*, much like the Mafia. The undercover men and women of the agency also have a code of silence and keep the details of their work even from their own families, in order to protect them, as well as to spare them from additional concerns that they are going to return home safely at the end of the day.

Dining at Daniel Boulud's CityCenterDC restaurant DBGB across the street from the agency, one notices that quite a few folks in undercover clothes—sporting beards and long hair in some cases—are regularly buzzed into the building. They are an elite group, associated with the Hunters, who look nothing like their colleagues, the polished Secret Service gentlemen, but use their disguises to infiltrate groups they surmise are prone to violence against government officials. They deliberately dress like misfits to blend in.

Researching a book on the Secret Service proved to be a daunting task for several reasons. The women and men of the agency take the word "secret" in the title very seriously. Most conspiracies that they snuff out, to keep the president and their other protectives safe, are never reported and never publicly discussed, and they like it that way.

A central tenet of the intelligence community agencies' philosophy is that discretion is their code, and is ultimately important to gain and keep the trust of the people they have pledged to protect. Countless harrowing incidents that would make headlines are filed under "all in a day's work." The details are then filed away and only discussed *sotto voce* among agents, over drinks when the day is done.

In my conversations with dozens of former and current agents, it was made clear to me that divulging methods and tactics is completely unacceptable, because it means giving away intelligence that can be used to the advantage of the bad guys.

The bottom line is that their daily work is dangerous and often violent enough, without making it worse by spreading loose talk.

In addition to an institutional culture that expects and rewards silence, the Secret Service made this official by requiring any agent hired after January 1, 1985, to sign a binding non-disclosure statement "at retirement debriefing."

I will be forever grateful for the candor and insight I was granted.

The Uzi that was ubiquitous for decades was replaced in 1991 by the also easily concealable, Belgian-manufactured, highly reliable NATO-standard automatic weapon, the FN P90, which fires 5.7x28mm rounds up to 900 per minute, though in interests of accuracy, agents are trained to fire in bursts of three.

The rifle weighs just over six pounds. Its ammunition will fully penetrate body armor and it comes equipped with infrared laser. It's a compact assault rifle, ideal for close-in urban warfare. The sight is adjustable for windage and elevation and can be used with night vision equipment.

The pistol version, the SS190, weighs just 1.5 pounds and has a magazine capacity of twenty rounds.

Standard equipment now also includes the 12-gauge Remington 870 semiautomatic shotgun and the .300 Winchester Magnum bolt-action rifle, as well as a KAC semiautomatic 7.62mm sniper rifle for counter-sniper situations.

For hand-to-hand confrontations, particularly in crowds, ASP twenty-six-inch Talon batons are issued, which retract to 9.5 inches and snap out when needed, making a sound very similar to the arming of a shotgun—a sound that speaks for itself. Other non-lethal weapons include pepper spray and tasers.

Former Agent Alswang said the Secret Service began making the difficult transition "from being the guys with buds in their ears, constantly looking around for suspicious activity, to soldiers who go hunting for the bad guys before they have a chance to strike."

"It took years to happen. It was very hard institutionally for an organization to change from purely defensive strategy to doing undercover work and seeking to disrupt plans before they were hatched. We had to hire a diverse group, including people with Middle Eastern roots, who spoke fluent Arabic and Farsi, as well as women and a broad range of minorities."

Because the Secret Service had never had their own intelligence service, they turned for help to the New York City Police Counter Terrorism Bureau, which they believed were farther advanced than even the FBI at the time. The NYPD were limited in both jurisdiction and funding, so the agency gladly helped with both."

The early days of the Hunters saw a number of agents reassigned to the various experimental groups, some of which turned out to be successful and some were discontinued. But what they all had in common was that agents who volunteered for special groups no longer had the relative luxury of working normal eight-hour shifts and having two days a week off. Instead, the new schedule, in the age of terror, required grueling twelve- to fifteen-hour days and subjected them to dangers unlike anything they had ever faced.

The agency's duty to protect visiting foreign dignitaries led to deadly encounters with terror groups from around the world trying to kill their own leaders during U.S. visits.

Former agent Scott Alswang said that some of his most dangerous assignments he carried out involved protecting visiting officials, which is a major part of the agency's duties. It's not politic to have a foreign leader slain in the U.S.—in fact it's very bad optics and badly hurts the world-wide image of American government and law enforcement. A government that can't protect its visiting world leaders isn't much of a government.

On one occasion Egyptian President Hosni Mubarak was speaking at the United Nations and staying with his entourage at the Waldorf Astoria.

Terror leader Ramzi Yousef, who was later a mastermind of the first World Trade Center bombing, had a murderous wrath toward Mubarak because he and some of his cohort had been charged with terrorist attacks in Egypt and claimed they were tortured.

"When our motorcade arrived at the Waldorf, Yousef's men were expecting us. They had remarkably good intelligence, broke through the thin layer of security and got into the hotel, and threw Molotov cocktails, which exploded and set fires all around the massive lobby. Our men struggled to make arrests, while the hotel staff did their best to control the flames until the fire department arrived. President Mubarak was rushed to a safe room and fortunately wasn't harmed on our watch."

Agent Alswang said that working on the first World Trade Center attack in February of 1993 was the closest he had come to death in the line of duty.

"We were working with the NYPD on information from undercover agents in the New Jersey Muslim community who tipped us there was a plan to bring down the WTC with a powerful bomb planted in a garage. It was of great concern to the Service because the WTC was frequently visited by foreign dignitaries and U.S. leaders."

Alswang went to the Twin Towers with a team to check out the vulnerability of the building, and was appalled to discover that the parking lots were open to the public and would be an ideal place to plant an explosive device.

"We told the building security people it should be closed and closely guarded, but they insisted they needed the revenue."

The former agent recalled that word from his Muslim community spies became increasingly alarming in February of 1993. He was told the plot to bomb the WTC was operational and that a bomb may have already been planted. The Hunters sprang into action on the morning of February 26, despite the obvious great risk to their safety.

"We arrived at the still virtually unprotected North Tower with a team of five or six. NYPD Terror had been alerted but we were first on the scene. We spread out and began searching the labyrinth parking garage in search of a suspicious truck that might contain the explosive device. Suddenly, there was a tremendous explosion. The entire building trembled, smoke and fire surged through the levels of the garage."

It later emerged that the bomb was a 1,336-pound urea nitrate-hydrogen gas enhanced device that had been hidden in a truck, once again the evil work of Ramzi Yousef (the nephew of Khalid Sheikh Mohammed, who planned 9/11 and is still in custody at Guantanamo Bay).

"We lost three men that morning. One of our guys was blown clear across the garage and landed under a car."

Dazed and in shock, unable to hear each other talk, nearly blinded by the tremendous flash, the surviving agents stumbled out into the daylight. Rather than wait for an ambulance, the wounded survivors stumbled out to the street and flagged down a cab to take them to the nearest hospital.

The tragic incident was one of the many heroic actions the agency has taken over the years that went largely unreported.

CHAPTER NINETEEN

Bloodied but Unbowed

The day Ranger returned from Afghanistan, bloodied but unbowed, their wedding plans were put in motion. He walked with a slight limp, his ankle having been grazed by an AK-47 round, but the joy of being home and having the wedding they had both long dreamed of assuaged the pain of the wound.

He presented Laredo with his Rangers ring, custom-encrusted with diamonds, as well as a traditional diamond engagement ring. She cried for joy

They married in Dallas, where both of their parents were then living. Ranger's dad had recently retired as a bird colonel, and Laredo's father, having received his general's star, naturally wanted to have a full military wedding.

They looked at various venues and decided on the Rosewood Mansion on Turtle Creek Blvd., with a beautiful, manicured Italian-inspired lawn, which was designed for weddings and other celebrations.

The guest list was almost all men and women in uniform, including some of the Army high command, who sat together at her father's table, as is traditional.

A military chaplain performed the ceremony, an American flag and the unit standard of the Army Rangers on display. Everyone was in full ceremonial dress uniform. Their unit friends wore white gloves, carried sabers, and formed an archway with their swords, as the newlyweds exited.

An Army band played triumphant, mostly martial music, even *Onward Christian Soldiers*.

The cake was cut with a special silver saber designed for that purpose.

The date was June 6th, to honor Ranger's grandfather and all the other soldiers and sailors who fought on D-Day. It went without a hitch. And to their surprise and delight, an Army fighter jet flew overhead, streaming red, white, and blue smoke.

Their honeymoon was in Key West, Florida, where they went snorkeling almost every day and drank at Hemingway's favorite bar, Sloppy Joe's, by night. Snorkeling with barracuda, and even the occasional shark, seemed perfectly safe compared to the company they had kept in Afghanistan.

Their first appointment post-honeymoon was at the H Street headquarters of the Secret Service, where they hoped to be accepted as members of the Proactive Response Group, Hunters Unit.

They were both prepared to be grilled, but the interviewer instead was trying to convince them to join. He explained what the jobs he wanted them to fill entailed.

He wasn't looking to hire people to follow the president while looking at open windows, searching for a rifleman, ready to take a bullet for the president if need be. He wanted soldiers who would probably seldom even see the president, soldiers who would hunt down bad guys who were plotting to do harm to the protectives of the service, whether ex-presidents or their families, or foreign dignitaries visiting the U.S.

He wanted Ranger to first be a member of the Hawkeye CAT, the organization tasked with being the secret weapon of the Secret Service: heavily armed combat soldiers who would spring into action if the presidential motorcade came under an organized terrorist assault.

The assignment would mean he would accompany the presidential entourage on all foreign trips where there could be potentially explosive situations that would have to be handled carefully. The interviewer was aware of Ranger's clandestine operations across the supposedly sovereign Pakistan border which, it was noted, were given high praise by his commanders.

The normal stint with Hawkeye CAT would be approximately two years because, since it was organized in the 1980s the Service had found there was burnout after that period, due to the fact that professional soldiers were programmed to take the fight to the enemy rather than spend their days waiting to be ambushed. Nevertheless, Hawkeye CAT was determined to be the last line of defense in a world that had grown increasingly menacing for the American president.

He was told frankly that the Hawkeye CAT was frowned upon by many in the regular Presidential Protective Service because they didn't see the need for a special ops team spoiling for a firefight. They still believed that a .38 revolver was all that was needed for a strong defense.

The addition of Hawkeye CAT to presidential motorcades had drastically changed the way the chief executive is transported. Each motorcade has two teams of five CAT men who are heavily armed with automatic weapons, including the rooftop electronic Gatling gun.

In practice sessions, the hood of the Suburban is covered with spent shells in a matter of seconds.

With all the explosive firepower and potential for havoc, the Secret Service determined that each of the vehicles be equipped with motion picture cameras that are always recording—much as police body cams record arrests—so there will be a record of any attacks on the motorcade and of the CAT response to the attacks. They are rather mordantly referred to as "death watch," or formally as "camera one."

The motorcade vehicles are equipped with night vision as well as infrared driving systems, in case of a total blackout caused by heavy smoke or other deliberate visual impairment by hostile forces. It also has remote detection and detonating devices to combat possible improvised explosive devices planted along the route. There are targeted jamming devices to prevent the remote detonation of an explosive.

The presidential "Beast" (also referred to as "the stagecoach") has its own independent air supply and detectors for nuclear, biological, and chemical weapons (or NBC).

Whenever a presidential motorcade is underway, Homeland Security has one or more helicopters in the air to warn of any suspicious activity, and to shadow the chief executive's parade from start to finish with a bird's eye view of the action, and the ability to see a possible assassin ahead of time.

On occasions when the president decides to visit numerous rural locations—making campaign stops or visiting disaster-damaged areas—a huge, armored, glossy black luxury bus is put into use. It is followed by Secret Service and Hawkeye CAT Suburbans equipped with heavy weapons to fend off any attempts to get the president. It is also given a police escort and is shadowed by Marine helicopters.

The top brass of the Secret Service were never convinced they should be responsible for two teams of five brawny soldiers ready to unleash a tsunami of automatic weapon blasts in a crowded American inner city. And while Hawkeye CAT is now fully established as a permanent section of the Presidential Protective Service, there is still indigestion about the awesome power of its weaponry that would have to be used in a congested inner-city environment.

Having been briefed for the first time about the above details, plus other secrets that can't be printed here, Ranger agreed to ride with the Hawkeye CAT for two years, as long as he could then be guaranteed a slot with the Hunters afterward. He was told that many of the Hawkeye CAT recruits were highly trained but lacked combat experience. The feeling was that a veteran of Afghanistan, familiar with heavy weapons like those the Hawkeye CAT men were issued, would benefit from Ranger's combat knowledge, gained under the deadliest of conditions.

The deal was sealed. Both jobs would keep him based largely in Washington, D.C. where at day's end, he would be home with his new wife, rather than on the other side of the world.

He knew his next assignment with the Hunters was going to be what he ultimately wanted though.

The interviewer said, "You both have good paper." He told Ranger that the job with the Hunters would require him to essentially do what he had done in Afghanistan: lead a small group on a mission with a tight deadline to prevent an assassination, or even a chemical or biological attack.

To Laredo he said that the Secret Service was receiving more and more threats, and actual attempts, to use biological and sometimes chemical weapons, and that he needed people like her who could recognize what the toxins are and contain them before the harm is done. "Your work on that Pakistani lab, which I have been given the clearance to study, despite that it's all classified, was superb. You saved a lot of lives and we would like for you to join us and do that domestically."

He told them both he didn't think either needed traditional Secret Service training. They both knew how to handle weapons and do the required job. But he wanted them to study the history of assassinations, and attempted assassinations, and familiarize themselves with Secret Service methods and operations, even though their jobs would be quite different: entailing responding to a massive assault, whether with arms or biochem, directed against the presidency.

Despite both having obligations to serve in the army for another year, the military had agreed to let them off to take on the new job with the Secret Service, and the Army had agreed to let Laredo continue to use the chemical and biological facilities at Aberdeen Proving Ground whenever she felt it necessary, though the Secret Service was going to provide her with a dedicated lab closer to D.C.

They both said, without reservation, they would like to sign up. Ranger felt a sharp twinge that it would mean hanging up the Ranger uniform he had worked so hard to earn, and was so hard to live up to in combat, but it was more important to him that he not suffer more long absences from his love and now wife. And he had the satisfaction of knowing he had earned the Ranger badge, had served in a hellacious war zone emerging with only an ankle wound, and had been awarded a captain's rank, a Bronze Star with a V for Valor, and a Purple Heart.

In studying the history of assassinations, they both realized that often the agent's worst enemy was the person whose life they were trying to save. If Jack Kennedy had agreed to let them put the metal roof on his limo in Dallas as the Secret Service had suggested, he almost certainly would not have died that day. But he was willing to take the chance to be seen by the voters, and to impress them with his youthful good looks and his elegant wife.

The lesson is that politics are always a consideration for the Secret Service, because the people they protect live and breathe politics. Being loved by the public is their mother's milk, and they can't survive without it, even if they put their lives on the line for it.

Ranger and Laredo learned that a Secret Service agent is trained to disarm bad guys as a matter of course, and to take a bullet for a protectee, also as an automatic response. They were also told that a safety decision is always in the end up to the president, except in a moment of imminent danger. Then, agents can politely argue and even plead, but the decision is up to the Commander-in-Chief, even if mingling in a crowd or riding in a topless limo is *ipso facto* almost a death wish.

President George H.W. Bush insisted on parachuting well into his dotage. Both his wife Barbara and the Secret Service strongly opposed it, but he insisted and neither were able to convince him otherwise.

But presidents are the kind of people who are risk-takers and probably hooked on danger, or they wouldn't work so hard to willingly put a bull's eye on their backs.

JFK was a war hero who refused to take an authorized and recommended survivor's leave after his PT boat was blown out of the water by a Japanese destroyer and he was very nearly killed. Instead, he insisted he be given command of another PT boat and get back in the fight.

Kennedy's favorite poem was Alan Seeger's "I Have a Rendezvous with Death." He had clearly come to grips with the fact that he probably wouldn't live "to comb gray hair," as his brother Ted said decades later, while eulogizing the equally reckless John Jr. after his fatal air crash near Martha's Vineyard—also the result of hubris.

Of course, both Laredo and Ranger had served in extraordinarily dangerous war zone situations and had danced with the grim reaper—he in combat and she with exposure to the world's deadliest pathogens.

They also learned that in recent years presidents get six to eight threats per day, or over two thousand a year, all of which require investigation. The presidents' wives and children also get threats; even parents, brothers, and sisters receive cyber and physical threats on a regular basis.

And there are actual attempts that are carried out. The office that screens mail sent to the president, which is far removed from the White House, regularly receives some chemical—but mostly biological—weapons that are sent through the mail. The real danger of such attempts is not to the president or the First Family, but to the mail handlers.

Laredo would come to be a regular visitor to the postal screening facility, investigating incidents and analyzing the contents of the dangerous packages and letters.

Each biochem weapon must be followed up and the sender tracked down, if possible, to find who created it, and to shut down any lab that was producing deadly poisons and sending them through the mail.

They also learned a Protective Mission Panel had been assembled to devise "an expansive, new set of counter measures aimed at finding and countering nascent threats" to the people and properties the Secret Service is charged with protecting, with their lives if need be.

The then-classified report laid out the new goals of the Secret Service in the 21st century time of terror.

It noted that many of the would-be assassination plots were concealed by the perpetrators "going dark"—that is, encrypting and double encrypting their nefarious schemes to prevent detection.

The job of the Service and the Hunters would be to work with private and public partners to break the codes and unravel the plots. The new policy was based on the obvious proposition that "the best way to stop an [assassination] incident is to prevent it from ever getting started."

The Hunters were to "provide critical and trusted support in identifying actors and methods *before* they pose an immediate danger"; in other words, to take down Lee Harvey Oswald before he gets his Mannlicher-Carcano rifle from mail order, or gets anywhere near his window-side lair in the Texas School Book Depository.

The other essential change in creating the new, proactive Secret Service was in "identifying future trends in tactics that adversaries may employ, which remains critical to mission success." That included chemical, biological, and radiological weapons that would inevitably be the weapons of choice for future would-be assassins, working with rogue nations and sophisticated terror groups.

The agency had no intentions of teaching Ranger about soldiering; his record clearly showed he had mastered that art in the hellscape that was Afghanistan and Pakistan. Nor did they feel a need to tutor Laredo on biochem detection and containment. She had received a Bronze Star from the army from her work in her field, and in a war zone.

What they wanted was to train them in the new very aggressive "stop the bad guys before they get started" philosophy, and in the latest scientific breakthroughs in detection and eavesdropping on suspects and architects of terror.

Ranger and Laredo were happy the Army was charging them once again with keeping the nation safe. They would still be facing great danger, but with the great new advantage of not having to be eight thousand miles apart for months on end, longing for each other. Giddy with joy over the next chapter in their lives, they studied the material the Service gave them and internalized the philosophy.

And they hired a real estate agent in Washington, D.C. and started hunting for their first real home together.

In the 1990s, the height of the fence surrounding the White House was doubled in size to thirteen feet and extended by one block to keep traffic further away, in an attempt to lessen the possibility of a car bomb attack. But even with the higher fence and other security precautions, intrusions onto White House property still occurred relatively regularly.

Finally, in 2020, the Secret Service got the funding and permission to change the look and security of the Executive Mansion, as well as the Treasury, Eisenhower Executive Office, New Executive Office, and the Winder Buildings—collectively known as the White House Complex—by building a new outer periphery fence.

A semi-joking suggestion that concertina wire be wrapped around the new fence was laughed off. It wouldn't be a good optic.

But most attacks don't even require the perps to get onto White House grounds: they simply fire a weapon through the fence.

On a warm autumn day in late October 1994, Francisco Martin Duran stood on the Pennsylvania Avenue sidewalk staring at the White House like any other tourist. Suddenly he reached inside his tan trench coat and brandished a Chinese SKS semiautomatic rifle and fired seven times at the White House.

He ran toward 15th Street, still firing, then paused to reload. Harry Rakosky, a tourist, saw an opportunity and bravely tackled him. Two other tourists joined in to disarm Duran and hold him until uniformed Secret Service agents could take him into custody.

Ranger commented, "We consider ourselves the last line of defense, but sometimes decent, concerned citizens fill the breach. There are a lot of good, brave people out there, who will get involved and can save lives, while risking their own."

In normal times there are lunatic assaults on the building. But with bin Laden and his evil deputy Ilyas Kashmiri dispatching wave after wave of fanatically committed assassins, it was the kind of pressure that sometimes leads Secret Service men and women to take early retirement, or apply for a desk job at Headquarters on H Street.

To avoid press notice and general panic, the dangerous crisis was kept as quiet as possible. But the nation's public safety units, from the FBI to local police, were placed on high alert. Immigration and Customs was ordered to be doubly careful about suspicious travelers. State and local police were informed of a possible presidential assassin taking orders from Al Qaeda operatives. The joint intel task force met daily and communicated hourly during the '90s. CAT men knew they were under strict orders during the Obama years to keep a low profile and not scare horses or children with their bellicose look, but they were actually spoiling for a flight if Al Qaeda should tread on their turf and menace their protectees.

A member of the team at the time told the author, "A foreign terrorist plot, hatched by Osama bin Laden, is exactly what we were designed to combat. We were and are the only outfit uniquely qualified for the job. All of our guys, from battle hardened veteran to the newest recruits have the attitude, 'Bring it on.'"

The Hawkeye CAT detail were disappointed in 2010 when they didn't get the s.o.b. in their death grip. But they continued the hunt, knowing he was gunning for President Obama, and finally, on June 3, 2011 at 3:56 a.m., Kashmiri was discovered by combined U.S. intelligence services to be in a South Waziristan, Pakistan safe house with eight other terrorist chiefs.

A drone pinpointed his position and control in the Nevada desert ordered a Hellfire missile released. Kashmiri and his coven were dispatched "with extreme prejudice."

On a cool zero dark hour in early May, Ranger and Laredo were lying in bed with the windows of their Capitol Hill townhouse open with a gentle breeze blowing.

Ranger's encrypted satellite phone came to life with a red light and a European-style siren ring tone. Ranger tried to gently disentangle from his wife, but she was already awake and quickly sat bolt upright in bed. The Secret Service never called at that hour without good reason.

It was the Dublin office of the Secret Service. The duty officer apologized for calling at 4:00 a.m. and cut to the chase.

Ireland's Special Detective Unit had arrested an Irish citizen, Khalid Kelly aka Taliban Terry, who was a known convert to radical Islam. He had given an interview to the *Sunday Mirror*, in which he said that Al Qaeda had plans to kill President Obama during his upcoming trip to Ireland. The trip was imminent, and it was clear Obama had no intentions of cancelling.

He said he would like to kill the president himself but was too famous for his pro-Taliban statements. "Personally, I would feel happy if Obama was killed. How could I not feel happy when a big enemy of Islam is gone?"

The counter-terrorism officers were holding him and would be glad for Ranger to come and participate in the interviews.

Ranger called agency transportation and was quickly booked on a C-17 Globemaster military transport plane from Joint Base Andrews non-stop to U.S. Naval Air Station Wexford, Ireland. He'd be in Dublin in time for the interrogation the next day.

As he threw a suitcase together, Ranger quipped that it wasn't going to much of a hunt, "with the prey already in the bag."

The challenge would be to sufficiently scare Taliban Terry to get useful intel about the Al Qaeda plot—if there really was one, and not just a figment of his fevered imagination. Still, a chance to interrogate a person with links to the terror organization was well worth losing a few hours of sleep and making an Atlantic crossing.

Taliban Terry was a curious character, even in the age of terror.

Raised in Dublin, he attended Catholic schools until quitting to work in a pub. In his early twenties he moved to London and trained as an intensive care nurse. Despite a nearly lifelong weakness for strong drink, he read the Koran and fell in thrall to all things about the Middle East, particularly radical Islam.

With his nursing credentials, Terry—as he still called himself—landed a job in Riyadh, Saudi Arabia. Ever the entrepreneur, he learned to make hard liquor, which fetched a handsome price because it was strictly prohibited under Islamic law.

He told *Religion News Blog*: "I got really good at making drink. I had three stills in my house, and then I got arrested...and sent to prison for eight months. The prison was 150 people in a dormitory with a mosque at the end."

A fellow inmate named Ali gave him a copy of the Koran in English. Terry was an instant convert, willing to kill other Britons for Islam and to willingly sacrifice his own life.

After serving his sentence, he was deported back to the U.K., where he attended sermons preached by the radical Islamist Omar Bakri Muhammed, who had a large and growing following in Britain.

He vowed to "kill those who insult the prophet" and fled for the Muslim world, where he hoped to become a jihadi and go to Afghanistan to "fight British soldiers." He came to believe that Barack Obama was the enemy of Islam and must be assassinated.

When Ranger entered the windowless interrogation room in the Irish Special Detective Unit where Taliban Terry was being held, he was surprised at how calm and worry-free he appeared. He later recalled Terry looked like a guy who had spent his life standing in a pub, "marinating in Guinness Stout."

Terry was interrogated for three solid days, with little or no sleep, and gave up a number of names, many of whom turned out to be dead. But he had little in the way of details of a plot to kill Obama when he came to Ireland, saying that if he were given instructions, he would carry them out "inshallah."

Ranger went with the Irish special detectives to search Taliban Terry's modest house in North Dublin.

When he called Laredo to tell her what was happening and his plan to search the house, she warned him that even though Irish detectives had done a cursory inspection of the house, there could be timed explosives and to be very cautious.

He took her at her word.

No weapons or bomb-making equipment were found—nothing that would merit serious charges and major jail time. There were volumes of radical Islamic propaganda, including tracts written by Ahlus Sunnah wal Jamaah, a leader of a British-based Islamist organization.

Most interesting to Ranger was a diary-like journal in childish handwriting, undated but clearly years old. It detailed Terry's childhood, during which he was beaten frequently by an abusive, hard drinking father; being forced by his father to quit school, which he wrote that he loved; and to work in the kitchen of a Dublin pub, washing dishes and mopping the floor to bring money home to pay for his father's drinking.

Ranger thought it helped develop a meaningful profile. Terry was damaged goods and was desperately searching for acceptance and redemption, blaming himself to some degree for the abuse he had suffered. Becoming an intensive care nurse was a way to prove he had value; turning to radical Islam was a quest for acceptance, a desperate attempt to find a place where he could be a member of something larger than his woefully diminished self.

The Irish detectives released Kelly because they found no specific crime with which to charge him. Threatening the life of the U.S. president was apparently not considered sufficient. He was simply put on the watch list.

Ranger was disappointed but knew he hadn't heard the last of Taliban Terry.

Ranger flew back to Washington the next day, planning to pay visits to two of the men Taliban Terry had fingered.

★★★

Part of the training to be a Hunter is learning the skills of studying and creating profiles of potential assassins, in order to read their motivations and predict their behavior.

Kelly reminded Ranger of Lee Harvey Oswald, JFK's killer. Neither man could be called a loner. They both married and had children (though both were spouse abusers). Oswald had two daughters, June, and Audrey. Kelly had Mohammed and Osama.

They were both neglected and abused as children and both sought to be a part of something greater than themselves. Oswald became a U.S. Marine, though he couldn't follow orders and was discharged. Kelly embraced radical Islam, though he continued to drink, which was considered blasphemous.

Oswald embraced communism and defected to the Soviet Union, though he was considered to have become a liability and soon deported. And they were both willing to kill and be killed to prove they were worthwhile people.

Kelly's serenity was the most disturbing aspect of his personality. Ranger had interviewed hundreds of people that were possible assassins, mostly under intense circumstances with sleep deprivation and relentless questioning, as was the case with Kelly. But a majority of the interviewees displayed signs of evasiveness and fear. They would perspire, sometimes twitch and tremble, be afraid to make eye contact, and would tell obvious, unimportant falsehoods. They lied for no good purpose, but rather out of the habit of concealing the truth from authorities.

Kelly displayed none of those common reactions. Despite knowing he was being questioned by Irish Federal Police and a U.S. Secret Service Agent, he remained calm and collected. He admitted freely that he wanted to kill President Obama, apparently aware that just saying this was not a crime in Ireland. He admitted that he was associated with Al Qaeda and would carry out any orders to kill or maim soldiers of the U.K. or the U.S.

Ranger marveled at how fearless and focused he was, and how his sense of humor remained intact. Speaking of incredibly violent desires, he was less animated than a man in a pub discussing his favorite football team.

Ranger's conclusion, after three days of almost non-stop interrogation, was that Kelly had found what he had been looking for all his life: serenity in the knowledge he would die a martyr. That would mean to him that his life would have been worthwhile, in a twisted, pathetic way.

Before leaving, Ranger had conversations with his superiors in which he begged them to do something to bring Kelly back to the states to be incarcerated, but was told it was impossible. The Irish authorities had been asked at the highest level and had responded in the negative. The U.S. could request extradition, but that would take a long time.

Ranger was utterly convinced that the Taliban Terry file was not going to end well, and that it was a grave error to let him go.

In the end Kelly got his wish. After floating around Iraq and Afghanistan for several years, he was given the order he had longed for in his warped mind. Taliban leadership fitted him with an explosive jacket and dispatched him to attempt to blow up a British army post in the desert.

He carried out the plan almost according to his orders, but failed to get close enough to kill anybody but himself. The explosion that atomized his body could be seen for miles around. He was a genuine nutjob martyr.

Ranger and Laredo were in the ninth floor Joint Operations Center when a video of the explosion was first aired on one of the giant screens. They tried not to smile too broadly.

One of the major concerns of the Secret Service, Hawkeye CAT, and the Hunters has been the possibility of rogue elements in the armed forces who may be sociopaths, who hate the current president and/or have their own radical political agenda. Sometimes they have formed well-trained cadres with access to military-grade weaponry and the training to use them effectively.

With about a million and a half active-duty soldiers in the U.S. military, there are obviously some with bad or even criminal intent. By the nature of their jobs, they are in proximity to protectees of the Secret Service. They are also entrusted with the care of the president's conveyance, including in some cases Air Force One and Marine One (the president's helicopter).

When Donald Trump was elected in 2016 and became president in 2017, the country was deeply divided and the animosity toward the Trump presidency palpable. Threats against him were part of daily chatter in much of the media, as well as among pundits and Hollywood stars, one of whom carried around a severed head resembling the new president. It was also popular loose talk in bars and dark backrooms.

Laredo studied statistics on the correlation between stunts like the actress holding the severed head that resembled Donald Trump, as well as thinly veiled threats made by so-called comedians on late-night television and actual attacks.

> We found that each time there was a highly publicized, scorching remark made about the president our incident board lit up with threats or even attempts. It gives unstable people ideas and awakens their well of venom.
>
> In June of 2016, when President Trump was the presumptive Republican nominee and the poison remarks about him started to fly, a British national named Michael Steven Sandford, who later admitted he had wanted to 'get' Trump for a year, was finally pushed over the brink.
>
> He drove hundreds of miles to Las Vegas, where there was a Trump rally. Unable to purchase a weapon without a U.S. driver's license, he entered the arena, and attempted to grab a police officer's weapon. The officer repulsed the attack and subdued Sandford. The would-be assassin later admitted he was under the impression that all Americans wanted Trump dead and thought he would be a hero if he carried out the assassination.

Another dangerous incident occurred in October of 2018, during the height of the heated rhetoric leading up to the mid-term elections.

Laredo continued, "William Clyde Allen III, a disturbed U.S. Navy veteran, sent a letter containing crushed castor beans—the main ingredient in ricin poison—to the White House, Secretary of Defense James Mattis, and chief of Naval Operations Admiral John Richardson.

"We, of course, inspected and intercepted the letters. But it was a dangerous ingredient to go through the U.S. Mail, and easily could have infected and possibly killed mail-screening personnel.

"Now we have people who carefully monitor incendiary remarks made on television or elsewhere, and ratchet up the alert level with other agencies, as well as local authorities in some cases."

In early 2017, the Hunters uncovered evidence that soldiers who worked in close proximity to both Air Force One and Marine One were overheard expressing violent opposition to President Trump, as well as the First Family.

"They weren't just guys who had too much to drink at an off-base bar and talked crazy. Evidence was found that several of them had hatched a plan to cause damage to Air Force One or Marine One that could have had catastrophic consequences had they not been stopped," said a source.

Another case had happened five years earlier at Fort Stewart in Georgia. Four soldiers—Private Isaac Aguigui, Private Michael Burnett, Private Christopher "Phish" Salmon, and Sergeant Anthony Peden—had shared a delusional plot to take over the U.S. Government and to assassinate President Obama, as well as a bizarre scheme to destroy a dam and poison apple orchards in Washington state.

Aguigui, the leader of the terror group, named it FEAR (Forever Enduring Always Ready) and tattooed the anarchy symbol of overlapping alpha and omega signs on his right shoulder.

His wife Deirdre, also a soldier, supposedly suffered an embolism in her femur when a grenade exploded near her in Iraq. He blamed the army for killing his wife and unborn child. But the Army Criminal Investigation Division theorized he had actually strangled his wife to reap a half-million-dollar survivor death benefit payment, which is routinely given to the spouse of a deceased active-duty soldier.

Before they could prove the strangulation theory, he received the five hundred thousand dollars and began organizing his crazy schemes, forming his FEAR group with other delusional soldiers.

With the payoff he launched the terror group, which was basically a haven for troubled soldiers with severe psychological problems, to some extent precipitated by war trauma, and a penchant for violent fantasies that quickly turned all too real.

Aguigui spent forty-eight thousand dollars buying at least thirty high-powered military-type weapons to arm his nascent terror group. Sergeant Anthony Peden, another troubled soldier who had been a sniper in Iraq, added deadly expertise, teaching the younger men the arts of improvised explosive devices and hunting humans. He happily gave instructions on building pipe bombs with nails and gun powder.

Aguigui confessed to Peden that he had sought to join militia groups in Washington State, but was rejected. He blamed racism for his rejection because he was a Pacific Islander.

From his prison cell in Savannah, after being sentenced to life without parole, he gave an interview to *The New Yorker* saying he feared the government might turn on its citizens, "in which case you need to protect yourself."

Isaac Aguigui fit the profile of a terrorist assassin quite well. His father had been a drill sergeant who treated his son like a fresh recruit. He was forbidden to date and was thrown out of the house when he started courting his first girlfriend. He was also forbidden to play video games and was kept on a strict diet.

But at eleven he was given his first gun, a Marlin .22, and taught to shoot by his grandfather, who was a Vietnam veteran. Strictly watched over by his father and mother, who deemed most of his school friends unacceptable, he was a solitary kid, who built an improvised fort in the backyard and said he "imagined myself a militiaman guarding the family house."

He became fascinated by all things military and wanted to go to West Point. But he had a dark side even as a kid, and became fascinated by guerilla fighters, fantasizing about being in "a struggle against repression."

Aguigui got accepted at a military school that was billed as a training ground for acceptance at West Point, but he dropped out, mostly over disciplinary problems.

He was also very interested in "active shooter situations, where a killer attacks in a confined area to maximize casualties." Displaying classic characteristics of a bipolar personality disorder with wild mood swings, he also had a penchant for torturing and killing small stray animals.

As a troubled adult, years later, he would often weep uncontrollably, moaning over the death of Deirdre and their baby, then fly into a rage, blaming the army for all his woes and swearing he would one day get revenge.

He later confessed, "We weren't out to change the government, we were out to destroy it."

Contacted by a friend he had served with in Afghanistan, at the time currently in the Army 3rd Infantry Division Criminal Investigation Department (C.I.D.), Ranger took the story as a four-alarm fire. Both C.I.D. and the Georgia Bureau of Investigation believed Aguigui and his cohort had committed multiple murders to stop disgruntled ex-members from squealing, that they had expertise with explosives, and that they had a plan—a delusional plan—to attempt to take over the Fort Stewart ammo dump. And they had discussed and hashed out a plan to kill President Obama.

"Is this maniac still on the loose?" he asked.

"Yes."

Naturally, the last point had Ranger heading for Andrews and a plane to Fort Stewart with a team.

On the short hop to Fort Stewart, Ranger studied reports of the Georgia Bureau of Investigation and the Army Criminal Investigation Command, and concluded Aguigui and his followers were classic sociopaths, with a taste for blood and hell-bound to wreak havoc if not stopped.

At one point Aguigui was quoted as saying, "You don't want to fuck with me. I'm nuts. I'm the nicest murderer you'll ever meet."

If the Army and Georgia authorities didn't put him on ice, and quickly, Ranger would. Aguigui had made a serious threat against the American president and that put him in Ranger's inbox.

At Fort Stewart, Ranger sat in on the interrogations with Aguigui and his ragtag militia, mostly to add to his profile base. It was obvious that they had no real beef with Barack Obama, other than the fact that he represented authority and the government, which they had loathed and feared all their lives.

Their criminal plans were utterly unfocused, but they were blood-thirsty and allegedly had murdered: there was strong evidence that Aguigui had strangled his pregnant wife and several members of the gang who had threatened to spill the beans.

But the talk of taking over the Fort Stewart arsenal or assassinating the president was delusional posturing. They all had less than average IQs and were likely incapable of planning a game of catch, let alone leading a rebellion against the U.S. Army and government.

It was anything but funny, still Ranger found it hard not to smile, in a grim way, at the Keystone Kops idiocy of their crazy deeds and grandiose pipe dreams.

He wrote a complete report on the Globemaster flight back to Andrews, satisfied that the C.I.D. and G.B.I. had the situation well in hand and the perps would spend the rest of their lives in prison, with no chance of parole for the so-called leader, and long sentences for his loony followers.

On the cold gusty night of November 11, 2011, Oscar Ramiro Ortega-Hernandez followed his orders from Al Qaeda to the letter, driving around the White House to Constitution Avenue, parking his nondescript black Honda in a closed lane, with a perfect, clear view of the family quarters of the presidential mansion.

His mission was to avenge Barack Obama's order to Navy SEAL Team Six to execute Osama bin Laden on May 2 of that year.

He climbed out of the car and discreetly trained his binoculars on the second-floor windows, which he had been told were his target. They were distant, nearly eight football fields away. With his sniper-scoped Romanian Cugir semiautomatic rifle it would be a difficult but not impossible shot. He had been trained to account for windage, noted the lulls in the approximately ten to fifteen mile per hour wind gusts, and planned to fire during lulls. In no hurry, he marveled at the bright white light that bathed the white building that housed his First Family targets.

Climbing into the passenger side, he retrieved his rifle from under a towel and rested it on the open window, with a clear view of the second story window of the formal First Family living room. The first round shattered the window and entered the First Family's quarters.

The next eight rounds were not as accurate, due presumably to his nervousness at having successfully sent his first round accurately through the window, and possibly wounding or killing a member of the Obama family. There was no response from the Secret Service men stationed on the White House roof armed with sniper rifles, nor from the agents on the south lawn of the building.

Ortega-Hernandez calmly hid his rifle in the back seat of the Honda, again covering it with a towel. He screeched away down Constitution Avenue toward the Roosevelt Bridge crossing of the Potomac River—similar to the escape route of John Wilkes Booth.

He had no way of knowing if a member of the first family had been wounded or killed, but had to know he had succeeded in the mission of firing potentially deadly bullets into the family quarters of the White House.

He had been assigned to commit an act of terror upon the U.S. President and had succeeded.

The Hawkeye CAT was huddling in the Secret Service office in the basement of the White House and received no alarms. A volley of high-powered semiautomatic rifle shots had struck the White House, one even entering the family quarters, but nobody seemed to notice.

Bin Laden would have been joyful that an act of terror had been committed to avenge his death. The American president's family wasn't safe, even in their own mansion.

By the time the Secret Service had unlimbered their P-90 assault rifles, the shooter had gotten six blocks away and wrecked his Honda. He fled on foot, leaving his weapon and about 180 rounds of ammunition in the back seat.

Over seven slugs had struck the walls and window of the family quarters.

No one was harmed, though not from lack of malign intent.

The youngest Obama daughter Sasha and Michelle's mother Marian Robinson were both in the family quarters at the time, and older daughter Malia was on her way home.

After hearing the rifle shots, Secret Service agents began searching the White House grounds for the shooter, and had unlimbered their weapons when a supervisor urgently ordered all hands to stand down, wrongly saying "no shots have been fired." He said the noise was construction vehicles backfiring.

It took almost four days to realize what had happened, and then only because a housekeeper pointed out a hole in a windowpane and debris from shots that had hit the window frame.

Days later one supervisor theorized—without evidence—that the shots were stray bullets from rival gang members in cars chasing each other near the White House, and had nothing to do with an attempted assassination.

It took four full days to realize what had happened, and to track down twenty-one-year-old Oscar Ramiro-Hernandez to a cheap hotel room in the little town of Indiana, Pennsylvania.

Hunters working with local police managed to make an arrest without incident.

Despite enhanced interrogation, Hunters were only able to get Ramiro-Hernandez to admit that he thought Obama was "the devil" and needed to be killed. He refused to identify who had put him up to the shooting, claiming it was all his idea and planning, but pled guilty to "terrorism enhancement" charges. By avoiding attempted assassination charges he escaped a mandated life sentence and instead was ordered to spend twenty-five years in prison.

The Hunters believed he had been influenced by terrorists, directly or indirectly associated with Al Qaeda. The consensus was that, while it was a clumsy attack, it would have been suicidal had law enforcement been awake and alert, so it was successful from a terrorist's point of view. A wingnut inspired by Al Qaeda, one way or another, had fired an

AK-47-style weapon into the White House while the president's family was home, and had gotten away to Pennsylvania, avoiding capture for five days.

According to a *Washington Post* account of the incident, published three years later in 2014, "the Secret Service fumbled response…infuriated the President and First Lady."

The paper quoted then White House chief of staff William Daley: "It was obviously very frightening that someone…was able to shoot and hit the White House and people here did not know it until several days later. The handling of this was not good."

Just as the Hunters and the Protective Service breathed a sigh of relief that Ortega had been captured and no member of the First Family injured, President Obama decided to go to Afghanistan to tour the war zone with General David Petraeus.

Apparently overjoyed, Kashmiri gave orders to his troops to blow the presidential plane out of the sky with a surface to air missile. That failed also.

The shooting incident caused despair in the Secret Service, as it emphasized the porous nature of White House security and displayed a woeful lack of judgement at the supervisory level. If the gun shots sounded like a truck backfire, why not put everyone on alert and begin an investigation, just in case? At the very least it would have been good practice. Instead, according to one member of the Secret Service staff, when the President and First Lady were out of town—they were enroute to Hawaii at the time of the Ortega shooting—the agents slipped into "casual Friday" mode, according to the *Washington Post* account.

Two D.C. police officers, William Johnson and Milton Olivo, were in their Chevrolet suburban near Constitution Avenue about fifteen yards from Ortega's Honda, and smelled the pungent odor of gunpowder. The officers filed an urgent report, yet no one seems to have taken their account seriously.

Also, a woman in a taxi noticed a "crazy man" with a gun aiming at the White House. She said the police "took a while to respond." But no one seems to have spoken to the Secret Service to report that there was a shooter aiming at the presidential mansion that night.

Signs were writ large that the agency needed a major overhaul in a hurry.

Despite raising the fence to thirteen feet and fortifying it, people—mostly mentally ill—continued to scale it and trespass on the White House grounds.

At one point a toddler strayed from his tourist parents, who were busy posing for pictures, squeezed his way through the fence, and ran in circles around the White House lawn before being caught and returned to his parents.

A sixty-six-year-old man managed to scramble over the fence just to show that he could.

A man who claimed he wanted to impress Chelsea Clinton, who no longer lived there, scaled the fence and quickly gave himself up.

A man who had been fired from his accounting job at the IRS made the climb, dressed in a suit and tie and carrying a brief case with a gun inside. He had a suicide note in his pocket blaming his ex-boss. He assumed that if you went over the fence with a gun you would automatically be killed.

He was wrong.

Another deranged individual scaled the fence and sprinted across the lawn, opened the unlocked door of the White House, and roamed around with a butcher knife until he was *finally* noticed and wrestled to the ground.

Anthony Henry made an almost surreal attempt to get to Jimmy Carter in October of 1978, trying, according to his confession, to convince the President to remove "In God we Trust" from U.S. currency. He scaled the fence dressed slightly inappropriately for a White House meeting—barefoot and wearing a karate outfit. He also happened to be carrying a Bible. When Secret Service agents surrounded him, he reached inside the

Bible and produced a dagger. He slashed two of the officers before being disarmed and wrestled to the ground.

In August of 2020, President Trump was in the middle of a press conference when the Secret Service interrupted and led him to a secure location. Myron Berryman, then fifty-one, was acting suspiciously outside the fence, and a uniformed agent thought he was pulling a gun and shot him in the torso. Unfortunately, it turned out to be a large black comb.

Subsequent police reports documented that Berryman had recently been discharged from a psychiatric hospital, which came as no surprise. He recovered from his wound and was charged with a misdemeanor.

During all the White House mini-invasions, Hawkeye CAT was present, poised like a wild cat ready to pounce, but was always restrained, letting the uniformed agents take on the unwanted visitors. Many CAT soldiers were champing at the bit, but their constant and skilled training spoke loudly that their volcanic power was best appreciated in the breach.

While the Obamas were on their way to a vacation in Hawaii, another threat loomed. A woman named Kristy Lee Roshia called the Boston office of the Secret Service, and after identifying herself announced she intended to "blow away" Michelle Obama. She was immediately taken into custody and held for psychological evaluation. It was noted that she often made long, rambling threats, which she telegraphed to the Secret Service and always left her phone number—presumably as a courtesy.

Ranger said,

> The majority of the people who phone in threats or post them on the internet are certifiably insane. The trouble is a lot of them also have guns and explosives and are poised to use them.

> You can rarely tell with certainty who are harmless nut jobs and who are sociopaths who are going to try to kill. Every threat has to be taken seriously, evaluated

and acted upon. About half of the people we take into custody wind up in a psychiatric facility. A lot of them are craving attention more than blood. But we use a lot of man-hours rounding up people with severe psychological problems. A lot of the training for agents is profiling and recognizing delusional behavior patterns.

None of it is a waste of time though. Every person who makes a threat, and particularly those who take a shot, or are even caught with a weapon and have made a threat are thoroughly interviewed to create additional profiles.

Those who actually shoot at a president or their security detail have an agent assigned to interview them multiple times, often over a period of years. John Hinckley had an agent assigned to his case, who spent years interviewing him and turned in thousands of pages of the interrogations for future profiling. Hinckley was an open book, giving great insight into the mind of an assassin. Whatever his motivation, he was very helpful, and contributed to the literature of profiling.

This is all done in an effort to hopefully allow us to draw a profile that will tell what type of person will actually carry out a threat and who won't, and maybe be able to proactively finger an assassin before he or she puts a plan into action.

The goal is to get inside the head of an assassin or attempted killer to find out if there really are worms crawling around in there. We often get warrants to access their private letters, diaries, interrogate friends, family, and neighbors to gain insight into motivation and methods. And most importantly to find out if they have confederates, and if they are being controlled or influenced by terror groups or foreign agents.

An interesting aspect is that often siblings, who grew up together, are often appalled and shocked that the guy they grew up with has turned into a potential or actual assassin.

We almost always interview ex-spouses, employers and even schoolteachers. Sometimes a middle school teacher will have an insight into motivation from years before.

But often the most useful interviews are with the mothers of assassins. Mothers of both assassins and serial killers often have terrible remorse over their lack of both love and parenting skills and want to confess for their child's sins.

We've learned that assassination attempts are almost never a spontaneous attack. Potential killers often plan for years. Sometimes the target changes, showing that it is simply because they don't like the policies or remarks of a certain leader. Most often that has nothing to do with it. They simply crave the fame and attention that comes with being an infamous assassin.

When the squeeze of a trigger can lift a person from the status of an obscure loser to a villain whose name is known to virtually everyone in the world is a powerful aphrodisiac to an unbalanced mind.

They also carry out dress rehearsals to see what the security looks like, to learn if the target is one who mingles in crowds and strays out of the security zone that we set up. There is even a counting of the number of agents who are protecting the subject and making of notes of how many appear to be alert and paying attention and how many seem distracted.

★★★

Legendary FBI profiler John Douglas writes in his book *Obsession* of his interviews with numerous political assassins, including Sirhan Sirhan, the slayer of Robert F. Kennedy; James Earl Ray, who murdered Martin Luther King; and Arthur Bremer, who grievously wounded George Wallace.

He compares these rogues to celebrity stalkers he has studied. "Both tend to be paranoid, lacking trust in other individuals. Usually loners, they are not relaxed in the presence of others and not practiced or skilled in social interaction. [But] they keep a running dialogue with themselves, often painstakingly detailing their thoughts and fantasies in a diary.

"It's like they're programing themselves to commit the crime, building courage to take action. Assassins are so focused on how people will receive them after they've acted...they don't always build in an escape plan."

He also points out that, like John Hinckley, who first targeted Jimmy Carter, then switched to Carter political nemesis Ronald Reagan, few have any loyalty to a political cause. They "needed the identity...gained by murdering [the] victim."

F rank Eugene Corder spent Sunday night September 11, 1994 in typical fashion, smoking crack cocaine and drinking beer with his brother in his room at Keyser's Motel in Aberdeen Maryland. He was depressed and grappling with suicidal thoughts. His third wife Lydia had dumped him and he had just gotten out of court-ordered drug rehabilitation after ninety days—which obviously didn't take. His trucking business was going belly up and he had no other prospects for employment. Even the bargain basement roadside motel where he was staying was about to evict him.

But as the crack kicked in, he was developing a plan.

He had read of a young man named Mathias Rust, who had checked out a Cessna 172 from his flying club and flown from Finland to Moscow, landing in the middle of Red Square. It was a sensational surprise and gained Rust ten minutes in the limelight, before he was frog-marched off to Lefortovo prison, part of the notorious Lubyanka (he was released a year later).

Corder explained to his brother that he was going to do the same thing, only landing on the grounds of the White House. He didn't necessarily intend to kill the Clintons, but was seeking fame, or rather infamy, and didn't particularly care if the plane exploded into the presidential mansion.

He didn't tell his brother that he was almost certain they would never meet again, because his plan was to go out "in a big way." He still hadn't made up his mind if he was going to crash into the White House or into the Capitol dome. He told other friends that either would be spectacular or hoped the deed would make him "somebody" in death. He hoped to make the front page of all the newspapers, and make all his detractors—especially his ex-wives—take notice.

On the night of September 11th, his equally drug- and drink-impaired brother thought the cockamamie idea sounded better than just sitting around waiting to die and volunteered to drive him to the Harford County Airport in nearby Churchville, Maryland, where he could probably steal a Cessna.

Corder had no aviator license, but his father had given him lessons the year before. The small airport had virtually no security and because it was before 9/11, he quickly found a fully-fueled Cessna 150 with the keys left in it and the door opened.

On Monday night at 10:55 p.m., he successfully lifted off, according to the plane's Hobbs meter, which automatically records a plane's running time.

Flight control at Baltimore/Washington International Airport picked the plane up on radar over York, Pennsylvania at 1:06 a.m., according to Federal Aviation Agency radar records, later studied during a Secret Service security review. The plane flew an erratic course, not surprising for the condition of the pilot, and eventually flew over Washington at approximately tree level—undetectable by radar. Six and a half miles north of the White House the plane suddenly turned and headed straight for the no-fly zone around the presidential mansion.

Meanwhile, then fourteen-year-old Chelsea Clinton had been in a foul mood all day. Her parents had told her that, due to a glitch in the White House circulation system, the First Family had to spend a few nights across the street at Blair House, where visiting dignitaries are normally housed.

Sounding like her mother when she is miffed, Chelsea said, "Why don't we open the damn windows."

Bill was in a good mood. It was a cool day, signaling the sizzling, swamp-like Washington summer weather was on the wane, and fall would soon be in the air. He would be able to jog outside again. He saw Chelsea and Hillary to the limo that would take them across the street to Blair House safely and retreated to the Oval Office, where a young lady was waiting for a quick liaison. He assured them he would finish his work and join them shortly, suppressing his naughty-boy smile.

Hillary told an old friend she has known since her college days at Wellesley, "Bill thought I didn't know he was meeting some sleazy semi-hooker while we were at Blair House, but I had spies and I knew about most of his shenanigans. He had no idea that I had Hillary spies throughout the White House who reported to me, because they trusted me and feared his sexually aggressive behavior. He harassed a lot of women."

Bill would be in the safety of Blair House before Corder made his early morning descent over Washington Circle and into the no-fly zone known as P-56. His "exact flight path...while known and verified, is not being detailed for security reasons," according to the report. As inexperienced as he was and as intoxicated, he still managed to completely elude radar, and for that reason details are still classified.

★★★

According to the security review, Corder scudded over the Ellipse, just south of the mansion, descended at a very steep angle at 1:49 a.m., apparently abandoning the plan he had told his brother, to land as safely as Mathias Rust had done in Moscow's Red Square. The review noted that the airplane's wing flaps were up, and the throttle was "full forward," indicating the pilot had no intention of making a safe landing.

According to the review, "the aircraft crashed into the White House lawn...skidded across the ground, struck a magnolia tree just west of the South Portico steps and hit the southwest corner of the first floor of the mansion."

Corder died instantly of "multiple, massive blunt-force injuries."

The National Transportation Safety Board concluded the crash was intentional and the D.C. medical examiner declared it suicide.

Within minutes of the crash, a swarm of Secret Service agents were in place at the White House and at Blair House, protecting the Clintons in case it turned out to be a wave attack, which they are trained to always assume will be the case. A perimeter was established, and the mansion emptied of non-security personnel. The Technical Security Division and the military's Explosive Ordnance Disposal team were searching for explosives in the wreckage.

An hour later, the FBI and a half dozen other agencies had teams in place on the scene.

When Laredo and Ranger returned from their tour in Afghanistan and were recruited to join the Proactive Response Group, they were immersed in the study of past protective failures.

One which caught their attention was the Corder case. They studied the still-classified dossiers on the crash, especially the actual flight path Corder's plane flew. The baffling aspect was: how could a man with almost no experience flying, who was intoxicated by drugs and drink, have eluded radar so skillfully and reach one of the most guarded and valuable sites in the capital?

He was clearly alone on the plane and no GPS navigation device was found on board. Plus, he had randomly stolen the plane because it was unlocked, fully fueled, with the keys still inside.

It was very hard to swallow the idea that it was just blind luck.

The most plausible answer had to be a conspiratorial one: He was trained by terrorists or potential terrorists who wanted to probe the weak underbelly of the nation's air defenses, and let the nation know that even the White House wasn't safe, despite the Secret Service, Park Police, Executive Protective Police, and D.C. Metropolitan Police.

If the theory was true, the conspirators would obviously have programmed him to crash-land and die, so that he couldn't talk. Corder was a perfect patsy. He was a complete failure as a human being, strung out on drugs, a convicted criminal with no one to care about him, save for a brother who was as screwed up as he was.

On the other hand, he had served successfully in the U.S. Army, was trained as a mechanic, and honorably discharged as a Private First Class. So he was teachable.

Ranger's theory was unprovable and probably irrelevant, since years had passed, but the conclusion that was important was that air defense of the White House, the Capitol, and other no-fly areas, had to be reinforced. That, of course, became more painfully obvious after 9/11.

He went to the Hunter heads and was told to come up with a plan.

Experts on radar and surface-to-air weapons were consulted and a new system was developed (the details are, of course, classified).

It would be several years before the Hunters were in full control of proactive protection and were able to install effective early warning radar in a wide circle around the White House, and had placed specially designed surface-to-air missiles capable of shooting down the next attempt on approach, with a minimum danger of collateral damage in position.

CHAPTER TWENTY-TWO

No Room for Cowards

Bill Clinton considered that he paid a high price to get Hillary the job of Obama's Secretary of State, but thought it worth the trouble to seriously burnish her credentials and hopefully grease the way to her presidency in 2016.

He reluctantly agreed to disclose the list of 205,000 donors who had contributed $492 million to the Clinton Foundation. The donors included Saudi and Indian billionaires. Other sources included Denise Rich—the wife of fugitive financier Marc Rich, the recipient of a Clinton pardon—as well as the China Overseas Real Estate corporation.

It was a tangled mess of conflicting interests. He also had to agree to turn down millions of dollars in speaking fees. But according to Hillary's former Wellesley classmate, Bill was willing to sacrifice for the prestige of having his wife become Secretary of State, and especially for the patina it would give to the Clinton Global Initiative and his standing in the world community.

Hillary's status with the Secret Service also changed. While they continued their umbrella of protection at her homes in Chappaqua, New York and at their Whitehaven mansion in Washington, D.C., her safety abroad would fall to the Diplomatic Security Service.

Bill was upset because he had less faith in the Diplomatic Service than he did the Secret Service. He still had a lot of influence because he had appointed the hierarchy of the agency, many of whom were still in place.

He was furious and blamed Barack, but had no intention of going to him hat in hand asking for a favor. The two men had never been friends, and even with Hillary coming into the Obama administration with a top post, Bill wasn't anxious to buddy up. Most of their meetings turned sour.

Determined to prevent Hillary's Secret Service protection from being cancelled, he went to his home office in a converted red barn, next to the couple's Dutch Colonial home at 15 Old House Lane in Chappaqua, a suburb of New York City. He put on his charming persona and worked the phone lines, calling higher-ups at Homeland Security and the Secret Service who owed him favors.

A few days later a young agent who had been assigned to the elite Hunters Group was ordered to travel with Hillary, and provide the Secret Service protection Bill had requested. He was a decorated veteran of Afghanistan and considered one of the nascent organization's rising stars. His code name was Ranger.

Ranger was reluctant at first, telling Laredo he "didn't join the Hunters to babysit some old lady." She laughed, but insisted Hillary was probably going to be president and she would be a good person to have as a friend.

"You'll travel the world with her, and if she likes you it will be a major asset to put on your C.V. You're a big strapping hunk and she might take to you. But I know I don't have to be jealous. Ha ha."

Naturally, he had heard horror stories about what a nasty, crazy bitch she could be, but there were other agents who said that if she took to you, she was personable and loyal. One of the cautionary reports from veteran agents was that Hillary was "known to fly into foul-mouthed fits of rage, hurl dangerous objects at people's heads…and diabolically tongue-lash Secret Service agents."

A staff member during the Clintons' White House years said, "Hillary's been having screaming, child-like tantrums that have left her staff members in tears and unable to work."

The Clinton staff were also problematic in the eyes of the Secret Service. Ranger had been told by some of the "old-timers" who had served in the early '90s, when the Clintons were first in the White House, that when the Service routinely walked drug- and bomb-sniffing dogs through the East and West Wings, they were often locked out of some of the offices, particularly those occupied by some of the younger "hipper" staffers. The agents doubted they were bringing explosives to work, so that left drugs. When the staffers did allow the dogs in their offices, it became routine for them to have doggie treats on hand to distract them. The Secret Service was accustomed to the White House being run by senior statesmen and women—this was a very surprising and unsettling change. The Woodstock generation had taken power.

Former agent Gary Byrne recalled that "Hillary's explosions grew worse as the Clintons' time in the White House went on. When she was running for the presidency in 2016, Byrne warned that she "is too erratic, uncontrollable and occasionally violent" to be president.

Hillary lashed back, demanding retaliation. "They f****d us, Bill. We need to get rid of these asses. They've had it out for us from the beginning," Byrne reported that Hillary said about the Secret Service staff who had stayed over from the George H.W. Bush administration.

On another occasion she ordered—improperly—that an agent carry her suitcases. "If you want to remain on this detail, get your ass over here and grab those bags," she said, according to *The First Partner* by Joyce Milton.

On a trip abroad, beginning with a presidential helicopter Marine One flight to Joint Airbase Andrews, Hillary realized she had left her sunglasses behind and demanded the pilot return to the White House in mid-flight, "Put this on the ground! I need those sunglasses. We need to go back!" she said, according to *Dereliction of Duty* by Air Force Lt. Col. Robert Patterson.

With all the dire warnings Ranger had been peppered with by veteran Secret Service agents about what an incredible she-devil Hillary was, it was with serious trepidation that he climbed aboard the Secretary's Air

Force Two Boeing 757. He wasn't easily intimidated, but he had been warned she was a man-eater and wielded her power wickedly.

She personally welcomed him aboard, shook his hand warmly, he thought, personally showed him to a first-class-type seat, and poured him a coffee from her own pot.

"I think you'll find this very easy duty. The Diplomatic Security does all the heavy lifting, coordinating with security in each country we visit and organizing transportation, hotels, and meals. Don't feel like you have to stay up—your seat lies flat, so you might as well get some sleep on these long flights to Asia. We're going to do six countries in twelve days, so you have to pace yourself for the marathon."

After that she largely left him alone. He remembers thinking, "what a goddamn pleasant surprise."

Clinton has been accused of "hammering humorlessness," but Ranger saw a side of her that was witty and self-deprecating. She cackled at her own jokes and when other people's jokes struck a chord, she could laugh until tears ran down her cheeks. But she occasionally walked around the plane with a satellite phone in the crook of her neck, and could occasionally be heard berating people in high places and low. She cursed like a sailor, and demanded that everything she wanted done was done post haste.

From her conversations with a person that he assumed from overheard snippets was Bill, she could sound loving at one point, then sometimes suddenly lose her temper and lash out with shouting and withering comments. He was told by one of her assistants that Bill was most often aboard his best friend Ron Burkle's private Gulfstream G650, probably surrounded by young girls and cruising around the world.

Ranger knew that he wanted to get past the assignment without getting on her bad side and experiencing her wraith.

Ranger was bored. Traveling the world in a luxurious Air Force Two plane was cushy, and several months into the gig Hillary was still respectful and friendly. Seeing the world, accompanying the U.S. Secretary of State would be a dream job to most, but Ranger had become an action junkie, as most Army Special Forces soldiers are.

There seemed no sense of danger, or of threats to be neutralized, on Hillary's trips. Ranger was a Hunter, not a security guard. He knew that Hillary sensed it and was likely to give him a pass when they returned to Washington, regardless of what Bill might say.

He kept in close touch with Secret Service command as well as the Defense Intelligence Agency, to keep up with the latest chatter around the world to monitor if any bad actors had plans to harm the Secretary.

After a time, he got the impression the bad guys frankly didn't give a damn about Hillary Clinton. Then out of nowhere, arriving in Kinshasa, Republic of the Congo, there was a coded report about a surprise for Clinton. "Surprise" in terrorist speak usually meant a bomb of some sort.

He looked over her schedule and saw that she was attending a luncheon to honor her presence in the country. It would be a busy event with over a hundred people. There was a scheduled motorcade through crowded, teeming streets of Kinshasa. It was all a perfect storm of danger. Plus, Defence Intelligence Agency also had reports that Al Qaeda was establishing a larger presence in the Congo. They had attacked an army barracks near Kinshasa, killing a number of soldiers, apparently to make a splash.

Killing the wife of a former U.S. president, who was now Obama's Secretary of State, would be seen as a huge victory and would instantly make them major players in the region.

He approached Hillary and asked to have an urgent private word. He was fully expecting she would laugh him off, as most leaders hated to show fear by cancelling an event, particularly in a foreign country that was welcoming her as a superstar. But she summoned her two top aides and asked if they could find a way to back out of the event. Ranger was again surprised at how reasonable Hillary could be, despite her nasty reputation.

In a few minutes it was done, and the event cancelled.

Hillary later told a long-time friend and former Wellesley classmate that the incident was a chilling reminder of Bill's 1996 near disaster in Manila.

When Air Force Two touched down at Joint Base Andrews, Hillary thanked Ranger for all he had done, said she had made arrangements for another agent to accompany her on trips, and said she knew he was bored and wanted to get back to the active duties of a Hunter, although she pretended not to have any idea what that entailed.

"Thanks for everything," she said. "I told your boss you did a great job."

Special agent Lew Merletti had been assigned to do intelligence work to protect then-president Bill Clinton, much as Ranger was specially assigned to travel with Hillary and guide her through the extreme dangers and uncertainties of travel, to places with spotty security and active terror cells.

Bill was attending the Asia-Pacific Economic Cooperation in the Philippines, along with most important world leaders. The Philippines was a hot bed of radical Islam, and twenty-six thousand police, soldiers, and other security personnel were assigned to protect the leaders and prevent a cataclysmic assassination disaster for the Philippine government.

On the motorcade taking Bill to the forum, tens of thousands of excited people lined the route, a recipe for trouble. Merletti was constantly monitoring the latest intelligence on chatter associated with known terror groups, as Ranger would be doing when he was warned of a plot to assassinate Hillary in the Congo.

Merletti's ears perked up when he got a message that included mention of "bridge" and "wedding," which could be code for a surprise attack. Reacting immediately, he ordered the motorcade to drastically alter course, meaning Bill would be late and miss his grand arrival moment.

The president bridled, saying the evidence was flimsy and could mean nothing. But the emergency decision was in the hands of Merletti alone.

For the rest of the trip Bill grumbled and sulked, which was his way when he was overruled.

Later that day, security discovered a bomb hidden under a bridge on the route, that could have killed President Clinton and his entourage.

Recalling that chilling near-miss incident, Hillary told her friend she had no intention of ignoring the advice of a Secret Service man assigned to protect her life, basically at the request of Bill. Hillary said she was also disappointed at missing a grand reception in a country the Obama administration was trying to influence.

She laughed with her friend over a glass of Chardonnay in the safety of her highly guarded Chappaqua home with her friend. "I didn't sulk or bitch. I acted like a grown-up, unlike silly Billy."

Hillary said that most of the incidents were unknown to the public, because the Secret Service always feared that news stories about thwarted attempts would encourage copycats, and they didn't want bad guys to repeat the formula over and over, until one of them got lucky.

She said that Bill and Barack Obama were both magnets for plots, even after they were both out of office.

"They both had bombs mailed to them, years after leaving office. Bill was told that was the second attempt made on an out-of-office president in over one hundred years when Teddy Roosevelt was shot, and that didn't count really count because he was running for president again. The Reagan break-in was the first.

"Bill and Barrack just piss people off for some reason," she laughed and toasted her friend.

Hillary Clinton turned out to be a friend and a great asset—much to Ranger's surprise and delight. He told Laredo he didn't think it was because he saved her from a potentially perilous situation, that was just him doing his job. Somehow, during the months he roamed the world with her, they had made a personal connection. In his opinion, she simply liked him.

Laredo and Ranger were frequently invited to parties at Whitehaven, the Clinton's Georgian mansion on Embassy Row, where they both made extremely useful contacts in government and politics, and where Hillary would whisper about important developments from around the government and around the world that impacted on Secret Service business.

Laredo had a woman's take on it. "Women always love to be rescued by a tall, handsome soldier boy. I think you are her hero and she wants you to be a friend. She's had bad luck with men. Her father was an angry drill sergeant, her husband is a lothario who shows her no respect, humiliating her before the world, time after time. I think you are the sort of man she has long wished was in her life.

"It [religion] was a very big part of her life until she met Bill and things came morally unglued. I think she is intrigued that you are openly religious and it's important to you."

Laredo was right that Hillary also grew up religious, and that it shaped her philosophic outlook. She had been involved and engaged with the youth group of the left-leaning wing of the Methodist Church.

"Plus, you're a war hero and I doubt that in her universe she's friends with many, or any for that matter, who are. Bill dodged the draft and said he loathed the military. You're the not-Bill."

At one outdoor/indoor gathering at Whitehaven in late summer of 2020, Ranger and Laredo were thrilled to be with the major movers and shakers in Washington. A tent had been erected on the landscaped grounds of the mansion and well over one hundred people were present. Many of the faces were instantly recognizable to anybody who watched the evening news.

There was free-flowing French champagne, catering by Washington's best restaurants, with a mostly vegan menu out of respect for Chelsea, who appeared to be a guest of honor at her parents' house. Another guest, a retired Court of Appeals judge, who advises Bill on matters legal, explained that Hillary and Bill were in the beginning phase of turning over the recently renamed Bill, Hillary and Chelsea Clinton Foundation to Chelsea, and the affair was an opportunity for her to mingle with some of the foundation's donors and supporters.

Chelsea had a suite of rooms in her parents' Washington house, which she had disappeared into before most of the guests arrived, and emerged in party clothes: a light green cashmere sweater, a black skirt, and black pumps.

Ranger and Laredo drifted through the living room, fluted crystal champagne glasses in hand. The living room was hung with abstract Vietnamese art, including a painting of Chelsea and Hillary wearing traditional Vietnamese conical hats made from bamboo and dried leaves, taken on a trip they had made to the Far East.

Bill was working the room, ever the consummate politician, remembering everyone's name, as well as the names of their children and even their dogs.

The ex-president stopped to say hello to Ranger and Laredo, calling them by their real names, not code names. They were not surprised; "the wily old guy knows everything," Laredo said later. Bill reached over and kissed Laredo on the cheek and said, "How's the general? Please give him my best." To Ranger he said, "How's Jim," meaning James Murray, the director of the Secret Service, a person Ranger had met but wasn't exactly on a first name basis with.

At one point, Hillary approached, welcomed them to Whitehaven and whispered in Ranger's ear that she had some major news he would surely be interested in. Naturally, his ears perked up. She told him a woman in Quebec was manufacturing ricin, and had sent several envelopes to law enforcement officers who had busted her in Texas years ago, and had sent one to President Trump. She slipped him a Post-it with the woman's address in the suburbs of Montreal.

It was a great tip; he thanked her profusely. Hillary smiled and said, "I have a pretty good incentive. The next letter could be mailed to my husband, or me."

On the drive to Secret Service headquarters, they marveled at how connected the Clintons were, with tentacles reaching through every department of government; even though they were out of office, a lot of officials had either been appointed or promoted by them. Ranger nodded, "For all the nasty stuff that is said about them, they're damn good friends if you're on their good side."

The information went straight up to the top with a message to "Jim" that Bill sent his regards.

An hour later they were at Joint Base Andrews boarding a Globe-master for Montreal. Ranger had already contacted a friend in the Royal Canadian Mounted Police and filled him in on what they knew. He immediately said they were welcome to join in the bust and for Laredo to examine whatever substances they found.

It turned out Pascale Cecile Veronique Ferrier had already fled Canada, and was arrested at the Peace Bridge border crossing in Buffalo. The Border Patrol knew nothing about the ricin attempts, but was holding her on a weapons charge for carrying a loaded concealed gun and a knife.

Laredo immediately recognized the castor beans that had been used to make ricin, and did a quick field test to see how potent the traces of ricin were. She declared it wasn't well made, but said, "It's good enough to make a person damn sick it they inhale it."

Meanwhile the ricin-laced envelope was intercepted at the White House mail-screening station in rural Virginia. The accompanying obligatory threatening letter had a hashtag #killTrump, called him an "Ugly Clown Tyrant," and said the letter was "a special gift for you."

When the fifty-three-year-old woman was placed in custody she mentioned that the FBI was searching for her, which was helpful to law enforcement, even though at that point the FBI wasn't yet on to her, though the Secret Service was.

The year before, Ferrier had sent four other ricin-laced letters to local police in Mission, Texas, where she had been arrested for carrying an altered driver's license.

U.S. Marshalls in Buffalo took her into their custody and remanded her to a federal prison, where she made her initial court appearance before U.S. Magistrate H. Kenneth Schroeder, Jr., who entered a not-guilty plea on her behalf, and ordered her held pending trial.

EPILOGUE

The Other Big Job

Protecting the life of the president and other top government officials has become the only job of the Secret Service, in the minds of most people. Certainly, that is a daunting assignment and extremely important to the continued functioning of our government, and that has been the theme of this book.

But, in truth, most employees of the agency are assigned to the other major charge, which is protecting the integrity of the American currency, economy and interstate trade. The vast majority of arrests and prosecutions by the agency are for violations of securities fraud regulations. If the government can't ensure that the nation's economy is protected and trusted by investors, almost nothing else matters.

A typical month of press releases on the Secret Service web site, of which there are hundreds, is typical:

> "Owner of India-based call center sentenced to prison for scamming U.S. victims out of millions of dollars."

> "Louisiana woman indicted in $4.8 million elder-fraud scheme."

> "Oklahoma residents plead guilty to mail and wire fraud in attempts to take titles to homes without owners' consent."

They are a federal police force with offices in every major American city and in every capital around the world.

Most of the members of the Secret Service division dedicated to financial deceit and fraud are accountants and financial examiners, not armed policemen. But if things get hairy with the bad guys, they can summon help from their colleagues in Hawkeye CAT and the Hunters, who act as the muscle behind the financial analysts.

If the crooks and fraudsters turn violent, the heavily armed enforcement wing of the service can get anywhere in the world quickly, bristling with weapons, and prepared to use them if need be.

Some of the schemes they unearth are fiendishly clever and generate Secret Service "Wanted" posters, offering up to a million dollars for their scalps.

In 2016, two Ukrainian nationals Artem Radchenko and Oleksandr Ieremenko were involved in a scheme to hack into the computers of the Securities and Exchange Commission's data system, to steal advance copies of their annual and quarterly reports before they were ready to be disseminated. Non-public information, including the corporation's confidential earnings figures, was included. The two men then dealt in trading the corporation's securities based on the illegally obtained secret information, and selling the information to others, who also profited.

The two men netted at least $4.5 million in a year from their international cybercrime, before their arrest.

The Secret Service had the million-dollar wanted posters printed in Russian and English and posted them world-wide, with pictures and descriptions of the men, to put maximum pressure on them and to hopefully flush them out. A million dollars for a tip as to where these men were living was a powerful incentive.

Then-director of the Secret Service, James M. Murray, practically exulted in the fact that the agency had finally organized internationally and could marshal the resources to put an end to such schemes. "For the first time in agency history, we are able to strategically leverage resources worldwide in the pursuit of wanted fugitives charged with the exploitation and manipulation of our financial systems."

A former agent said:

The integrity of our major, multi-national corporations is essential to the American economy, and the government, which relies on the corporations to produce the weapons of war and the tools of commerce.

The health of these entities is directly related to our standing in the world. Keeping our corporations safe from hacking and stolen proprietary secrets is a major national security issue, up there with keeping government leaders safe, and that's why the Secret Service is one of the agencies tasked with enforcement, including State and Justice, both of which were deeply involved in the battle.

The Secret Service's first assignment in 1865, from President Lincoln, was to stop the flood of counterfeiting that was threatening to destroy world-wide confidence in the dollar, and they are still protecting the economy, as well as the presidents.

END

ABOUT THE AUTHOR

Leon Wagener was born in Washington, D.C. His father Leon Sr., a veteran of World War II, was in finance. His mother Shirley worked in the Richard Nixon White House and was one of the first female press secretaries. She was proudly an "unindicted co-conspirator."

Wagener first started as a copy boy at the *Wall Street Journal* in Washington, D.C.; he then worked as a news assistant at the *New York Times* Washington bureau. From 1968 to 1974, Wagener served in the U.S. Coast Guard Reserve. After leaving the Coast Guard, he studied journalism at the University of Maryland. He joined the *National Enquirer* in the early seventies and worked as the chief for the Washington and Miami bureaus.

Wagener is the author of bestselling biographies of Neil Armstrong and Jodie Foster and wrote and contributed to eight political books about the Clintons and Obamas, including *The Amateur*, *The Truth About Hillary*, and *Blood Feud*, which were *New York Times* bestsellers.